Mao Tse-tung and the Chinese People

Mao Tse-tung and the Chinese People

Roger Howard

MONTHLY REVIEW PRESS

New York and London

Library of Congress Cataloging in Publication Data
Howard, Roger, 1938-
    Mao Tse-tung and the Chinese people.
    Bibliography: p. 371.
    Includes index.
    1. Mao, Tse-tung, 1893-1976. 2. Heads of state —
China — Biography. 3. China — History — 1900-
4. China — History — 1949-1976. I. Title.
DS778.M3H68   951.05'092'4 (B)   77-70969
ISBN 0-85345-413-2

Monthly Review Press
62 West 14th Street, New York, N.Y. 10011
47 Red Lion Street, London WC1R 4PF

Manufactured in the United States of America

10   9   8   7   6   5   4   3   2   1

50947

Contents

MAP

Routes of the Long March

Acknowledgements

I am indebted to the authors and publishers mentioned in my list of references for the use of the material indicated. In particular I must record my thanks for permission to use longer extracts from published works to Lois Wheeler Snow and to Victor Gollancz Ltd. and Random House for Edgar Snow's *Red Star over China*, reprinted by permission of Grove Press, © Edgar Snow, 1968; to Monthly Review Press for Agnes Smedley's *The Great Road*; to Jerome Ch'en and Oxford University Press for *Mao Papers*, edited by Jerome Ch'en, reprinted by permission of the publisher; to Jerome Ch'en, and the editors of *The China Quarterly* for the translation of Mao's poem *Chingkangshan Revisited* appearing in *Mao* (Great Lives Observed), © Prentice-Hall, 1969; to Jerome Ch'en and Prentice-Hall Inc. for *Mao* (Great Lives Observed), © 1969, reprinted by permission of the publisher; to Stuart R. Schram and Praeger Publishers, New York, and Pall Mall Press, London, for Stuart Schram's *The Political Thought of Mao Tse-tung*; to Harvard University Press for Mark Selden's *The Yenan Way in Revolutionary China*; to International Publishers, New York, for Agnes Smedley's *Chinese Destinies*.

Acknowledgements are due to Lindsay Drummond Ltd, the publishers of *China Fights for Freedom* by Anna Louise Strong. Thanks are also due to Eastern Horizon Press, Hong Kong; the People's Publishing House, Bombay; Gunther Stein; the editors of *Chinese Literature*; and the Foreign Languages Press, Peking, for the use of material.

Jerome Ch'en's *Mao and the Chinese Revolution* (Oxford University Press, 1965) and Stuart R. Schram's *Mao Tse-tung* (Penguin Books, 1966) remain useful and detailed accounts of Mao's life from angles different from my own. Any biographer of Mao must acknowledge a debt to these scholars.

I should also like to acknowledge the help and encouragement of many comrades and friends in both Britain and China in the preparation and writing of this book.

Preface

I am concerned in this book with seeing Mao Tse-tung in his relationship to the Chinese people. I have tried to show the closeness which I believe existed between him and the masses of workers and, especially, peasants. But I am aware that what I will reveal is still very much Mao and China as outsiders have seen them. The Chinese people, as distinct from their officials, are even now largely silent on paper: it is their acts that speak.

There is a small amount of documentation of Chinese life by foreign visitors. I have used these records extensively. What has been published in China about the revolution, apart from Mao's writings, is now mainly repudiated there. What remains is often arch and gauche and gives an idealised and non-Marxist presentation of Chinese life and people. It is still acts that speak, so I have relied heavily on witnesses of them.

That those who have written as witnesses have mainly been foreign visitors to China is an accident of history, at least until the Chinese themselves develop a considered view of the events of past years. As one of my students at Peking University said to me, 'Visitors often know more about the details of China than we do, since they have the opportunity to travel and visit factories, communes and schools, while we have not.' His comment reflects the paucity of informational writing in China.

But observations by visitors hardly constitute a record of the life and breath of China. Few are the witnesses of the great events, who have managed to get beneath the surface and felt life as it was lived during the great changes. My student also commented, 'But visitors often miss the essence: they cannot get the feel of the broad movement of politics

and ideas that we Chinese people are involved in every day.'
Given the segregation of most foreigners in China from the
ordinary people that is hardly surprising.

If foreign impressions of China remain very much on the
surface, so too do Chinese impressions of other countries. In
their great work of transforming nature and society, the
Chinese have kept their heads down, intent on their work,
their soil, their depths. This is a strength, since it has led to
a remarkable concreteness of aim, and a pertinence of
thought, in the Chinese revolution. It is also a weakness. The
Chinese peasant — and now the commune member — has had
no time and little inclination to explore broader, and even
alien, territories of the revolutionary spirit. Many Chinese
regard this lack of vision as a fault. As the woman party
secretary, Chiang Shui-ying, in the Peking opera *Song of the
Dragon River*, says to a parochial fellow commune member:

> Raise your head, expand your chest,
> Fix your eyes on distant vistas,
> Don't let 'Hand-Palm' your view impede,
> A world-wide vision is what you need.

The mass study of the major works of Marx, Engels, Lenin
and Stalin from 1970 onwards is the first time in Chinese
history that any foreign thinking has reached the masses of
the people (as distinct from their officials) other than through
monks and priests.

Mao has frequently pointed out to the Chinese people that
the struggles of the world's peoples are also their own. Objec-
tively, this is true, but it is a point that has yet to sink in
deeply, though China is not alone, of course, in this short-
coming. A passionate international concern, which is in the
interests of educated young workers everywhere, may yet
keep China away from chauvinism and along the path of
internationalism. As Mao said in 1970,

> It is not necessary to make foreigners accept Chinese
> thought. We should only require them to apply the

principles of Marxism-Leninism in the concrete conditions of their own countries ... We still have great
nation chauvinism in our party and state ... It must be
overcome.

If it is overcome, and the meaning of the Chinese revolution
really reaches the working people of the world, while at the
same time knowledge of other struggles becomes as immediate
to the Chinese people as involvement in their own, China's
revolutionary experience of the past fifty years and more
will have begun in word as it already has in deed to join the
great mainstream of modern revolutionary advance.

I hope this book will make a certain, though small, con-
tribution to this popularisation of revolutionary history. I
know, however, that an author dealing with a subject of
this complexity and obscurity and moreover writing for
English-speaking readers about a person and a country very
different from their experience, is bound to make some
mistakes of presentation or viewpoint which his Chinese
friends would not have made. I hope that despite inevitable
shortcomings, my work will serve the cause of better understanding between the two peoples.

A chronicling of Mao's part in China's revolution is inhibited
by several factors. One is the extraordinary hatred with which
many western scholars viewed him and the Chinese revolution
for so many years, a hatred which coloured their marshalling
of the facts and which is only now in recession. In consequence, and despite the efforts of more recent observers,
there is still a backlog of misconceptions to put right.

Second, there is the extreme remoteness of the life of a
Chinese peasant to life in the twentieth-century West.
Memories of similar lives in Britain, for example, are preserved
in stories which country people tell about their ancestors of
150 years ago, though the real equivalent is perhaps even
further back, in the break-up of feudalism. But they are
stories and have little more bearing on the British people's

present lives than have their present lives on the experience of China's hundreds of millions of peasants. The incomprehension is reciprocal.

The third difficulty stems from the careful secrecy with with the Chinese Communist Party (CCP) works. It is still a party living under threat and it acts like one. The result is that only the end-result of a series of inner debates and decisions is ever published, often in somewhat generalised formulations. The processes by which the results have been reached are not referred to. Much of the CCP's inner history, especially recently, and of Mao's role in it, will remain conjectural in China and the West for some time to come.

I have not therefore been able to use a dialectic in my treatment of the life of Mao as much as I would have wished. The dialectical approach is, to say the least, difficult with only limited, and frequently one-sided, information available. My approach has had to be to use dialectics as a basis, and to use an illustrative method to go deeper into parts of the wide panorama of events as they affected the people's lives. Hence my lengthy use of extracts from the reports of eye-witnesses.

The broad pattern of struggle, both in the party and in the country, has emerged in the past few years. It became clearest in the Great Proletarian Cultural Revolution, when there was a short burst of 'extensive democracy'. Publications, especially by Red Guard groups, revealed, along with what the struggle itself showed, a number of matters which had previously been unclear concerning intra-party debate. I have taken the opportunity of studying a number of these documents. But it is perhaps of more importance that the broad pattern of struggle, and the people's responses to it, should be known than that every secret of Communist Party life should be broadcast. It is among the people that the party's policies are made or broken. At its best, the party is the agent of change; it is not change itself. If we are to study the great changes in China, we should look among the people.

I have had the benefit of a number of interviews with a

cross-section of Chinese people in the preparation of this book. I have incorporated my findings into the text. In the four years I lived in China, I have also talked to many hundreds of Chinese in many different jobs in factories, communes, mines, construction projects, schools, universities and offices, in the course of my travels across fifteen provinces. But my study of China has benefitted most from the work I have done alongside my Chinese friends, briefly in factories and communes, mainly in universities with worker, peasant and bourgeois students. If there is anything at all of the spirit of Mao Tse-tung and the Chinese people in this book it is from what they have transmitted to me. If there is not, it is because the listener was at fault.

Peking, January—August 1973
London, September 1976

Hard is the Journey,
Hard is the Journey,
So many turnings,
And now where am I?

LI PO

Introduction

China at Mao Tse-tung's birth in 1893 was already a country in change. In this land of peasants, centuries of small-scale farming and home handicrafts had created the material wealth underpinning the Emperor's power. These were the traditional modes of production. Capitalism hardly existed. A few porcelain and silk factories had developed small-scale mass production and created a nation-wide market for their goods, but Chinese industry as a whole had not reached the stage of manufacture by the time the Opium War 'opened' China to the West in 1840.

In that war, British capital intervened to defend her fifty-year-old export trade of opium to China. The war secured for Britain the Treaty of Nanking in 1842 which ceded Hongkong and opened five seaports to British trade, the first of a series of unequal treaties imposed on a weak Chinese imperial government by European and Japanese merchants. This was China's brutal initiation into the modern world.

At first the foreign firms used their privileges merely to dump their goods on the Chinese market. By the 1890s, however, foreign capitalists had begun to consolidate their positions by exporting capital itself into China. They sent their personnel to run factories, open mines, build railways and set up banks. They thus obtained control over China's industry and banking, either directly through their own personnel, or indirectly through the Chinese comprador class. China's economy became reliant on the imperialist economies of the foreign powers and China was reduced to the level of a semi-colony.

The penetration of China by foreign capital and trade had important results which were later to be turned to the advantage of the revolution Mao Tse-tung was to lead. First of all, it shattered China's small-farm and handicraft economy in the countryside. It accelerated the emergence and growth of indigenous capitalist industry tied to foreign interests, and it forced peasants to depend more on the market as their home-produced handicrafts were crowded out by machine products. Furthermore, the indemnities extorted from the imperial government by foreign powers in part-settlement of conflicts, added to the tax burdens laid on the peasants and handicraftsmen, many of whom went bankrupt and left their villages for the towns and cities, where their presence created a labour market for capitalism. At the same time, imperialist interference in China began to re-awaken the sense of cultural and historical identity of the Chinese people and so created the spiritual as well as material conditions which the revolutionary movement could use to unite the masses of the people against foreign capital and its Chinese apologists. All these factors helped to undermine the rural base of the semi-feudal economy.

The communists, including Mao, later identified various contradictions which they held were characteristic of Chinese semi-feudal, semi-colonial society. There were two outstanding ones. On the one hand they pointed out the contradiction between the interests of the foreign powers and the interests of the Chinese nation. On the other hand they underlined the contradiction within China itself between the semi-feudal landlords in the countryside (and their urban capitalist counterparts) and the masses of the people. These two contradictions, they maintained, underlay the whole period of 109 years of struggle from the Opium War to the establishment of the People's Republic in 1949.

Which was the primary contradiction? Obviously, according to Mao, when China's very existence was threatened (as when the Japanese army began to overrun her in the 1930s) the national interest of China was paramount, for without a China, how could the Chinese people have a social revolution?

At such times, the contradiction between the interests of the foreign powers and the interests of the Chinese nation was the main one.

Even so, Mao maintained, the underlying and determining contradiction was at all times the one within China itself, between semi-feudalism and capitalism on the one hand and the masses of the people on the other. The four wars in China since 1919 have essentially been class wars and the revolution has been born of class contradictions and only secondarily of national contradictions.

The revolution since 1840 falls into three main periods. The eighty years prior to the May 4th Movement of 1919, when the revolution was of a bourgeois-democratic type, were followed from 1919 to 1949 by a bourgeois revolution of a new-democratic type, as defined by Mao; this was led by the working class, effected largely by peasant armies, and sought the co-operation of the revolutionary intelligentsia of the Chinese bourgeoisie. After the communists took power in 1949, the revolution turned to what the Chinese Communist Party called socialist construction. It sought to use the technical skills of the 'patriotic' bourgeoisie in the socialist transformation of industry, led by the working class and the Communist Party. After 1949, too, the revolution began to socialise agriculture by a mobilisation of peasant consciousness and endeavour. The objective of this construction and reconstruction was socialism, which itself marked a transitional stage between capitalist and communist modes of production.

Mao's part in this protracted revolution began at the time of the overthrow of the Ching dynasty in 1911. His political initiation came during that anti-imperial revolution, but his active political life began in earnest after the May 4th Movement of 1919, and broadened in the First Revolutionary Civil War against the warlords of 1924-7. His political understanding deepened in the Kiangsi Soviet of 1928-34 and the Long March of 1935 (the Second Revolutionary Civil War, against the Kuomintang nationalists, the KMT). It matured at Yenan in the anti-Japanese war of 1937-45 and the War of Liberation of 1945-9. His political life came to fruition in the years of socialist construction under the government of the People's Republic. His maturity spans more than fifty years of continuous war and social upheaval, and for forty of those years Mao was in the forefront of the nation's politics.

In his talk with Mao in January 1965, the journalist Edgar Snow, as reported in his book *The Long Revolution*, remarked that he could not recall any man in Chinese history who rose from rural obscurity not only to lead a successful revolution but 'to write its history, to conceive the strategy of its military victory, to formulate an ideological doctrine which changed the traditional thought of China and then to live out the practice of his philosophy in a new kind of civilisation with broad implications for the whole world.' Mao commented that he had begun life as a primary school teacher. He had no thought of fighting wars then or of becoming a communist. He was more or less 'a democratic personage'.

The factor which changed this 'democratic personage' into a revolutionary communist was the actual condition of China. Mao's thinking is rooted deep in the Chinese soil. It is therefore rooted in famine and flood, disease, and oppression of the poor peasants. It is rooted in natural and man-made disaster. His political work may best be summed up as an attempt to make order out of chaos by destroying the roots of chaos. His method of doing this may be called the method of using the disunity of the classes to forge unity amongst the masses of the people.

In the China of Mao's birth, disasters were normal. Flood, drought and resultant famine were frequent, expected and regarded as inevitable. Famine was an aspect of life, neither more nor less surprising than birth, speech, work and death. A famine factor was built into China's death rate: if you were a peasant, famine was one of the things you might expect to die of, as likely as sickness or old age.

Living thus close to famine was not particular to the nineteenth and twentieth centuries in China. Between 108 B.C. and 1911 A.D. there were 1828 famines, or one nearly every year, in one or more of the provinces. From 620 to 1619 A.D. there was insufficient rain in one or more provinces in 610 years, and great or severe drought in 203 years. A drought might last six years.

Loss of life and food resources were huge. In the three year drought of 1876-9 which affected five northern provinces, between twelve and thirteen millions died of hunger, disease and the consequent rural violence. A break in the embankment of the Yellow River in Honan caused the floods of 1887-9 which inundated nearly the whole province south of the river: more than two million were drowned or died of starvation. Huai River floods of disaster proportions affected Anhwei and Kiangsu provinces on average once every six or seven years and a minor flood came every three of four years. These provinces, together larger than Belgium, contained some of the best farmland in China: as a result of even a minor flood, food enough to feed six million adults for a year was lost. In Mao's own province of Hunan in 1906 a great famine killed three million people when he was 12 years old.

Warlords and corrupt officials did nothing to change the siuation. Their avarice even made it worse. Hallett Abend gave an illustration of this in the book *Tortured China*, of the period under Kuomintang rule.

In the early spring of 1928 there was a famine in Shantung ... Into Tsinanfu, the capital of Shantung, more than 28,000 refugees from the famine districts had trooped for shelter. They camped in the ravines and gullies near the city — camped in little tents made of woven straw, and slept on the bare ground despite the cold winds which brought alternate snow squalls and drenching showers. Once each day each of these 28,000 wretches was given one bowl of hot millet gruel, salted but made without the addition of meat or vegetables.

Marshall Chang Tsung-chang was then governor of Shantung province . . . Even while these 28,000 shivered in rags at the gates of his capital, Chang Tsung-chang was host at a great banquet, given to celebrate the installation of a $50,000 central heating system in his spacious *yamen*. At that banquet the guests were served on a dinner set of cut glass — a special order from Belgium which had cost $40,000.

There was no actual shortage of food in Shantung as a whole, and at that time rice was cheaper in the not distant Yangtse Valley than for ten years. But there had been no rains in a portion of the province the summer before, and crops had been bad the year before that. Then Chang Tsung-chang's tax gatherers descended upon the drought-stricken areas. The people had no money. Their grain reserves were taken in lieu of cash, and when they had not sufficient grain reserves the soliders tore from their mud houses the wooden beams and rooftrees — for wood is worth money in China. Whole villages were abandoned, their roofless houses standing open to the skies, and it was money wrung from these people which paid for that central heating plant and for that cut glass dinner service.

With such disasters and injustices forming part of the normal pattern of life, it is hardly surprising that the traditional Chinese greeting is not 'How are you?' but 'Have you eaten?'

The disasters were in fact the result of the injustices. They were avoidable. While the rich lined their pockets from taxes, centuries of deforestation and lack of proper water conservation measures at the headwaters of the great rivers of central and northern China had brought problems of flooding on the great plains as silt built up the beds of the rivers to a level higher than the surrounding fields. The small-scale farming economy, an individualistic form of exploitation of the soil, could do nothing to alter this situation. Neither could the central government tackle this problem at its source, lacking both the technical ability and the social consciousness (and, in the nineteenth century, largely the authority) to provide more than dykes and irrigation canals on the plains. It was not until 1949 that national plans of river control and afforestation began to overcome man's long neglect.

In taking a measure of Mao's mind, we must not underestimate these facts, common to the Chinese people. Living with famine as a normal condition for a lifetime leaves an indelible mark on the spirit. For a people to live with it for centuries is to mark every new generation with a history of bitterness that paralyses the soul. But extreme passivity, the numbed fatalism of the destitute, turns into its opposite — revolt — immediately 'a method, an organisation, leadership, a workable programme, hope — and arms', in Edgar Snow's words, are offered. An abject population, given the means of regeneration, becomes as bold as it was formerly listless. Where before they could do nothing, they rise up and learn that they can accomplish much. Mao himself had to learn this simple lesson before he could teach it to millions.

The fertility of the ricelands of Mao's home county of Hsiangtan in Hunan province, in southern China, and the comparative well-being of his own rich peasant family, only served to highlight the general poverty in a mind alert to the existence of imbalance and harmony, of chaos and order, and hence of contradiction. As Dr. Sun Yat-sen, the Kuomintang leader, remarked of the peasantry: 'In China what is called inequality between poor and rich is only a distinction between the very poor and the less poor.'

Certainly, Mao's family was not rich by contemporary western standards. He and his brothers ate meat three or four times a year. His father owned just twenty-two *mu* at his wealthiest (one *mu* being about 0.15 of an acre), and employed no more than one or two labourers. But his father ran a grain transport business, and that was remunerative in a countryside where only human carriers could be used for transportation in most parts: men could use footpaths where four-legged animals could not pass. As late as 1922 there were only 1,700 miles of road in China, including dirt roads.

The normal insecurity of life of the poor peasant and his total lack of control over his own future was a harsher element than the destruction resulting from famine, because it was longer lasting. In good times, a peasant rented land from a landlord, 3.3 acres on average. The landlord took about half of the wealth the peasant created, grain being extracted as rent. What was left was not enough for the tenant and his family, and he was forced to borrow from a money-lender, paying interest as low as thirty percent in good years and as high as one hundred percent in famine conditions.

Between a third and three-quarters of the farm population of China were such tenants and the numbers increased throughout the 1920s and 1930s. Taxes were levied by the central government, and by provincial warlords and local landlords. Land tax was extorted in advance: in 1929-30 in Kiangsi and Fukien provinces, it was being collected for as far ahead as 1943 and in some parts of Szechuan for ninety-nine years in advance.

To pay such taxes the peasant was frequently forced to sell every single possession, including his wife and children. A steady supply of such folk fed the city factories with labour and the maritime brothels with girls. If this was not sufficient to meet his debts, the peasant sold the roof over his head and wandered as a beggar. If famine struck, he sold his clothes before dying.

While still able-bodied he might be drafted to join a bandit rabble or be shot or tortured by them if he refused. Press gangs might force him into a warlord's army where he was made to act as carrier or soldier. For such masses of people, the prospect of eating leaf-dust, tree bark and stone ground into 'flour', the fare of those hit by famine, was neither frightening nor surprising: it was food.

Mao's thinking, and the appeal of Mao's thinking to the Chinese peasant, was born of this life. Previous uprisings, such as the Taiping Revolution, which was crushed only thirty years before Mao's birth, had grown from a similar soil.

The Taipings rose against the central imperial government and set up a capital in Nanking. Their revolution lasted fourteen years from 1851-64 and its influence extended to seventeen provinces. It was a peasant rising of the old type, imbued with superstition and lacking an analysis of feudal rule. The Taipings neglected to establish solid bases in the areas occupied by their armies. Their programme was weakened by its equalitarian vagueness and by a tendency to think in terms of a small peasant economy: its ideal was an equal allotment of land, trees and livestock to each peasant family. The leaders quarrelled among themselves and did not co-operate with other peasant rebels. Some of their leaders adopted a luxurious style of living, leaving their supporters to a spartan existence. The Taipings were thus open to annihilation by the forces of the Ching emperor, aided by American, British and French troops. The killings as a result of this uprising and of its suppression, and all the great peasant risings of the nineteenth century, ran to 30 to 40 million. All these points Mao noted when the time came for him to lead a new peasant-based movement.

A greater lesson for Mao, however, came in his youth with the failure of the 1911 revolution. Although this revolution overthrew the Ching dynasty (the imperial rule of the Manchus) and the monarchy was abolished, state power soon fell into the hands of the warlord Yuan Shih-kai. Dr. Sun Yat-sen's Alliance Society and the Kuomintang (KMT) that came after failed to solve the land question, the basic problem in any democratic revolution in China where eighty-five percent of the 400 million people lived on the land. In general, Sun Yat-sen wanted the land to go to the tiller and its products to be shared more equitably. But his KMT — the National Party — tried to further its ends by conspiracy and arrangements between individuals and cliques. The people whom the revolution's reforms were supposed to benefit —

the tillers of the soil — were not mobilised or even consulted. Sun himself realised his mistake, but it was left to the communists, acting on their own analysis, and allying with members of the revolutionary wing of the KMT, to lead a new peasant revolution beginning with the formation of peasant associations in 1923.

Sun's programme of 'equalisation of land ownership' in a bourgeois democracy would have created a peasant market and fostered capitalist forces, but such a reform was impossible on a wide scale while China's capital was controlled by foreign interests. Bourgeois revolution was emasculated in China by the foreign powers' reduction of the country to a semi-colony; the indigenous bourgeoisie was not allowed to grow in competition with foreign masters. Leadership of the new-democratic revolution had to pass to a new class and its political party before the liberation from semi-feudal rule in the countryside and from imperialist domination in the cities could be accomplished and the new transition to socialism begin. This class was the working class; its effective army, according to Mao, was the masses of the peasantry; and its party was the Chinese Communist Party, the Kungchantang, or 'Sharing Wealth Party'.

This liberation was not to be effected without a terrible toll, equal to, and probably far surpassing, the losses sustained in the crushing of the revolutions of the nineteenth century. Rewi Alley, a New Zealander who lived in China throughout this period, estimated, in answer to an enquiry from Edgar Snow, that in the two civil wars between the CCP and the KMT alone (that is, excluding the First Revolutionary Civil War against the warlords, and the anti-Japanese war) total casualties on both sides add up to some 50 million dead.

If Mao's thinking was grounded on poverty and suffering, his life shows a part of the Chinese people's long battle to throw off those chains and aspire to a better order of things. The story of Mao's life is embedded in this rich people's movement. To discover its significance, one must dig deep into the condition of modern China as known by its poorest inhabitants, and into the actions of those who rose in revolt against its misery.

1 We Pointed the Finger at Our Land

Early Years, 1893-1923

> I was still confused, looking for a road ... I became more and more convinced that only mass political power, secured through mass action, could guarantee the realisation of dynamic reforms.
>
> Mao to Edgar Snow, *Red Star over China*

Mao Tse-tung was born in the village of Shaoshan in Hunan province on 26 December 1893, one of four children — three sons and a daughter — of Mao Jen-sheng and his wife Wen Chi-mei.

> Shaoshan Chung, a village of Hsiangtan County ... stretches about ten *li* in length. It commands a lovely view, the hills and waters around all having that indefinable touch of the South which travellers find so pleasing. The houses are few and far between; the inhabitants are mostly honest, hard-working peasants. Among the local families is that of Mao.
>
> Shaoshan Chung has an 'Upper South Bank' and a 'Lower South Bank'. On the Lower South Bank is a road leading to the town of Hsiangtan and the adjacent Hsianghsiang County. Along the Upper South Bank is a stone bridge with a few shops clustering around selling meat, salt and other daily necessities. A stream runs under the bridge and meanders on by Shaoshan. Near this stream is a plain, tile-roofed house with two wings in which two families, one named Tsou and the other Mao, used to live. Each occupied half of the house, with the boundary line passing neatly through the middle of the living room. [1]

Mao's father was stern and autocratic; beginning poor, he was thrifty, and when he had saved a little money from trading in pigs and rice he bought an acre or two of land which by careful management brought him more savings. He lent these savings at high rates of interest. Later he turned to buying, transporting and selling grain. Little by little he passed from 'poor', through 'middle' to 'rich' peasant. This lesson in social advance, a cruel man lifting himself by diligence and usury to the relative wealth of a trader, was not lost on Mao Tse-tung.

> My father was in his early days, and in middle age, a sceptic, but my mother devoutly worshipped Buddha. She gave her children religious instruction, and we were all saddened that our father was an unbeliever. When I was nine years old I seriously discussed the problem of my father's lack of piety with my mother. We made many attempts then and later on to convert him, but without success. He only cursed us, and, overwhelmed by his attacks, we withdrew to devise new plans. But he would have nothing to do with the gods . . . Then one day he went out on the road to collect some money, and on his way he met a tiger. The tiger was surprised at the encounter and fled at once, but my father was even more astonished and afterwards reflected a good deal on his miraculous escape. He began to wonder if he had not offended the gods. From then on he showed more respect to Buddhism and burned incense now and then . . . He prayed to the gods only when he was in difficulties. [2]

His mother gave, and received from Tse-tung, more affection. She was kindly and hard-working, and had strong moral feelings. 'There were two "parties" in the family,' Mao said. 'One was my father, the Ruling Power. The opposition was made up of myself, my mother, my brother, and sometimes even a labourer. [But] my mother . . . criticised any overt display of emotion and attempts at open rebellion against the Ruling Power. She said it was not the Chinese way.'

When Tse-tung was about ten, his father cursed him one

day and was going to beat him for his 'laziness' and 'useless-ness'. Tse-tung rushed out in a fury and, saying he would drown himself in a pond, demanded that his father withdraw the threats. He did so, and Tse-tung, too, apologised. This incident, though not untypical of families everywhere, taught Mao about the nature of power, 'When I defended my rights by open rebellion my father relented, but when I remained meek and submissive he only cursed and beat me the more.'

Between the ages of five and seven years he worked on his father's land. Then he went to a local primary school to be taught reading and writing so he could draw up business letters and keep accounts. He knew the classics but preferred the old romances about peasant rebellions which he and his schoolmates read in class, covering them up with a classic when the teacher walked past; they were discussed and redis-cussed. These romances were banned by the old teachers yet loved by the villagers. Education, it seemed, did not include the people's culture. Mao said that for two years he wondered about this. When he analysed even the old romances and tales he found the chief characters were warriors, officials and scholars, though they became bandits. There was never a peasant hero. They glorified those who ruled, 'who did not have to work the land, because they owned and controlled it'.

Mao's teacher used harsh methods.

His repertoire included many forms of corporal punish-ment such as flogging, beating on the palm, head, feet and thighs and 'incense kneeling'. This last required the offender to kneel on a cash-board with sharp ridges or on a patch of gravelly earth for the length of the time it took a whole stick of incense to burn out. Naturally, Mao Tse-tung resisted. The first time he adopted the line of passive resistance, *ie* truancy. He ran away from school and went down the hill in the direction of an imaginary city. After a three-day journey, he discovered he had been going around the valley in circles and was only about ten *li* from home. Eventually, his family found him and brought him back. Upon reaching home he found his father no longer so hot-tempered as before, nor was the teacher so severe. The effect of this resistance left a deep imprint on his young mind. As he himself later on put it, borrowing a new term, he had carried out a successful 'strike'. [3]

At thirteen he left school and hoed the fields and kept the cattle and pigs on the farm during the day and read books at night, covering up the window of his room so his father would not see the light.

I succeeded in continuing my reading, devouring everything I could find except the Classics. This annoyed my father, who wanted me to master the Classics, especially after he was defeated in a lawsuit because of an apt Classical quotation used by his adversary in the Chinese court ... I read a book called *Sheng-shih Wei-yen* [*Words of Warning*, by Chung Kuang-ying], which I liked very much. The author, one of a number of old reformist scholars, thought that the weakness of China lay in her lack of Western appliances — railways, telephones, and steamships — and wanted to have them introduced into the country. My father considered such books a waste of time. He wanted me to read something practical like the Classics, which could help him in winning lawsuits.' [4]

He quarrelled with his father and, disgusted by his labour for him, ran away from home to the house of an unemployed law student where he studied for six months.

That year, 1906, there was a flood in Hunan, causing a famine. The starving sent their spokesmen to the civil governor to beg for relief. He replied, 'Why haven't you any food? There is plenty in the city. I always have enough.' The people were angry at this and they held meetings and demonstrated, finally attacking the government offices and driving out the governor. Later, a new governor arrived and ordered the execution of the leaders of the uprising, whose heads were displayed on poles as a warning.

At the same time, in a dispute at Shaoshan between a local landlord and the secret society, the Ke Lao Hui, the landlord bought a decision in a court of law. The society members rebelled, withdrew to a nearby mountain and built a stronghold. Troops attacked them, and their leader, Pang the Millstone Maker, was captured and beheaded.

During a food shortage the following year, the poor requested that the rich farmers help them. But the rich were selling their rice to the city, so the poor started a movement called 'Let's eat at the big house,' that is, 'Let's take the rice free of charge.' When one of his own consignments was seized Mao's father was angry. Mao did not sympathise with him. On the other hand, he thought the villagers' method was wrong, too. What lasting good would it do them? They would still be as poor the next year.

> These incidents, occurring close together, made lasting impressions on my young mind, already rebellious. In this period also I began to have a certain amount of political consciousness, especially after I read a pamphlet telling of the dismemberment of China. I remember even now that this pamphlet opened with the sentence: 'Alas, China will be subjugated!' It told of Japan's occupation of Korea and Taiwan, of the loss of suzerainty in Indochina, Burma, and elsewhere. After I read this I felt depressed about the future of my country and began to realise that it was the duty of all the people to help save it. [5]

Returning home again, Mao was given a wife six years older than himself, a marriage he refused to consummate. 'I had never lived with her,' he said in 1936, 'and never subsequently did. I did not consider her my wife and at this time gave little thought to her.'

He worked three more years for his father before a cousin told him about the Tungshan Primary School in the neighbouring town of Hsianghsiang. The course was 'modern', laid less emphasis on the Classics and more on the 'new knowledge' from the West, and the teaching methods were 'radical'. At sixteen Mao registered there and lodged at the school for a year, his father finally agreeing after friends had pointed out that 'higher' education would increase his son's earning powers.

> I had never before seen so many children together. Most of them were sons of landlords, wearing expensive clothes; very few peasants could afford to send their children to such a school. I was more poorly dressed than the others. I owned only one decent coat-and-trousers suit. Gowns were not worn by students, but only by the teachers, and none but 'foreign devils' wore foreign clothes. Many of the richer students despised me because usually I was wearing my ragged coat and trousers. However, among them I had friends, and two especially were my good comrades.
>
> I was also disliked because I was not a native of Hsianghsiang. It was very important to be a native of Hsianghsiang and also important to be from a certain district of Hsianghsiang. There was an upper, lower and middle district, and lower and upper were continually fighting, purely on a regional basis. Neither could become reconciled to the existence of the other. I took a neutral position in this war, because I was not a native at all. Consequently all three factions despised me. I felt spiritually very depressed. [6]

Mao's course included the classics, essay-writing, natural sciences, history and geography. He learnt something of foreign 'great men' and of the rulers of ancient China. As for the death of the Empress Dowager in 1908 he heard about it two years after the event. And he learnt of America for the first time.

> One evening when the children had finished playing and were crowding into the study-room at the sound of the

bell, Mao Tse-tung found himself in the company of
another boy as he made his way towards the second gate
of the school. The boy was holding a book in his hand.
'What book do you have there?' asked Mao Tse-tung.
'Heroes and Great Men of the World.' 'May I have a
look?' A few days later, Mao Tse-tung returned the
book. His manners were apologetic: 'Forgive me for
smearing your book.' The curious student opened the
book and found many passages marked out with
circles and dots. The most heavily marked were the
biographies of Washington, Napoleon, Peter the Great,
Catherine the Great, Wellington, Gladstone, Rousseau,
Montesquieu and Lincoln. Said Mao Tse-tung: 'We
should strive to make our country strong and prosperous, so as not to follow in the footsteps of Indochina,
Korea and India. You know the ancient Chinese proverb:
"One overturned chariot serves as a warning to the next."
We should all rally together. Ku Yen-wu was perfectly
right in saying, "Every common man has a hand in determining the fate of his nation!"' Then, after a brief
pause, he continued: 'China's decline did not begin
yesterday. Therefore, to make her rich, strong and independent will also take a long time. But we shouldn't let
the length of time worry us. Look here,' he opened the
book and pointed at one page, 'Victory and independence only came to the United States after eight
years of fighting under Washington, eight long, bitter
years . . .' [7]

I made good progress at this school. The teachers
liked me, especially those who taught the Classics,
because I wrote good essays in the Classical manner. But
my mind was not on the Classics. I was reading two
books sent to me by my cousin, telling of the reform
movement of Kang Yu-wei. One was by Liang Chi-chao,
editor of the *Hsin-min Tsung-pao* [New People's Miscel-
lany]. I read and reread these books until I knew them
by heart. I worshipped Kang Yu-wei and Liang Chi-chao.'
[8]

Kang and Liang were reformers, the 'intellectual godfathers' of the 1911 revolution that was about to break out.

At the age of seventeen, in the summer of 1911, Mao walked and boated the forty miles to the city of Changsha, the capital of Hunan province, to take the entrance examination to the Hunan First Middle School. When he arrived in Changsha, the country was on the eve of revolution, the overthrow of the Ching (Manchu) dynasty and the founding of the Republic.

> Changsha ... lies on the Hsiang River in a magnificent setting of hills growing to mountains, of lush fields and dense woods. It was, like all Chinese cities, a maze of small dark houses and twisted mud lanes, yet it held fine temples and residences, parks and great schools. It was, in the early 1900s, more than a provincial capital, a centre of intellectual radicalism ... The hunger and misery of the countryside, despite the fertile soil, filled even 'the scholars' street' with beggars and the corpses of those who had died of starvation.' [9]

The republican uprising broke out on 10 October 1911 in Wuhan. Twelve days later at Changsha the white banners of the revolutionary army proclaimed 'Long live the Great Han Republic.' In a few hours the old imperial administration in the city was swept away. Mao was caught up in the excitement.

> Rebels were approaching the city along the Canton— Hankow railway, and fighting had begun. A big battle occurred outside the city walls of Changsha. There was at the same time an insurrection within the city, and the gates were stormed and taken by Chinese labourers. Through one of the gates I re-entered the city. Then I stood on a high place and watched the battle, until at last I saw the Han flag raised over the *yamen*. It was a white banner with the character *Han* in it. I returned to my school, to find it under military guard. [10]

As a result of reading *The People's Strength*, a publication of Dr. Sun Yat-sen's Alliance Society, he had already written a political essay heralding the republic and stuck it on the wall at school, his first *tatsepao* or big-character poster, a traditional form of public protest which was to become familiar the world over during the cultural revolution in 1966. He had joined with a friend in cutting off their queues, symbolising their rejection of the alien Manchu imperial rule. Now he joined the regular army to 'help complete the revolution.' But there was little fighting to do.

> My salary was seven *yuan* a month and of this I spent two *yuan* a month on food. I also had to buy water. The soldiers had to carry water in from outside the city, but I, being a student, could not condescend to carrying, and bought it from the water peddlers. The rest of my wages were spent on newspapers, of which I became an avid reader. Among journals then dealing with the revolution was the *Hsiang Chiang Jih-pao* [Hsiang River Daily News]. Socialism was discussed in it, and in these columns I first learned the term. I also discussed socialism, really social-reformism, with other students and soldiers. I read some pamphlets written by Kiang Kang-hu about socialism and its principles. I wrote enthusiastically to several of my classmates on this subject, but only one of them responded in agreement. There was a Hunan miner in my squad, and an ironsmith, whom I liked very much. The rest were mediocre, and one was a rascal. I persuaded two more students to join the army, and came to be on friendly terms with the platoon commander and most of the soldiers. I could write, I knew something about books, and they respected my 'great learning'. I could help by writing letters for them or in other such ways. [11]

Sun Yat-sen, whose Alliance Society grouped together numerous anti-Manchu societies, was forced to resign the presidency of the new Republic to the militarist Yuan Shih-kai on 15 February 1912. Mao thought that the revolution was over and left the army to return to his studies and seek a career. Tempted by a number of alluring advertisements he put his name down for a police school, then for courses in soap-making and law, before entering a commercial college. He had assumed he would be taught economics there, a useful subject for helping China's modernisation, but he left after a month because much of the teaching was in English, of which he knew no more than the alphabet.

He spent the next six months at Hunan First Middle School whose restricted curriculum and objectionable regulations convinced him he would be better off studying alone. He drew up a course of his own and went to read at Hunan Provincial Library. His family refused to support him, accusing him of drifting.

I was very regular and conscientious about it, and the half-year I spent in this way I consider to have been extremely valuable to me. I went to the library in the morning when it opened. At noon I paused long enough to buy and eat two rice cakes, which were my daily lunch. I stayed in the library every day reading until it closed.

During this period of self-education I read many books, studied world geography and world history. There for the first time I saw and studied with great interest a map of the world. I read Adam Smith's *The Wealth of Nations*, and Darwin's *Origin of Species* and a book on ethics by John Stuart Mill [Mill's *Logic*]. I read the works of Rousseau, Spencer's *Logic* [*Sociology*], and a book on law written by Montesquieu [*The Spirit of the Laws*]. I mixed poetry and romances, and the tales of ancient Greece, with serious study of history and geography of Russia, America, England, France and other countries.

I was then living in a guild house for natives of Hsianghsiang district. Many soldiers were there also, 'retired' or disbanded men from the district, who had no work to do and little money. Students and soldiers were always quarrelling in the guild house, and one night this hostility between them broke out in physical violence. The soldiers attacked and tried to kill the students. I escaped by fleeing to the toilet, where I hid until the fight was over. [12]

He decided he was most suited to being a teacher. In the spring of 1913 he enrolled at a teachers' training school in Changsha, the Hunan Provincial First Normal School. He found this school more to his liking, and he stayed there until 1918, finally obtaining his degree.

There were many regulations in the new school and I agreed with very few of them. For one thing, I was opposed to the required courses in natural science. I wanted to specialise in social sciences. Natural sciences did not especially interest me, and I did not study them, so I got poor marks in most of these courses ... Fortunately my marks in social sciences were all excellent ...

A Chinese teacher here, whom the students nicknamed 'Yuan the Big Beard', ridiculed my writing and called it the work of a journalist. He despised Liang Chi-chao, who had been my model, and considered him half-literate. I was obliged to alter my style. I studied the writings of Han Yu, and mastered the old Classical phraseology. Thanks to Yuan the Big Beard, therefore, I can today still turn out a passable Classical essay if required. [13]

These years were formative in Mao's intellectual development. They coincided with the decline of Yuan Shih-kai's rule and the start of the warlord period after Yuan's death in July 1916. Between 1913 and 1918 Hunan saw warfare in every year but 1914. Each battle led to the closing of Mao's school until peace returned. From his years studying in this battle-ground, Mao took the moral that it was important to be strong, physically, militarily and in understanding, or else there was little point in being virtuous, for no-one would gain from it. He began to see warfare as a means of consolidating

sufficient strength to allow virtue, and hence good government, to reign. He linked learning to ethics and to virtue. The
notes he made to his careful reading of Paulsen's *A System of
Ethics* reveal his conviction that China's decline would be
ended by a complete reconstruction in which the political
system and the people's characteristics would change. 'Let
destruction play the role of a mother in giving birth to a new
country,' he wrote in the book's margins.

He read fast, showed great powers of concentration, and
wrote lucid essays which he dated precisely on the last page.
He was quiet and preferred to listen, but he was roused to
boldness by irrational rules and by injustices done to his
friends. He successfully disputed his Chinese master's rule
that he should leave out the date on his essays. When a
schoolmate was threatened with an arranged marriage, Mao
made the bride-to-be's uncle, a headmaster, stop the wedding.
In 1915 his school wanted to collect money from its pupils
towards expenses: Mao drafted a manifesto attacking the
headmaster's mismanagement, and came near to being expelled
as a result.

Once, when defeated troops wanted to make their headquarters in the school buildings, Mao led a group of students
at night, armed with real and dummy rifles, and bluffed the
troops into surrendering by shouting that their leader had
fled, thus freeing the school for the students who had nowhere to go after study had been suspended.

His reading of foreign ethics did not lead him especially to
admire western thought. He wanted neither western nor
Chinese traditional civilisation, but a better one, which would
learn from both sources. He tied this ambition to his life's
search. He was encouraged by his philosophy teacher Yang
Chang-chi, whom he described as 'a man of high moral
character'. Yang had studied in Britain, Germany and Japan,
and held idealistic views on self-cultivation, regarding education not as a means to a good career in the civil service but
as a way of breaking out of the restrictions of the self to

some greater life. Yang warned that 'the culture of one country cannot be transplanted in its entirety to another country', meaning that the study of things foreign should be made in order to renovate one's own heritage and stir it to movement. At the same time, Mao met Yang's daughter, whom he was to marry in 1921. His whole memory of his teacher was imbued with a warmth that denoted a strong intellectual, as well as familial, attachment.

Yang Chang-chi's influence was not confined to study but extended to student life styles too. He was opposed to 'the corrupt feudal type of living' and advised his students to live 'in a new, democratic and scientific manner'. The new manner included doing away with breakfast and going in for deep breathing, meditation and cold baths all the year round. Mao Tse-tung, Tsai Ho-shen (one of Mao's best friends, later a communist executed in Canton in 1931) and others imitated Yang with some enthusiasm. For almost two years they went without breakfast.

Mao built up his health with walking, climbing and swimming, agreeing with Yang that exercise was an aspect of mental and spiritual training. He lived frugally and dressed simply from a necessity that did not go against his inclinations.

One year, during the summer vacation, Mao, Tsai and a student named Chang Kun-ti shared a pavilion on top of the Yuehlu Mountain, on the river bank opposite Changsha . . . Their diet consisted largely of fresh broad beans . . . They went to the hilltop to meditate in the morning and then came down to bathe in a cold pond or in the river. This went on until the end of the vacation . . . They also enlarged what the term 'bathing' usually connotes, often stripping and exposing their bodies to the elements: sun, wind and downpours. Mao Tse-tung referred to these practices facetiously as 'sunbath', 'windbath', and 'rainbath' . . . All this was intended to help build up a strong constitution.

Another hobby of theirs was 'voice-training'. They

would go to the hills and shout or recite the poets of the Tang dynasty; or climb up the city walls and there inflate their lungs and yell to the roaring winds ... During their stay in the pavilion, each of them had only one towel, one umbrella and some clothes. Mao was always clad in a long grey gown which distinguished him from the rest. At night they slept out in the open, in a meadow, keeping far apart from each other, to give themselves plenty of fresh air. When they later went back to school they continued to sleep out in the playground right up to the cold season. In recalling these days, Mao once wrote the following words in his diary:

'To struggle against Heaven, what joy!

To struggle against Earth, what joy!' [14]

In April 1917 Mao published an essay which attempted to lay a practical basis to this cult of the body.

Our nation is wanting in strength. The military spirit has not been encouraged. The physical condition of the population deteriorates daily. This is an extremely disturbing phenomenon. The promoters of physical education have not grasped the essence of the problem, and therefore their efforts, though prolonged, have not been effective. If this state continues, our weakness will increase further. To attain our goals and to make our influence felt are external matters, results. The development of our physical strength is an internal matter, a cause. If our bodies are not strong we will be afraid as soon as we see enemy soldiers, and then how can we attain our goals and make ourselves respected? Strength depends on drill, and drill depends on self-awareness ... Physical education complements education in virtue and knowledge. Moreover, both virtue and knowledge reside in the body. Without the body there would be neither virtue nor knowledge ... Physical education really occupies the first place in our lives. When the body is strong, then one can advance speedily in knowledge and morality, and reap far-reaching advantages. It should be regarded as an important part of our study. [15]

Mao's disposition was already towards turning such military discipline and will to the service of revolt against injustice. His month's 'investigation tour' of the villages near Changsha during the summer vacation in 1917 had broadened his knowledge of peasant conditions.

On the evening of the autumn festival in 1917, a picnic was held by some of the college students at a famous spot on the outskirts of Changsha. As usual their conversation turned on 'saving the country'. Which was the best way to save the country?

'To build a large army,' said one student.

'To learn science, build railways and factories,' said another.

'To become a politician and sweep away corruption,' said someone else.

Mao Tse-tung was silent, his eyes fixed on the ground. He appeared to dream. Someone turned to him. 'What do you think?'

'It takes money and influence to become a politician,' Mao Tse-tung replied. 'As to learning science or becoming a teacher, that also requires money and influence and time. To build an army . . . what kind of an army that would not oppress the people could one build . . . unless one does like the heroes of Liang Shan-po . . .'

At this the others laughed, and the talk turned to heroes of old.

The heroes of Liang Shan-po are the heroes of the Chinese people. In *Water Margin*, Mao's favourite book, 108 rebels, called 'bandits' by the ruling power, gather in a mountain fortress to fight for justice against tyranny. [16]

Out of such musings and debates between friends came more serious societies and study groups, all critical of the warlord misrule. One such, the New People's Study Society, which Mao helped to found, came into being on 18 April 1918. Many of its members were to take leading parts in the growth of the Communist Party. The purpose of these student societies was to resist unreasonable authority in college, to study the new ideas and assist national regeneration.

Mao taught an evening class at the First Normal School where senior students passed on their learning to workers. Here he discovered that the literary language was difficult for workers to understand. He lectured in the vernacular on history and current affairs, read the newspapers to the workers and led them in discussion. He advertised the course on posters saying, 'Do come and listen to some plain speech.' He later told Edgar Snow, 'At this time my mind was a curious mixture of ideas of liberalism, democratic reformism and utopian socialism. I had somewhat vague passions about "nineteenth century democracy", utopianism, and old-fashioned liberalism, and I was definitely antimilitarist and anti-imperialist.'

He made the acquaintance of a student, Li Li-san, who was later to oppose him politically, and he began to correspond with two other men whose names would become famous in the history of the Communist Party, the scholar Li Ta-chao, and Chen Tu-hsiu, Dean of the Faculty of Letters at Peking University, then the country's main intellectual centre.

Some members of the New People's Study Society in Changsha wanted to go to France as students on a work-study scheme. Mao travelled with them to Peking in September 1918 but decided not to go on to France: 'I felt that I did not know enough about my own country and that my time could more profitably be spent in China.' In the next six months in Peking the intellectual stimulus he received turned him from a politically conscious provincial student into an embryonic revolutionary activist.

In Peking he worked as a minor assistant to Li Ta-chao, the librarian of Peking University, who, as professor of political economy on Mao's arrival, was just beginning to hail the Russian revolution and to assimilate its ideas. Chen Tu-hsiu, on the other hand, at that time advocated parliamentary democracy and thought highly of the French system. His articles impressed Mao, who admitted to a third line of influence, anarchism, through the writings of Bakunin, Kropotkin and Tolstoy. He was 'confused, looking for a road'.

My own living conditions in Peking were quite miserable, and in contrast the beauty of the old capital was a vivid and living compensation. I stayed in a place called San Yen-ching ['Three-Eyes Well'], in a little room which held seven other people. When we were all packed fast on the *kang* [bed] there was scarcely room enough for any of us to breathe. I used to have to warn people on each side of me when I wanted to turn over. But in the parks and the old palace grounds I saw the early northern spring, I saw the white plum blossoms flower while the ice still held solid over Pei Hai ['the North Sea' – a lake in the former Forbidden City]. I saw the willows over Pei Hai with the ice crystals hanging from them and remembered the description of the scene by the Tang poet Chen Chang, who wrote about Pei Hai's winter-jewelled trees looking 'like ten thousand peach trees blossoming'. The innumerable trees of Peking aroused my wonder and admiration. [17]

His lowly job led him to experience, too, the arrogance of intellectuals. To most of them, 'I didn't exist as a human being.' Famous names of the newly emerging national renaissance movement with whom he tried to speak when they visited the library 'had no time to listen to an assistant librarian speaking southern dialect'. But as a member of the philosophy and journalism societies at Peking University, he listened in on lectures, though he was not a student, and joined Li Ta-chao's Marxist Study Group.

Mao returned to Changsha via Nanking and Shanghai in March 1919 and took up a teaching post in a Changsha primary school. The great student demonstrations of 4 May 1919 in Peking and the movement they supported, with its demands for national independence, democracy, reform of the language, science and a break with traditions including Confucianism and superstition, gave impetus to the rising ferment in Hunan.

Mao later wrote that the May 4th Movement marked the dividing line between 'old democracy' and 'new democracy' in China. Before the Movement, he said, the political guiding force of the Chinese bourgeois-democratic revolution of the 'old type' was the intelligentsia of the Chinese petty-bourgeois and bourgeois classes. After it, he claimed, political leadership of the 'new-democratic' revolution fell to the proletariat.

Mao lectured on Marxism and the revolution, wrote articles and helped form a United Students' Association for Hunan province. When arrests of students in Peking in June were followed by strikes of merchants and workers in other cities, Mao's Hunan group welcomed this first sign of solidarity among 'the popular masses' by forming a wider provincial association open to all social classes, not merely students.

Mao published articles celebrating 'the union of the popular masses' in the weekly *Hsiang River Review*, which he began to edit in July, in which he showed that a huge progressive force was latent in the Chinese people. This *Review*, in common with most of the new political writing that summer, was written in a reformed language easier for the uneducated to understand, and consequently had a far wider circulation than previous literary-political journals. The Changsha authorities soon closed down the *Review* and its successor *New Hunan*.

Mao wrote in the *Review*,

What is the greatest question in the world? The greatest question is that of getting food to eat. What is the greatest force? The greatest force is that of the union of the popular masses. What should we not fear? We should not fear heaven. We should not fear ghosts. We should not fear the dead. We should not fear the bureaucrats. We should not fear the militarists. We should not fear the capitalists ... If we do not speak, who will speak?

If we do not act, who will act? If we do not rise up and fight, who will rise up and fight? . . . Our Chinese people possesses great intrinsic energy. The more profound the oppression, the greater its resistance; that which has accumulated for a long time will surely burst forth quickly. The great union of the Chinese people must be achieved.

If we study history, we find that all the movements that have occurred in the course of history, of whatever type they may be, have all without exception resulted from the union of a certain number of people. A greater movement naturally requires a greater union, and the greatest movement requires the greatest union . . . Why is the great union of the popular masses so terribly effective? Because the popular masses in any country are much more numerous than the aristocracy, the capitalists, and the other holders of power in society . . . If we wish to achieve a great union, in order to resist the powerful people whom we face who harm their fellow men, and in order to pursue our own interests, we must necessarily have many small unions to serve as its foundation.

We are peasants, and so we want to unite with others who cultivate the land like we do . . . The interests of we who cultivate the land can only be protected by ourselves! . . . How do the landlords treat us? Are the rents and taxes heavy or light? Are our houses satisfactory or not? Are our bellies full or not? Is there enough land? Are there those in the village who have no land to cultivate? We must constantly seek answers to all these questions . . . We are workers, we wish to unite with others who work like ourselves in order to pursue the various interests of we workers . . . We cannot fail to seek a solution to questions concerning us as workers, such as the level of our wages, the length of the working day, and the equal or unequal sharing of dividends . . . We are students, we are already living in the twentieth century, and yet they still compel us to observe the old ceremonies and the old methods. The country is about to perish, and yet they still paste up posters forbidding us to love our country . . . We want our own union . . . We are women, we are sunk even deeper in a sea of bitterness, we want to carry out our union. [18]

Mao helped organise a strike of primary and secondary school students in December 1919 but the repressive climate became stronger. He was sent to Peking in January 1920 as a representative to the New People's Study Society and other democratic groups who opposed the warlord rule of the Hunan governor Chang Ching-yao. In Peking he read Kautsky's *Class Struggle*, Engels' *Socialism: Utopian and Scientific*, *The Communist Manifesto* and Kirkup's *History of Socialism*, all just translated into Chinese, and he headed a news agency which promoted anti-militarism. In April he went to Shanghai and met Chen Tu-hsiu, whose development was also now towards Marxism. Mao worked there as a laundryman and in July, with the expulsion of Governor Chang from Changsha, he returned to Hunan, where he was made director of the primary school attached to Changsha's First Normal School.

By then he counted himself a Marxist in theory and 'to some extent in action.' Although supporting the movement towards a bourgeois democracy for Hunan as an interim improvement, he did not believe the 'gradual method' of revolution through trade unionism and through education in school and propaganda would succeed. While the ruling class controlled these channels for their own consolidation, how could socialism dominate? When Bertrand Russell spoke against Bolshevism in Changsha at the end of 1920, Mao expressed scepticism that socialism could be achieved without armed struggle against the ruling class.

In his lecture at Changsha, Russell . . . took a position in favour of communism but against the dictatorship of the workers and peasants. He said that one should employ the method of education to change the consciousness of the propertied classes, and that in this way it would not be necessary to limit freedom or to have recourse to war and bloody revolution . . . My objections to Russell's viewpoint can be stated in a few words: 'This is all very well as a theory, but it is not feasible in practice.' . . . Those who have charge of education are all capitalists or slaves of capitalists. In today's world, the schools and the press, the two most important instruments of education, are entirely under capitalist control . . . If we teach capitalism to children, these children, when they grow up, will in turn teach capitalism to a second generation of children. Education thus remains in the hands of capitalists . . . If the communists do not seize political power, how could they take charge of education? . . . [My] second argument is that, based on the principle of mental habits and on my observation of human history, I am of the opinion that one absolutely cannot expect the capitalists to become converted to communism . . . If one wishes to use the power of education to transform them, then since one cannot obtain control of the whole or even an important part of the two instruments of education — schools and the press — even if one has a mouth and a tongue and one or two schools and newspapers as means of propaganda, this is really not enough to change the mentality of the adherents of capitalism even slightly. How then can one hope that the latter will repent and turn toward the good? [19]

Mao sided with those of his friends who favoured forming a Communist Party as the nerve-centre of the revolutionary and labour movements. Alternative power could only be built by forming a counter-attractive force, a party whose growth would weaken and finally overthrow the rulers. In this Mao began to show the dual nature of his thinking, containing elements of destruction and creation, and his goal of releasing the latent energies and political creativity of the people. He wrote to a friend in the New People's Study Society,

The old atmosphere of China is too heavy and suffocating. We certainly need a new, powerful atmosphere in order to be able to change it. We must have a group of people, fearless of hardships and strong willed for the creation of this new atmosphere; what we need more is commonly accepted political philosophy. No new atmosphere can be created without such a political philosophy. I think our Society must not remain merely a gathering of men based on personal feelings, but rather it should be transformed into an association based on a political philosophy. A political philosophy is like a banner which gives hope and a sense of direction, once it is hoisted. [20]

Mao set about choosing candidates for party membership. He opened the Culture Bookshop for Marxist literature, whose proceeds later went to the Chinese Communist Party (CCP) and which was not closed until the 1927 'Horse Day' mass-acre in Changsha. In August 1920 he helped sponsor a work-study scheme for students to go to Russia. In September or October he formed the first communist group in Changsha and he began party work as a labour organiser. He started more study groups and a socialist youth corps, and circulated the first issues of the Shanghai *Communist Party Monthly* amongst students and in the local party group.

In the winter of 1920-1 he married Yang Kai-hui. He had met her again in Peking and they had fallen in love. For a year and a half they rented a small isolated cottage amongst fields of vegetables on the outskirts of Changsha. Marxist groups met secretly at their house. Their marriage was known as a model among Hunan radical youth. Yang Kai-hui became a youth leader and an active communist before her capture by the Kuomintang police in 1930. She refused to renounce her marriage to Mao or her communist principles and was exe-cuted by Ho Chien, then governor of Hunan. Mao always mourned 'my proud poplar'.

In these 'crowded months and years of endeavour', Mao

and his colleagues nevertheless found time to get together a
'Weekend Club' which visited scenic spots in and around
Changsha on Sundays. One autumn evening they boated
down the Hsiang River near the city, viewing the moon and
discussing the future. They spent the best part of a night in
this way, circling Orange Island west of the city and returning
home only in the small hours. This outing and the whole
period was recalled by Mao in his poem *Changsha*, which he
wrote when he came back to Changsha in the autumn of
1926.

> Alone I stand in the autumn cold
> And watch the river northward flowing
> Past the Orange Island shore,
> And I see a myriad hills all tinged with red,
> Tier upon tier of crimsoned woods.
> On the broad stream, intensely blue,
> A hundred jostling barges float;
> Eagles strike at the lofty air,
> Fish hover among the shallows;
> A million creatures under this freezing sky are striving for
>   freedom.
> In this immensity, deeply pondering,
> I ask the great earth and the boundless blue
> Who are the masters of all nature?
>
> I have been here in days past with a throng of companions;
> During those crowded months and years of endeavour,
> All of us students together and all of us young,
> Our bearing was proud, our bodies strong,
> Our ideals true to a scholar's spirit;
> Just and upright, fearless and frank,
> We pointed the finger at our land,
> We praised and condemned through our writings,
> And those in high positions we counted no more than dust.
> But don't you remember
> How, when we reached mid-stream, we struck the waters,
> How the waves dashed against the speeding boats?

In the early summer of 1921, Mao travelled incognito to

Shanghai for the founding conference of the Chinese Communist Party which took place in July, in the face of police intimidation. The ten years of the Republic that succeeded the old Empire in 1911 had been dominated by warlords, with no sign of effective rebuilding of political institutions and central administration. The country was divided, torn apart by warlord ambitions. China, like Mao, was looking for a way: 1 July 1921 marked the birth of a party that proved able to chart that way.

The First Congress, attended by only thirteen delegates and two Comintern representatives, committed the communists to remain independent of other parties and to bring about the overthrow of the capitalist class with the 'revolutionary army of the proletariat'. It is probable Mao argued against this decision and inclined to a policy of a united front with Sun Yat-sen's Kuomintang (KMT).

Mao was made secretary of the party's Hunan branch. He continued organising the province's labour and youth movements upon his return from Shanghai. He and Yang Kai-hui established a 'Self-education University' and an adult education movement. He wrote school textbooks whose first lesson taught the words 'labour', 'worker' and 'exploitation'. He set up clubs for Anyuan miners and Hankow-Canton Railway workers, being joined in this work by Li Li-san and Liu Shao-chi. The clubs at first did little to improve conditions. A strike in September 1922 was suppressed by troops who killed six strikers and wounded seventy. Wages were then raised for a while and trade unions permitted. But, more important, Mao taught the miners *they* were the masters of their destiny, not the pit owners.

After interviewing Anyuan miners in 1970, Han Suyin wrote:

> Old miners still remember how Mao talked to them, how incredible it all seemed that an 'educated' young man should go down the pits, blacken his hands, crawl through the narrow tunnels where stunted waifs of ten

or twelve pushed the coal carts, sit in their hovels, take notes of what they said, then tell them to take fate in their hands ... Mao made them recall how they had risen with the peasants, in the previous famines, against Japanese imperialism in 1915. 'History is in your hands,' said Mao Tse-tung. 'History is yours to make.'

A sense of their own power spread to workers in other industries, and by the end of 1922 more than twenty unions in Hunan combined into an association headed by Mao.

By 1923 Changsha was no safe place for Mao, the governor Chao Heng-ti having ordered the arrest of this troublesome organiser. In April that year Mao left Hunan again for Shanghai. He arrived there at a time when the militarists had shown their power, and the workers' weakness, in the 7 February 1923 massacre of striking railwaymen on the Peking—Hankow Railway.

It was also a time when the CCP was debating the merits of joining in a temporary alliance with the bourgeois democratic forces of the KMT against the warlords. The CCP's Second Congress in July 1922, which Mao missed, had adopted the alliance policy. Mao believed, with Lenin, that such an alliance must preserve the independence of the proletarian movement. For their part, the KMT, under Sun Yat-sen, aimed to carry out the Three People's Principles of nationalism, democracy and socialism, and agreed to admit communists to membership of their party as individuals.

At the Third CCP Congress in June 1923, which Mao attended, the Central Committee finally approved Stalin's strategy of going further than alliance. The communists were to form a '*bloc* within' the KMT. On the left of the party, Chang Kuo-tao opposed any alliance with the KMT. On the right, Chen Tu-hsiu, reversing his previous attitude, argued in favour of the united front since it would allow revolutionary elements of both the bourgeoisie and the working class to fight together against the warlords. He was even prepared to relinquish the leadership of the revolution to the bourgeoisie until such time as the bourgeois Republic could be replaced by the dictatorship of the proletariat. Mao opposed both lines and proposed a united front that would preserve the CCP's autonomy. Yet he was ready to give a very important role in the national revolution to the merchants, since there were signs many of them were rising to oppose the warlords. He appealed in July 1923 to all those 'who suffer under a common oppression' to bind together into 'a closely knit united front'.

Mao's view was accepted by the party but Chen Tu-hsiu's leadership continued to vacillate on this issue after the Third Congress. Mao was elected to the Central Committee. The communists began to build a left wing within the KMT and to use the KMT's organisational structure to make contacts and spread propaganda. Sun Yat-sen agreed to the appointment of Borodin as Russian adviser to help the KMT in reorganisation and to provide it with a modern army.

Thus the period began of the first united front with the KMT. It was also the period when Mao decided to turn to the countryside, rather than to industry, to find the mass base for a successful proletarian-led revolution in China.

2 Who are Our Enemies? Who are Our Friends?

The First Revolutionary Civil War, 1924–1927

> But after all, ours was then still an infant party; it lacked experience concerning the three basic problems of the united front, armed struggle and party building. It did not have much knowledge of Chinese history and Chinese society or of the specific features and laws of the Chinese revolution, and it lacked a comprehensive understanding of the unity between the theory of Marxism–Leninism and the practice of the Chinese revolution.
>
> Mao Tse-tung, *Introducing 'The Communist'*

On 1 January 1924 the first national congress of the Kuomintang opened in Kwangchow (Canton) and Mao attended as a Hunan delegate. The composition of the leadership elected there suggested that the left wing would be more influential than the right in implementing policy decisions, though they were not in a majority as regards policy making. Rifts soon showed between left and right, and after Sun Yat-sen's death in March 1925 they quickly deepened, although in outward form the united front between the two parties lasted until 1927.

Mao became secretary of the organisation department of the Shanghai branch of the KMT in February 1924, but he could achieve little to coordinate KMT and CCP propaganda. To him it was clear that one or the other party must be dominant in the front and at that time it was evidently not the CCP. He claimed that there was little contact between the people and the 'high-level functionaries sitting in posts in Kwangchow and doing nothing'. The national revolution lacked leadership. High bureaucrats gave orders 'empty of significance'. The leaders were divorced from the people: they had not investigated conditions.

The Shanghai in which Mao worked in 1924 was already the foreign merchants' and the Chinese compradors' paradise — a 'pearl of a city', a high British official was to call it. The report of the Shanghai Child Labour Commission (1924) described a feature of this pearl:

> In many mills the conditions during the night shift are, according to Western ideas, most unusual. Rows of baskets containing babies and children, sleeping or awake, as the case may be, lie placed between the rapidly moving and noisy machinery. Young children, who are supposed to be working, but who have been overcome by fatigue or who have taken advantage of the absence of adequate supervision, lie asleep in every corner, some in the open, others hidden in baskets under a covering of raw cotton.

The English editor of the *Peking and Tientsin Times*, H. G. W. Woodhead, commenting on the report in his book *The Truth about the Chinese Republic*, said, 'Appalling though conditions are in many of the factories, they are the outgrowth of the peculiar conditions existing in a country where life is held so cheap, where the average earnings of the unskilled adult worker amount to only a few pence a day, and where, over large areas, it is cheaper to use human porters than beasts of burden.'

In the opinion of the Chinese Cotton Mill Owners' Association, 'The employment of children by mills is a matter of charitable nature towards the parent workers; for so long as their children are employed it adds to their income, relieving the burden of supporting their children, and also removes their anxiety for the safety of their children, who, from the parents' point of view, are safer and more comfortable in the mills than they would be if left to run wild on the street.'

These were Chinese-owned mills: in the Chinese factories of the Foreign Settlement in Shanghai, thirteen percent of the workers were boys and girls under twelve. Higher percentages were employed in foreign-owned factories: sixteen percent in American, seventeen percent in British, forty-five percent in Italian, forty-seven percent in French. There were generally two twelve-hour shifts for these children, day and night. In the British-owned Yangtszepoo cotton mill 700 out of 2,800 employees were children under twelve.

Liberal factory regulations had been passed by the KMT government in Kwangchow to improve labour conditions but they were unknown to, or ignored by, the local authorities throughout the country. Its inability to enforce its own laws gradually created the impression that the Republic and its institutions were a myth.

Mao drew attention to bureaucratic corruption in his scheme for the reorganisation of the KMT party structure, a report he drew up in Shanghai in 1924. While the report recommended a purification of the KMT's methods of work, Mao drew the conclusion in private that the rightists in the KMT, allied to the compradors and the militarists, would never support a revolution to the extent of throwing out the warlords, corrupt landlords and foreign factory owners. The demands of capital, most of all foreign capital, and the influence of rural feudalism, were too strong. The journalist Arthur Ransome, reporting from China in 1926 in his book *The Chinese Puzzle*, concluded that 'the interests of the large class of compradors and other Chinese working for or in connection with foreign firms are identical with foreign interests'. Or as Mao put it, 'When one of our foreign masters farts, it is a lovely perfume.'

When he finally made his *Analysis of the Classes in Chinese Society* in 1926, Mao described the landlord and comprador classes as 'wholly appendages of the international bourgeoisie, depending on imperialism for their survival and growth ... Their existence is utterly incompatible with the aims of the Chinese revolution.'

The propagandists of the 'foreign masters' similarly admitted the unreality of the Republic under the warlords.

'She has never been a republic in aught but name since the abdication of the Manchus in February 1912,' wrote the same editor of the *Peking and Tientsin Times*. 'China, a country in which, until recently, the military profession has been held in disrepute, has now become the prey of rival militarists, who have expanded their armies until they have become a veritable incubus, absorbing every cent of the national revenues on which they can lay their hands.' But he doubted the Chinese people's ability to resist the warlords. 'The Chinese is not noted for moral courage. He can easily be worked up into a state of hysteria against foreigners, but he is more likely meekly to submit to, or to attempt to buy off, oppressors of his own race. Successful resistance to oppression might have been organised in the days when the Chinese soldier was equipped with spears and bows and arrows. It is a different matter to resist a tyranny enforced by coolies equipped with rifles, automatic pistols and artillery.'

The foreign firms' economic intervention in the Republic, on the other hand, was held to be exemplary; it was in no way connected with China's chaos under the warlords. The same commentator wrote,

> It has become customary, since the inception of Bolshevik propaganda in China, to describe foreign commerce in that country as the 'economic exploitation' of the Chinese worker. Nothing could, in reality, be further from the truth, unless the development of any legitimate commerce is thus to be described . . . It is to foreign enterprise that China owes the development of her important export trade in pigs' bristles.

And he quoted 'an obviously well-informed writer' in his own newspaper,

> As for 'exploitation' in the selfish manner charged against foreign firms by Moscow nursery rhymes, it simply does not exist. In the main part foreign firms, compradors, dealers and producers have worked together

in the interests of trade . . . Prices that foreigners obtain
are governed by the same law that rules the world's
markets, supply and demand . . . If there is any selfish
exploitation in connection with the export trade it takes
place long before the article reaches the godowns of the
Treaty Port foreign buyer. Whatever unfair profits are
made in the deal are made by the Chinese themselves. It
is not denied that many foreigners make, or have made,
their 'pile' in the China trade, but their total fortunes
are a mere bagatelle compared with what is made by the
Chinese from the ultimate producer down to the comprador, and the Chinese Government Customs.

The editor concluded that 'it would take far greater shrewd-
ness than the average foreigner possesses to "exploit" the
Chinese, who are "born traders", and have nothing to fear
from any western competition in their own field.'

Nevertheless, it was sometimes necessary to back up this
friendly competition with something more impressive. While
pointing out, 'We cannot coerce China into trading with us,'
Lloyd George made it clear in 1927 that 'in so far as the
[KMT] leaders are inexperienced and at times incompetent
to control the emotions they have aroused in their followers,
we may be compelled to use force to protect our rights until
saner councils prevail', the force being in 1927 a battalion of
the Coldstream Guards. British Liberal and Conservative
leaders were united in uttering such threats.

The British regarded reforms in China essentially as
measures to protect their own merchants. The system of
extraterritoriality (by which foreign nationals in China were
subject to the jurisdiction, not of Chinese courts, but of
judicial authorities maintained there by foreign governments)
had inflicted 'time-honoured indignities' upon China. This
Lloyd George admitted, and the KMT were now 'resolved to
cast them off'. He agreed with the Foreign Secretary, Sir
Austen Chamberlain, that extraterritoriality must go because
it 'no longer provides security and protection for the peaceful

avocations of our merchants'. Arthur Ransome reported, 'It must be realised that the British troops, though illegally in China, are part of Sir Austen Chamberlain's conciliatory policy.' And Lloyd George gave a broad hint for the future, 'With prudent handling [the KMT] may prove our best friends.' Ransome agreed, and concluded that the revolution of the KMT in 'trying to shrug off whatever in their opinion impedes [China's] economic development', namely, feudalism and imperialism, was no different from all 'respectable "bourgeois" revolutions'.

This was exactly Mao's analysis too, and he went further in ascribing these respectable intentions to some of the CCP's policies also. He saw that the CCP lacked an analysis of classes and neglected the peasantry. It seemed the CCP hoped to effect a revolution from above through a clique of leftist KMT and rightist CCP officials without seeking the widest support among the people. Mao insisted on the importance of recruiting and training cadres for rural work. It was, he felt, in the countryside that the fight against landlords was of immediate significance – the peasants had already begun to rise – since in the countryside lay the possibility of gaining an effective mass power base for the revolutionary movement.

But the CCP's Fourth Congress in January 1925 decided to concentrate on spreading the party's influence in the trade unions. Party membership increased*, especially among workers, as a result of the shooting of strikers in Shanghai and Kwangchow by the Japanese and British in May and June 1925. The shootings provoked a nationwide series of strikes and protests and gave further impetus to the peasant uprisings.

---

*The CCP's membership in 1921 was about 60. By 1923 it was 400, by May 1925 about 1,000 and by November 1925 over 10,000. In 1926 at least sixty-six percent of the CCP's 30,000 members could be classified as proletarian. Another twenty-two percent were termed intellectuals. Only five percent were peasants and two percent soldiers. By early 1930, after the KMT betrayal and Mao's withdrawal to the Kiangsi hills, workers totalled only eight percent of the membership, of whom two percent were industrial workers. The remainder were peasants and soldiers.

Mao's view, that the focus of the revolutionary movement was slowly changing to party work in the countryside, was regarded as rightist by the leaders who dominated the Fourth Congress, and he was not re-elected to the Central Committee.

After the Congress Mao retired to his native Shaoshan to recover from an illness. He was chastened by his experience in the KMT's organisation department and unhappy at the preponderance of city-oriented intellectuals in the CCP. He spent the following months studying the extent and growth of rural unrest and laying the foundations of a Hunan peasant movement.

The first peasant association had been organised in Haifeng, Kwangtung province, early in 1923. Its leader, Peng Pai, the son of a shopkeeper who had married a poor peasant woman, 'addressed meetings of peasants at the crossroads,' according to the story told by his mother after 1949, 'composed simple songs in folk tunes but with new content, distributed leaflets with no writing but printed with photographs, cartoons or woodcuts which would convey his message to the illiterate peasants'. Peng Pai ran the KMT's Peasant Movement Training Institute when it was set up in Kwangchow in 1924.

In 1925-6 Peng Pai mobilised a peasant army which defeated the local warlord. When the KMT turned against the communists in 1927, Peng Pai established a workers' and peasants' government in his Haifeng county. Under pressure from Chiang Kai-shek's forces, he retreated into the hills, only to reappear four months later when he re-established soviets (people's representative councils) in Haifeng and Lufeng counties. They were again short-lived. Chiang Kai-shek succeeded in crushing them and Peng Pai was captured in Shanghai, betrayed by a traitor. He was arrested, tortured for many days (one by one his ears, tongue, feet and legs were cut off) and finally was killed by a bullet through the heart.

After his death, his mother 'could not even cry aloud except at night' since KMT assassins were searching for Peng's family. His two brothers and his wife were ambushed and killed in Macao by KMT agents. Seven children of his and his brothers were starved to death in a KMT jail and six other members of the family were executed, all because they were related to Peng Pai. The entire family property in Haifeng was confiscated and their houses burnt. Only his mother lived, and became a much-honoured figure after liberation in 1949. This story was typical of many after the KMT betrayal.

When Mao reached Shaoshan at the end of January 1925, the united front was officially still in operation and it was as a KMT party worker as well as a communist that Mao began his rural investigations. He divided the population around Changsha into landlords and rich peasants (ten percent), middle peasants (twenty percent) and poor peasants (seventy percent). He further subdivided the categories:

> No matter where you go in the villages, if you are a careful observer, you will see the following eight different types of people: big landlords; small landlords; peasant landholders; semi-landholders; sharecroppers; poor peasants; farm labourers and rural artisans; *éléments déclassés*. These eight types of people form eight separate classes. Their economic status and standard of living differs, this in turn influences their psychology, so that their attitudes towards revolution also differ. [1]

Of the poor, the poorest obviously had most to gain:

> The poor peasants do not have sufficient farm implements nor do they have any circulating capital. They are short of fertilisers and reap only a meagre harvest from the fields. After paying the rent, very little is left for them. During years of famine or difficult months, they beg from relatives and friends, appealing for a few measures of grain to tide them over for four or five days. Their debts pile up like the burden on the backs of draught oxen. They are the most miserable among the peasants and are most receptive to revolutionary propaganda.
>
> The farm labourers, or agricultural proletariat, include

those hired by the year, the month, or the day. These farm labourers possess neither land nor tools, nor do they have any circulating capital. Hence they can subsist only by their labour. With their long hours of work, their low salaries, the treatment they receive, and the insecurity of their employment, they are worse off than the other workers. This group of people is the most distressed in the rural areas and should be given the greatest attention by those who are organising peasant movements. [2]

The *éléments déclassés*, known generally as the *lumpen-*proletariat (and to the gentry as riffraff), numbered some 20 million in China at that time;

[They] consist of peasants who have lost their land, handicraftsmen who have lost all opportunity of employment as a result of oppression and exploitation by the imperialists, the militarists, and the landlords, or as a result of floods and droughts. They can be divided into soldiers, bandits, robbers, beggars, and prostitutes. These five categories of people have different names, and they enjoy a somewhat different status in society. But they are all human beings, and they all have five senses and four limbs, and are therefore one. They each have a different way of making a living: the soldier fights, the bandit robs, the thief steals, the beggar begs, and the prostitute seduces. But to the extent that they must all earn their livelihood and cook rice to eat, they are one. They lead the most precarious existence of any human being ... These people are capable of fighting very bravely, and, if properly led, can become a revolutionary force. [3]

Mao summed up the approach of the peasant associations:

Our work of organising the peasantry involves gathering the five kinds of peasants into a single organisation: the peasant landholders, semi-landholders, sharecroppers, poor peasants, and farm labourers and handicraftsmen.

In principle, the peasants should adopt the method of struggle in their relations with the landlord class, demanding from them economic and political concessions. In special circumstances, when one encounters particularly reactionary and bad gentry and local bullies who exploit the people savagely, as in Haifeng and Huangning, the peasants should overthrow them altogether. As for the *éléments déclassés*, one should exhort them to side with the peasants' associations and to join the big revolutionary movement to help solve the problem of unemployment; one should never force them to go over to the side of the enemy and become a force in the service of the counter-revolutionaries. [4]

When he published his *Analysis of the Classes in Chinese Society* in the magazine *Chung-kuo Nung-min* (*The Chinese Peasant*) in February 1926, based on these investigations, Mao combined the various classes into five main categories, so that it was easier to recognise 'Who are our enemies? Who are our friends?' These five categories were the landlord class and the comprador class (the big bourgeoisie), the middle (or national) bourgeoisie, the petty-bourgeoisie (including the middle peasants), the semi-proletariat (mainly the poor and lower-middle peasants) and the proletariat.

Representing the new productive forces, the industrial proletariat, 'though not very numerous . . . has become the leading [or major] force in the [national] revolutionary movement'. As for the middle (or national) bourgeoisie, representing capitalist relations of production in town and country, it was a vacillating class which, like the petty-bourgeoisie, would side with counter-revolution rather than revolution when forced to choose between the two. It would try to fight imperialism in the name of the nation, while a few individuals from that class would side with the revolutionary wing of the nationalist movement and would join the revolution rather than betray it.

This outline class analysis of Mao's, the listing of the five categories, remained valid for him up until 1949. But it was originally written, according to a note in the *Selected Works*,

> to combat two deviations then to be found in the party. The exponents of the first deviation, represented by Chen Tu-hsiu, [who refused to print Mao's *Analysis* in the party press] were concerned only with co-operation with the KMT and forgot about the peasants; this was Right opportunism. The exponents of the second deviation, represented by Chang Kuo-tao, were concerned only with the labour movement, and likewise forgot about the peasants; this was 'Left' opportunism. Both were aware that their own strength was inadequate, but neither of them knew where to seek reinforcements or where to obtain allies on a mass scale. Comrade Mao Tse-tung pointed out that the peasantry was the staunchest and numerically the largest ally of the Chinese proletariat, and thus solved the problem of who was the chief ally in the Chinese revolution.

Before the *Analysis* was published, Mao had to flee from Hunan under pressure of the province's governor and leave his work of forming peasant party cells and peasant associations. He went to Kwangchow in September 1925 and took the job of instructing organisers of the peasant movement at the Peasant Institute, which had begun operating the previous summer under the initial direction of Peng Pai. Although the Peasant Institute was nominally under the KMT's peasant department, each of its directors was a communist, culminating in Mao in the sixth and final term when 318 trainees from eight provinces graduated as organisers. Here Mao instructed future cadres in the nature of the classes in the countryside and the methods and aims of the peasant associations. The Peasant Institute helped to build the framework of a communist movement in the countryside to complement the urban movement and provide it with a mass base.

At the second congress of the KMT in January 1926 it was

clear the left wing now held a majority. On 20 March Chiang Kai-shek, the leader of the KMT after Sun's death, moved against the left in a coup which placed the Russian advisers under surveillance and arrested many communists. By this action Chiang halted the advance of the communists' activities within the KMT and at the same time allowed him to lead the Northern Expedition, a revolutionary war supported by the communists against the semi-feudal warlords which Chiang intended to use to unify the country under his rule.

The expedition was launched from Kwangchow northwards in July, and in the same month Mao went to Shanghai to set up the Peasant Department of the CCP, using cadres just graduated from the Kwangchow Peasant Institute. While in Shanghai he took trips into the countryside to investigate conditions. He summarised his findings in an article, *The Bitter Sufferings of the Peasants in the Provinces of Kiangsi and Chekiang, and Their Anti-feudal, Anti-landlord Movement*, published in November 1926.

> Tzu Hsi is located in Chekiang, east of Ningpo. In recent months there occurred a great insurrection in the Shanpei area of this *hsien* [county]. The peasants of this Shanpei area are violent by nature, and frequently indulge in armed combat. On top of this, in recent years the officials and police have been unreasonably oppressive and the bad landlords have stepped up their exploitation. So the accumulated exasperation of the peasants was already deep. By chance the climate this year was unstable, and as a result the rice and cotton crops failed, but the landlords refused to make any reduction whatever in their harsh rents. The peasants' insurrection against famine thereupon exploded. Once the farmers' insurrection broke out, all the *éléments déclassés* joined them very courageously. In the morning of 13 September, there assembled more than 2,000 people, who went to the police station to report the famine, and clashed with the police. They burned down the police station, and distributed the arms of the police among themselves.

They then turned to go to the homes of the village gentry landlords to 'eat up powerful families'. After eating them up, and out of anger at the evils of the village gentry landlords, they destroyed the landlords' screens, paintings, and sculptured ancient doors and windows. They did this every day; they did not listen much to others' exhortation, but let off their steam in this manner. The day after [each such outburst], the landlord in question ran to the city to report, and soldiers and police came down to the village and turned everything upside down, but the leaders of the peasants had already mostly escaped. There was widespread propaganda about 'violation of the law' and 'crimes'; the farmers became fearful, and thus the movement was suppressed. The reason for the failure of this movement is that the masses did not fully organise themselves, and did not have leadership, so that the movement got started and then failed. [5]

The Northern Expedition passed through Hunan and Mao returned in the late summer of 1926 to his home province now freed from the tyranny of Governor Chao Heng-ti. The next stage of Mao's work with the peasant movement in the province, which occupied him from August 1926 to May 1927, included the first serious study of the politics of the peasant unrest, his *Report on an Investigation of the Peasant Movement in Hunan*, written in February 1927.

As the armies of the Northern Expedition extended anti-feudal rule, the membership of the peasant associations grew from one million in June 1926 to nearly ten million a year later. The Haifeng peasant association was composed of ten percent farm labourers, twenty percent self-employed farmers (middle peasants), thirty percent self-employing farmer tenants (lower-middle or semi-poor peasants), and forty percent tenants (poor peasants). Beside these land workers there were 500 artisans, 300 unemployed, 400 boatmen, 30 students, 30 small merchants, 10 small landowners, 10 village schoolteachers and 1 magician.

The Hunan peasant association, led by Mao, had 2 million members by 1927. It confiscated land, checked accounts, tried officials for embezzlement and conducted economic struggles against the entire gentry while attacking individual rich tyrants for murder, rape and kidnapping.

Mao addressed the first Peasants' and Workers' Congress of Hunan, held in Changsha from 20-29 December 1926. He cautiously defended the gains of the uprisings against the criticisms of those in the CCP who wanted to curb them for the sake of preserving good relations with the rightists of the KMT. But his *Report on an Investigation* nearly two months later went over to the attack and castigated the critics, saying,

> The present upsurge of the peasant movement is a colossal event. In a very short time, in China's central, southern and northern provinces, several hundred million peasants will rise like a mighty storm, like a hurricane, a force so swift and violent that no power, however great, will be able to hold it back ... Every revolutionary party and every revolutionary comrade will be put to the test, to be accepted or rejected as they decide. There are three alternatives. To march at their head and lead them? To trail behind them, gesticulating and criticising? Or to stand in their way and oppose them? [6]

In the *Report* Mao went further than in his *Analysis* in attributing the main political force in the countryside to the poor peasants. He nowhere said that the peasants would prove the leading force in the national revolution as a whole. That role he understood to belong to the urban proletariat.

The *Report* was based on a tour from 4 January to 5 February 1927. 'I called together fact-finding conferences in villages and county towns, which were attended by experienced peasants and by comrades working in the peasant movement, and I listened attentively to their reports and collected a great deal of material.'

The main targets of attack by the peasants are the local tyrants, the evil gentry and the lawless landlords, but in passing they also hit out against patriarchal ideas and institutions, against the corrupt officials in the cities and against bad practices and customs in the rural areas . . . With the collapse of the power of the landlords, the peasant associations have now become the sole organs of authority and the popular slogan 'All power to the peasant associations' has become a reality.' [7]

This revolt 'disturbed the gentry's sweet dreams'. It was, he said, 'fine' and not 'terrible'. Were the peasants 'going too far'?

True, the peasants are in a sense 'unruly' in the countryside . . . They fine the local tyrants and evil gentry, they demand contributions from them, and they smash their sedan-chairs. People swarm into the houses of local tyrants and evil gentry who are against the peasant association, slaughter their pigs and consume their grain. They even loll for a minute or two on the ivory-inlaid beds belonging to the young ladies in the households of the local tyrants and evil gentry. At the slightest provocation they make arrests, crown the arrested with tall paper-hats, and parade them through the village, saying, 'You dirty landlords, now you know who we are!' . . . But they [the tyrants] have themselves driven the peasants to this. For ages they have used their power to tyrannise the peasants and trample them underfoot; that is why the peasants have reacted so strongly. The most violent revolts and the most serious disorders have invariably occurred in places where they [tyrants] perpetrated the worst outrages. The peasants are clear-sighted. Who is bad and who is not, who is the worst and who is not quite so vicious, who deserves severe punishment and who deserves to be let off lightly – the peasants keep clear accounts, and very seldom has the punishment exceeded the crime . . .

A revolution is not a dinner party, or writing an essay, or painting a picture, or doing embroidery; it cannot be so refined, so leisurely and gentle, so temperate, kind, courteous, restrained and magnanimous [the Confucian virtues]. A revolution is an insurrection, an act of violence by which one class overthrows another. A rural revolution is a revolution by which the peasantry overthrows the power of the feudal landlord class. [8]

Mao then listed 'fourteen great achievements' of the peasants in 'accomplishing their revolutionary task'. The peasantry were organising themselves, hitting the landlords politically and economically, overthrowing feudal rule and laws, including superstition and ancestral rites and 'the masculine authority of the husband'. They were defeating landlord armies and forming their own. They were prohibiting gaming, gambling, opium-smoking and other 'bad practices and customs'. They were eliminating banditry, abolishing levies, spreading education and starting co-operatives, building roads and repairing embankments.

Mao illustrated how he had used ridicule as a weapon against worship:

While I was in the countryside, I did some propaganda against superstition among the peasants. I said: 'If you believe in the Eight Characters, you hope for good luck; if you believe in geomancy, you hope to benefit from the location of your ancestral graves. This year within a space of a few months the local tyrants, evil gentry and corrupt officials have all toppled from their pedestals. Is it possible that until a few months ago they all had good luck and enjoyed the benefit of well-sited ancestral graves, while suddenly in the last few months their luck has turned and their ancestral graves have ceased to exert a beneficial influence? . . . How strange! The Eight Characters of all the poor wretches in the countryside have suddenly turned auspicious! And their ancestral graves have suddenly started exerting beneficial influences! The gods? Worship them by all means. But if you had only Lord Kuan and the Goddess of Mercy and no peasant association, could you have overthrown the local tyrants and evil gentry? The gods and goddesses are indeed miserable objects. You have worshipped them for centuries, and they have not overthrown a single one of the local tyrants or evil gentry for you! Now you want to have your rent reduced. Let me ask, how will you go about it? Will you believe in the gods or in the peasant associations?' My words made the peasants roar with laughter. [9]

Lastly, turning again on the right-wing critics, Mao said,

It is reported from Nanchang that Chiang Kai-shek . . . and other such gentlemen do not altogether approve of the activities of the Hunan peasants . . . [They all say,] 'They have simply gone Red.' But where would the national revolution be without this bit of Red? To talk about 'arousing the masses of the people' day in and day out and then to be scared to death when the masses do rise — what difference is there between this and Lord Sheh's love of dragons? [10]

Lord Sheh, according to the story, was so fond of dragons he covered his entire palace with drawings and carvings of them, but when a real dragon heard of his fondness and paid him a visit, he was frightened out of his wits.

Naturally, the rise of the peasant associations frightened the landlords and their military backers. It was at the point in the national revolution of the seizure of land by the organised peasants of Hunan and the capture of Shanghai in mid-March 1927 by armed workers (under the direction of the General Trade Union) that the ruling classes decided to prevent the people's movement taking possession of the entire revolution.

A wave of reaction was stirred up against the peasant associations and against the communists inside the KMT in the spring of 1927. Intellectuals like Li Ta-chao (executed by strangling in Peking) and thousands of labour and peasant leaders were murdered or arrested throughout the country. The peasant associations were suppressed. Mao's capture was once more ordered. Chiang's soldiers recaptured Shanghai in

April 1927, massacring thousands of workers there in the following months. Rival KMT governments were set up, the right in Nanking under Chiang, the left in Wuhan.

At the Fifth Congress of the CCP, held in Wuhan on 27 April 1927, Chen Tu-hsiu, in the face of the KMT repression, failed to support the peasants' struggle that had erupted with such unexpected force. This failure weakened the revolutionary forces and exposed the working class and the CCP to further KMT assaults. Mao's opinions, favouring a stepping up of the peasant struggle and organising it effectively, were not discussed; instead he was charged with 'responsibility' for some of the Hunan 'excesses'. The trust the CCP leaders placed in the rightists of the KMT (which Stalin shared, although at the same time he supported 'pushing the peasants in the revolution') was proved unrealistic. Instead of bringing generals and funds to the side of the revolution, the rightists pulled the First Revolution away from its base in the people and towards its culmination in an anti-democratic coup.

Mao stayed in Wuhan and directed the Peasant Institute there. Set up along the lines of its predecessor in Kwangchow, it trained 2,000 cadres for rural political work in less than a year. Mao remained isolated from the party leadership. He wrote bitterly in a poem, *Yellow Crane Tower*, in spring 1927, that two hills, the Snake and the Tortoise, stand over the Yangtze River near Wuhan. Between them the river squeezes through with huge force, the narrower banks only succeeding in making the river run deeper. Whatever the restrictions and curbs the party's leaders placed on the mass movement, Mao affirmed,

> With wine I drink a pledge to the surging torrent;
> The tide of my heart rises high as its waves!

The continued redistribution of land by peasants near Changsha led to General Ho Chien's troops shooting some hundreds of communists before that city on 21 May 1927, the Horse Day Massacre. This opened a campaign of killing that was responsible for 30,000 deaths in Hunan in three months. Mao backed a protest movement against the terror but the Wuhan party leaders hesitated, calling for a toning down of the revolution and the disarming of workers.

Repression intensified everywhere and street executions of communists and their sympathisers became commonplace. Finally the communists withdrew from the Wuhan government, though not from the KMT. The Wuhan government, under Wang Ching-wei, retaliated by declaring the CCP completely outlawed on 13 July 1927. The KMT 'left' went over to Chiang Kai-shek in Nanking. The White terror continued, forcing communist leaders and activists into hiding. Land which had been seized in the countryside was restored to the landlords.

The betrayal of the First Revolution by the KMT convinced Mao that if there were to be alliances in future the CCP should keep the initiative in its own hands and that CCP policy must be based on the concrete class conditions existing in China. He saw that a much deeper investigation and analysis of the military necessities stemming from those conditions must be carried out by the CCP. He began to conceive the idea of a Red Army to provide the people's movement with a firm backing.

3 The Army of the Poor

The Second Revolutionary Civil War:
The Kiangsi Base, 1927–1934

In the ten years from the defeat of the revolution in
1927 to the outbreak of the War of Resistance against
Japan in 1937, it was the Communist Party of China,
and the Communist Party of China alone, which continued in unity to hold aloft the great banner of anti-
imperialism and anti-feudalism under the counter-
revolutionary reign of extreme terror and which led
the broad masses of workers, peasants, soldiers, revolutionary intellectuals and other revolutionaries in great
political, military and ideological struggles. During these
struggles the Communist Party of China created the Red
Army, established the government of Councils of
Workers, Peasants and Soldiers, set up revolutionary
bases, distributed land to impoverished peasants and
resisted both the attacks of the reactionary Kuomintang
government and, after 18 September 1931, the aggression
of Japanese imperialism.

> Mao Tse-tung, *Appendix*:
> *Resolution on Questions in Party History*

In August 1927, the Central Committee of the Communist
Party, guided by Chu Chiu-pai after Chen Tu-hsiu's removal,
issued orders for uprisings in Hunan and Hupeh, at first in the
cities and later to extend to the countryside. From July to
September, Mao directed the Autumn Harvest Uprising in
Hunan. Here he spread the idea of soviets, or people's representative councils, consisting of workers, peasants and
soldiers. He advocated raising the red flag and lowering the
'black' flag of the KMT in the peasant movement. On 20
August, in a letter to the Central Committee, he wrote,

We really cannot use the Kuomintang flag. If we do, we will only be defeated again. Formerly, we did not actively seize the leadership of the Kuomintang, and let Wang Ching-wei, Chiang Kai-shek, Tang Sheng-chih [the militarist governor of Hunan] and the others lead it. Now we should let them keep this flag, which is already nothing but a black flag, and we must immediately and resolutely raise the red flag. [1]

Mao also favoured a radical solution of the land question, meaning confiscating and redistributing all land without exception. The Central Committee replied by ordering him not to establish soviets, that he must retain the KMT flag, and he was to organise confiscation of land only from big landlords. On the first two issues, Mao later forced a change of decision; on the last, he soon changed his tactic.

The uprisings were defeated. The Central Committee's desire for a popular insurrection, at a time when the communists' numbers had been more than halved by the terror, was not backed by adequate military preparation. Mao saw the need to build a military force to give a firm basis to the revolutionary actions of the workers and peasants, or else the movement would invite a series of defeats in the face of superior armies.

As a result, Mao marched with 800 survivors of the Autumn Harvest Uprising to the Chingkang Mountains. In October he and his peasant and Anyuan miner comrades set up the first Red base in that remote area on the Hunan–Kiangsi border. Joined by bandit soldiers, and in January 1928 by Chu Teh's forces from the defeated Nanchang Uprising, they trained in political and military affairs, set up local soviets, and expropriated the wealth of rich merchants and big landlords. They tried to win over the intermediate class of peasant proprietors to the side of the poor and landless peasants.

Chingkangshan was the general name for a mountainous area some 150 miles in circuit. Great forests of pine and spruce and bamboo rose on every hand, great flowering creepers wrapped trees in their embrace, and spring flowers cast their fragrance on the breeze. It was a region of great loveliness, yet shrouded in fogs for most of the year.

In the midst of this wild and relatively unproductive mountain region was a broad, circular valley surrounded by wooded slopes. In past ages, 'bandit peasants' whose descendants now numbered fifteen hundred souls had founded five villages, each of them grouped around a well, so that the valley was known locally as the 'Five Big and Little Wells'. [2]

Mao organised and began the training of the peasants in the valleys and mountains with the consent and help of the bandit leaders. The local peasants lived off their vegetable patches and sold bamboo shoots, tea and medicinal herbs. This had proved insufficient for existence, and so to make ends meet they had gone marauding in distant towns. As Chu Teh explained,

Banditry and landlordism have always gone hand in hand in China. Landlordism breeds poverty and ignorance, so that peasants often become bandits for at least part of each year. When, as in the Chingkangshan region, these banditised peasants are organised under leaders, the landlords make agreements with their leaders. Before we arrived on the mountain, Wang Tso and Yuan Wen-tsai received a little tribute from the landlords and in return left them in peace. The landlords said, 'Don't raid us – raid others.' All this changed after we began the agrarian revolution, with the confiscation of the land and goods of the landlords and their distribution among the peasants. Then the landlords called in Kuomintang troops against us.' [3]

The First Party Congress of the Border Area, held at Maoping on 20 May 1928, elected Mao as secretary of the local party organisation, and party representative in the Fourth Red Army (commanded by Chu Teh) which totalled 10,000 men.

The 'Chu–Mao Army', as it came to be called, held off KMT attacks by concentrating their forces.

Efforts were made to educate the army to serve the people. Mao's *Eight Points for Attention* showed how differently Red soldiers were expected to behave compared with the bandit and KMT marauders.

1 Speak politely to the people.
2 Pay fairly for what you buy.
3 Return everything you borrow.
4 Pay for anything you damage.
5 Replace all doors [planks of wood were easily unhinged, and used for sleeping on] and return all straw on which you sleep.
6 Dig latrines away from houses and fill them with earth when you leave.
7 Do not take liberties with women.
8 Do not ill-treat captives.

Of even greater significance, soldiers began to help the peasants with sowing and planting and to open up wasteland. This was the first effort of the Red Army to become not only a military but a productive force.

The failure of the urban uprisings, especially of the Canton (Kwangchow) Commune in December 1927, led the Communist International to condemn Chu Chiu-pai's policy of city insurrections. Instead, the Sixth Congress of the CCP, held in Moscow in August and September 1928, endorsed the use of soviets and rural base areas from which guerrilla attacks could be launched, though it saw their function as holding operations until the revolutionary forces in the cities, bled by the terror, could build up strength and resume their fight.

Mao, on the other hand, was using the year the Red Army spent on the Chingkang Mountains to develop his theory of 'people's war'. 'Without a people's army the people have nothing,' he was to say in 1945. It was in 1928 he began to realise this. Conversely, without the support of the people, Mao argued, an army turns into a bandit gang or a wing of landlord repression: if the army does not serve the people, it will serve the landlords. The Red Army must therefore be strong or else the base (the revolutionary power established locally by each military victory in the guerrilla war that was beginning) could not be consolidated. The fruits of each victory could not be held by the people unless the army was directed by the party and did not degenerate into a purely military force, and unless the party's own policy was consonant with the needs of the poor peasants in the countryside and the workers in the towns and cities.

Again, in defending the poor, Mao pointed out, the Red Army must not antagonise the petty bourgeoisie, its ally or potential ally, which even in the countryside was an intellectual and economic force. The petty-bourgeoisie's respect must be earned and yet its attempts to infiltrate the Communist Party and to dominate its policy must be thwarted. On the Chingkang Mountains Mao was feeling his way towards a position in the creative centre of the revolutionary movement which he would occupy thereafter, defending the core of the revolution against what he came to regard as distortions by both right and 'left'.

Mao started from the fact that the revolution under way was still a bourgeois democratic revolution though later he identified it as of a new type, 'new-democratic', which 'we must go through . . . before we can lay a real foundation for the transition to socialism.' He also felt that in 1928 the tide was on the ebb in the country as a whole. In his report of the Chingkangshan Front Committee to the party's Central Committee of 25 November 1928, he said:

> While Red political power has been established in a few small areas, in the country as a whole the people lack the ordinary democratic rights. The workers, the peasants and even the bourgeois democrats do not have freedom of speech or assembly, and the worst crime is to join the Communist Party. Wherever the Red Army goes, the masses are cold and aloof, and only after our

propaganda do they slowly move into action. Whatever enemy units we face, there are hardly any cases of mutiny or desertion to our side and we have to fight it out ... We have an acute sense of our isolation which we keep hoping will end. Only by launching a political and economic struggle for democracy, which will also involve the urban petty-bourgeoisie, can we turn the revolution into a seething tide that will surge through the country. [4]

But the urban insurrections had all been crushed. When workers and petty-bourgeois revolutionaries seized control of Kwangchow and set up the Canton Commune on 11 December 1927, the uprising was drowned in blood after only three days. Six thousand rebels were massacred by KMT troops. A woman revolutionary described the slaughter,

The White officers killed every working man or student they met. Sometimes they halted them, then shot them dead; or they had them captured, forced to their knees, and beheaded or sliced into bits. Every girl with bobbed hair who was caught was stripped naked, raped by as many men as were present, then her body slit in two, from below upwards. Often the girls were no more than fifteen or sixteen, and officers, giving interviews to eager British journalists from Hongkong, said: 'The bobbed-haired girls are the worst; they are very arrogant and talk back defiantly. We have had to kill hundreds of them.' [5]

The regime of the big bourgeoisie and militarists was re-established in Kwangchow and the semi-feudal order was restored throughout the parts of China that had been liberated during the Northern Expedition. In Kwangchow,

All labour unions except the yellow Mechanics Union, a semi-official union whose officers had helped the reaction, were disbanded. The merchants of the city, whose armed volunteer corps had been dissolved by the revolutionary government and even by Dr. Sun Yat-sen years before, now reorganised and heavily armed it. The

Peasant Leagues [associations] throughout the province were smashed and thousands of peasants killed in the struggle ... Opium dens flourished ... gambling, banquets, prostitutes again became the chief amusement of the officials. The traffic in girl slaves again flourished, ... [and so did] the buying and selling of girls from the peasantry into the homes of the merchants and official classes, as household drudges, as concubines ... [Tax collectors] with their own armed forces, were turned loose upon the peasants to levy and collect taxes. [6]

At a time of such urban repression, Mao considered it the duty of the Red Army to stand firm in its Chingkang Mountain stronghold. In a poem written in the autumn of 1928, he referred to the blockade the KMT forces were tightening around the mountain fastness:

> Below the hill were our flags and banners,
> To the hilltop sounded our bugles and drums.
> The foe surrounded us thousands strong,
> But we were steadfast and never moved.
>
> Our defence was strong as a wall already,
> Now did our wills unite like a fortress.
> From Huangyangchieh came the thunder of guns,
> And the enemy army had fled in the night!

Mao laid down the basic conditions he thought should underlie the firm establishment of 'separate armed Soviet bases'. In his report of 25 November 1928 to the party's Central Committee, he said the first condition of an independent regime was that it had a mass base. A land reform programme must arise from the needs of the local poor people. Second, there was a need for a strong party leading the work of reform and directing the army. Without a sense of direction and the organisation to implement it, the rural movement might fragment and again open itself to annihilation by the KMT. The third condition was the existence of a strong Red Army. The defence of areas already won became a necessary accompaniment to the process of agrarian reform. The fourth condition was the control of a strategically suitable base area, preferably on the borders of a number of provinces, to provide a nucleus of influence that could gradually be extended outwards into the surrounding areas. Fifth, the base area should be, or should become, self-sufficient enough to maintain its population.

The Chingkang Mountain base, with Ningkang as its centre, fulfilled most of these conditions, Mao claimed, though he drew attention to one drawback, which was indeed to prove fatal. The base, he said, was 'confronted by the enemy's large "encirclement and suppression" forces, [and] its economic problems, especially the shortage of cash, are extremely difficult'.

Two episodes in the life of the Red Army of the time related in *China's Red Army Marches* by the American writer Agnes Smedley, who travelled in the base area, illustrate Mao's methods of impressing the peasants that this army was an army different from all others.

During one assay from their Chingkang Mountain base, Red Army soldiers looted some villagers' homes, led by their company commanders, in clear contradiction of Red Army rules. Mao ordered the looters to explain their actions to a mass meeting of peasants. One looter defended himself by saying, 'What shall a man do if his own commander leads in the looting? I would have stopped if they had ordered me to.' Another said, 'Shoot us for what we have done wrong! Our commanders led us, but we followed like sheep.' At the vote of the massed assembly, the soldiers went free but the commanders were executed.

The second incident occurred in midsummer 1928 when some local Kiangsi warlords sent agents to try to bribe Mao and Chu Teh. They asked for a private meeting with the two leaders, intending to pay them large sums to desert from the army. But Mao led the messengers to a great mass meeting in Ningkang.

'Comrades,' Mao is supposed to have said to the crowd, 'the Whites have sent these agents to bribe Chu Teh and myself. They have offered us great sums of money and positions of command in the militarist armies. To me they have offered fat political jobs in Nanking and Shanghai. We could become little running dogs of Chiang Kai-shek. Some of us could put on foreign clothes, wag our tails and aspire to drink tea and play bridge with the wives of the imperialists on big occasions! We might even go to the dog races with the imperialist diplomats in Shanghai! We could buy many concubines, deal in opium, and banquet with the gang leaders in Shanghai. We could, in short, become the bloodhounds of the counter-revolution and hunt down our comrades fighting for the revolution. Well, comrades, the offer has been made us. Tell us now, what shall be our answer to the Whites?

The reply came from an angry peasant: 'Chop off the heads of these running dogs and return them to their masters in a basket!' A Canton railway worker protested, 'We let them come in, we must let them go out. We are fighting against a whole system. Our answer must be this: Fight for the worker-peasant-soldier soviets! Organise and arm the masses! ... But let these little pigs in their suits fit for a Shanghai sing-song house never dare stick their tails into our soviet region again!'

Mao turned to the sweating messengers: 'Now we'll take you to the border. Take care of yourself after that, and if you aren't shot by the peasants beyond, it'll be a pity!'

While the Red Army began to create a favourable impression on the poor peasants, economic conditions in the Chingkang Mountains deteriorated. Food and clothing were especially scarce. Chu Teh and Mao, and later Peng Teh-huai with his Fifth Red Army, who had moved up to join them after the Pingchiang Uprising, decided to break the KMT blockade and descend from the original base to gather their forces around Juichin in a more fertile area of South Kiangsi. By the time they arrived there in April 1929, their numbers had been reduced to 2,800 by desertion and attacks.

Agnes Smedley described the blockade of the Chingkang Mountains and how it was broken:

> More and more enemy troops came up to tighten the blockade. The Red troops swarmed down the mountain on night raids for weeks, but these soon cost more ammunition than they were worth and resulted in heavy casualties. The mass movement in the countryside beyond had been crushed or driven underground. Rice was rationed on Chingkangshan where the troops had put in fields of squash. Week after week squash was their only vegetable.
>
> From the end of September onward the fighting front was frozen and by December the Red troops began to starve. Five thousand men filled the hospitals and barracks. Some were wounded, but most of them were suffering from hunger and some had pneumonia and tuberculosis. It was wet and cold and they had little warm clothing.

Chu and Mao led their 4,000 men out along a mountaintop route known only to the bandits. They left Peng Teh-huai behind with 1,500 men and the sick and wounded, to follow later.

> At dawn on 4 January 1929, the column of gaunt and ragged men and women began creeping single file along the jagged crest ... The stones and peaks were worn to slippery smoothness by fierce winds, rains and snow. Snow lay in pockets and an icy wind lashed the bodies of the column that inched forward, crawling over huge boulders and hanging on to one another to avoid slipping into the black chasms below. [7]

By nightfall they had reached a small plateau where they ate half of the pound of cooked rice each had taken with him. Linking arms, they huddled together to sleep. Next day they passed down the mountain along an overgrown trail to the village of Tafen, which they surrounded, overpowering the garrison. As Chu Teh recalled, 'We ate that night!'

They marched on to the town of Tayu where, after stopping to call a mass meeting with workers, they found an enemy regiment had crept up on them. In a confused battle, hundreds of Red Army soldiers were killed.

Chu and Mao ordered a retreat. For ten days the small army fought a running battle through freezing mountains, constantly attacked by the enemy who traced them by the blood they left behind them in the snow.

At Tapoti, said Chu Teh, 'We had run enough, and in a conference we decided to get rid of our pursuers once and for all. We selected our own battlefield. Our troops discussed the plan of battle until everything was clear, then met in a mass meeting and with raised fists swore to destroy the enemy or die in the attempt.'

A young commander, Lin Piao, led one regiment into the rear of the enemy column by night. From dawn to noon the battle raged. At the end, they had completely destroyed the enemy division and taken about 1,000 prisoners. A hundred poor peasants taken captive were asked to join the Red Army. The rest, 'old mercenaries and opium smokers', Chu Teh let free. 'We didn't want such men.'

With the pressure off them, Chu and Mao advanced to the walled city of Ningtu, took the food and possessions of the landlords, distributed the surplus to the city poor and opened the prison. The march west toward the mountain base at Tungku became a triumphal procession, peasants flocking to help carry the wounded and the supplies.

The market town of Tungku was on a high fertile plateau dotted with small villages. Here the army rested, mended their clothes, boiling them to kill the lice, and made themselves new sandals with rope soles.

The troops received military education at conferences where the plans of battle were discussed and criticised; the individual conduct of any commander or fighter could also be criticised. Mao attached great importance to such democratic education since it was in changes in the consciousness of the poor peasant soldiers, which would make them feel they could control their destiny, that the future of the revolution lay. Mao explained the stage of the revolution at these meetings, and outlined the reasons for the present strategy and tactics. 'We are weak and small,' he told the soldiers, 'but a spark can kindle a flame and we have a boundless future. With time and under certain conditions the people's power will be extended to areas that include large towns. From the liberation of a small part of the country we will thus advance to larger and still larger areas; and eventually we will liberate all China.'

He wrote in a poem that spring;

> Soon the dawn will break in the east,
> But do not say we are marching early;
> Though we've travelled all over these green hills we are
>   not yet old,
> And the landscape here is beyond compare.

> Straight from the walls of Huichang lofty peaks,
> Range after range, extend to the eastern ocean.
> Our soldiers, pointing, gaze south towards Kwangtung,
> So green, so luxuriant in the distance.

On their arrival at Tungku in the spring of 1929, the soldiers of the Chu–Mao army, the 'poor man's army' according to the peasants, were,

> lean and hungry men, many of them in their middle or late teens, with big hard hands and thickly calloused feet, to whom life had been nothing but a round of toil and privation, insecurity and oppression. Most were illiterate. Each man wore a long, sausage-like pouch long enough to encircle one shoulder and tie at the opposite hip, a pouch now filled with enough rice to last for two or three days after which it would have to be replenished from the bins of landlords, or with rice

captured from the supply columns of the enemy. Their second article of equipment consisted of a cloth cartridge belt long enough to wrap around each shoulder, cross in front and back, and go around the waist. The belts of men with rifles now held a few rounds of ammunition each, but those worn by men with spears were empty. [8]

On the eighth night after reaching Tungku, Chu and Mao, developing their tactics, led 3,000 men east to draw a threatening KMT force off the mountain, divide it and destroy its parts one by one. Sending swift troops in opposite directions to their main force to make feints at large towns and draw the KMT force after them, the Chu–Mao main force occupied itself in distant villages, arousing and arming the peasants and placing cadres in position to organise resistance. At the same time, they made surprise attacks on the KMT troops, quickly retiring after each raid.

A conflict began between Mao and Li Li-san over these tactics. Li Li-san was chairman of the organisation bureau of the CCP and the most powerful member of the Central Committee. He called for 'pure' guerrilla warfare, small roving agitational bands who would awaken the peasants but would await the revolutionary signal from the urban proletariat. Mao's tactics, on the other hand, aimed at the formation and growth of the Red Army as a military and propaganda force to defend and widen the bases.

Mao's theory was that when the ruling class was weak from its own splits and wars, the Red Army could be comparatively adventurous in carving out a base, but while the ruling class was united against them, as in 1928-9, the revolutionary forces should conserve their strength. Mao worked out his tactics with Chu Teh. He characterised them thus:

Divide our forces to arouse the masses, concentrate our forces to deal with the enemy.

The enemy advances, we retreat; the enemy camps, we harrass; the enemy tires, we attack; the enemy retreats, we pursue.

To extend stable base areas, employ the policy of advancing in waves; when pursued by a powerful enemy, employ the policy of circling around.

Arouse the largest numbers of the masses in the shortest possible time and by the best possible methods.

These tactics are just like casting a net; at any moment we should be able to cast it or draw it in. We cast it wide to win over the masses and draw it in to deal with the enemy. [9]

Successfully applying these tactics, the Chu—Mao army evaded a large force concentrated against them and camped near Tingchow in south Fukien province, a walled city held by a great landlord and Kuomintang general, Kuo Fang-ming. They enticed Kuo's bandit and opium-smoking troops out from the safety of the walls by the ruse of spreading a rumour that a small force of badly armed 'Red bandits' was encamped a little way away. Two enemy regiments, followed by their commander in a sedan chair borne by four carriers, marched out in single file along a footpath through the valley over-looking which the Red troops had stationed themselves. The Chu—Mao troops fired at random and ran up the mountain-side, the enemy troops in hot pursuit. The main force then broke out from their hiding places and the enemy turned and tumbled downhill with the Red soldiers at their heels.

Kuo, 'a big fat fellow in a fine uniform' with a huge gold watch and chain and wearing rings on his fingers, was killed trying to escape in a boat. Tingchow was taken and Mao set to work reviving the people's organisations and establishing soviets. The landlords fled or were captured and the land was soon being divided up by village and town committees.

At a conference in Juichin, two or three days' march from Tingchow, the Red Army was divided into three parts headed by Mao, Chu and Peng Teh-huai (who had managed to fight his way off the Chingkang Mountains as planned). They were to move against the counter-revolution in the way Mao had marched through the countryside, taking the towns just as

Tingchow had been taken, and destroying the landlord and KMT power in the villages and military centres, with the aim of establishing a central revolutionary base in south and central Kiangsi.

Chu Teh told Agnes Smedley of the conditions of the peasants in the areas through which he and Mao marched:

> The peasants lived in small villages surrounded by crumbling walls in which there was only one gate. Inside these walls were two rows of squalid thatch-roofed mud hovels bordering a street which became a quagmire in the rainy season. In dry weather the open gutters on either side of the street were filled with decaying refuse.
>
> The dark hovels had one door and no windows. Inside, the beds consisted either of pallets of rice straw on the earthen floor, or of boards stretched across trestles and heaped with rice straw which served both as mattress and as covering . . . The people slept in the only clothing they owned, loose trousers and jackets with many generations of patches. There might be a crude wooden table with benches, for family meals. The stove, made of mud, was fed through a vent beneath an iron vat, which was the only cooking vessel; fuel was dried grass and twigs gathered from the hillsides by children. Rice bowls were of clay with broken pieces riveted in place. Chopsticks were whittled out of bamboo.
>
> Rents (as high as 70 percent or more of the crops), usury, crop failures and requisitions by provincial and local armies kept the death rate high and the peasant families small . . . At least 70 percent of the population consisted of poor peasants – tenants – and land labourers, and almost all were illiterate . . .
>
> The 'hundred-headed' landlords, as the peasants called them, lived in the large towns and cities, safely enthroned behind strong walls. Here they acted as officials, judges, juries and executioners . . . They used the local garrison troops to supervise the reaping of the harvests lest the peasants bury some of the grain which the landlords claimed as their due. [10]

Such conditions created a widespread peasant eagerness to know who this ordinary man called 'Chu Mao' was, who wore the same clothes as they did and led the poor to attack the rich. When they learnt, they marched with him. According to Chu Teh,

> We never had to lay seige to any village. Whole villages poured out and often walked for miles to wait for us, but the strongholds of the landlords had to be taken by storm. Our miners, whom we had organised into an embryonic engineering corps, would excavate holes in the walls of such towns or cities and fill them with the black powder that the peasants manufacture and sell to make firecrackers. If the explosion failed to blow a hole through which our troops could enter, the peasants would bring bamboo ladders which we used to scale the walls. Often women and children marched along, carrying baskets and shoulder poles, to clean out the rice bins of the landlords.

In the prisons which they opened, they found,

> poor men unable to pay their debts or taxes, or those who had been jailed for petty crimes against private property. We always found at least some prisoners who were suspected of belonging to peasant or workers' organisations, or to the Communist Party, though most such men had already died or been killed. Those left alive were shackled, and the chains had worn sores in their legs so that they often could not walk at all. All were covered with lice, their hair was long and matted, and many had tuberculosis, heart ailments, or were dying of dysentry or typhoid. The prison-keepers furnished no food; this had to be supplied by the families of the victims. The prison authorities kept most of this food themselves, so that the prisoners were like skeletons. [11]

Mao's forces entered Fukien province and harassed the KMT with lightning strikes at their powerful garrisons in the cities and towns. In the autumn of 1929 Mao fell ill of malaria. Chu and Lin Piao led an attack on the walled city of Shanghang in south Fukien. After its fall, Mao was carried into the city on a stretcher. From his sickbed he directed the political work that had become customary whenever, as he wrote in a poem,

> A part of the realm has been recovered
> And the land is being actively redistributed.

Peasants poured into the city to celebrate the victory, take part in land redistribution and accuse the hated landlords.

> Their cry was, 'Where is my son? Where is my brother? Where is my father?' Receiving no reply, they attacked them with their bare hands. The Red Guards, set to maintain order, refused to obey orders of their commanders to protect the prisoners. [12]

The Red Army Medical Corps sent a man to Shanghai to buy quinine for Mao. He returned with some and was sent for more. On the second journey he was captured and beheaded. But Mao's life was saved and by December 1929 he had recovered sufficiently to speak at a conference of party representatives in the Red Army, held at Kutien.

The Kutien conference adopted Mao's report, *On Correcting Mistaken Ideas in the Party*, which called Li Li-san's tactics 'putschism'. Bases had to be established and expanded, he said in the report, and once areas had been liberated the Red Army had to learn to defend the peasants' gains. 'Some people', said Mao, 'want to increase our political influence only by means of roving guerrilla actions, but are unwilling to increase it by undertaking the arduous task of building up base areas and establishing the people's political power'.

He criticised those who 'regard military affairs and politics as opposed to each other and refuse to recognise that military affairs are only one means of accomplishing political tasks'.

Mao was beginning to identify the characteristics which distinguished the Red Army from the armies of the old type. If the task of the KMT army was 'merely to fight', with the result that its soldiers showed a mercenary mentality, destroying and plundering wherever they went,

> the Chinese Red Army is an armed body for carrying out the political tasks of the revolution . . . Beside fighting to destroy the enemy's military strength, it should shoulder such important tasks as spreading propaganda among the masses, organising the masses, arming them, helping them to establish revolutionary political power and setting up party organisations . . . Without these objectives, fighting loses its meaning and the Red Army loses the reason for its existence. [13]

In attacking various forms of purely military individualism and organisational indiscipline, Mao laid the basis of an army whose tactics and strategy would reflect and respond to the political needs of the revolution. He had already learnt the lesson of the failure of the KMT's 'revolutionary' armies to defend the gains of the Northern Expedition. Those armies, starting out as harbingers of liberation for the peasants from semi-feudal landlord oppression had become oppressive in their turn, fighting to preserve landlord power and attacking and plundering the poor.

In a letter dated 5 January 1930 and addressed to Lin Piao, then the twenty-two-year-old commander of one of the Fourth Red Army's regiments, Mao criticised his young colleague. Lin believed that mobile guerrilla methods were themselves enough to spread the revolution's political influence to the point where a nationwide insurrection broke out. He seemed to think it was 'a waste of effort to do the arduous work of establishing political power' at local levels and building up the power step by step.

Mao's long-term strategy, on the other hand, was to use mobile guerrilla methods to establish local Red power bases. The political power built up in the bases would then expand the revolution's influence, with the army as its tool, finally generating 'a revolutionary high tide' which would advance over the whole nation in a series of waves.

Mao's point was that while 'a single spark can start a prairie fire', in the sense that even small Red bases could generate the rapid spread of political forces, the revolution's political power itself could only develop 'through wave-like expansion' outwards from the base areas. Given the lack of unified state power in China that could be seized at a blow, the local revolutionary power would have to grow to the point where it could finally unite its various base areas, assume state power and itself unite the country. Mao's letter concluded,

> In saying that you want to spread our political influence through mobile guerrilla methods, I am not accusing you of having the purely military viewpoint or roving bandit ideology. You clearly have neither of these, which both involve no intention of winning over the masses; you advocate going all out to win over the masses — and besides advocating it, you actually do it. Where I disagree with you is in that you do not believe deeply in establishing political power, without which the tasks of winning over the masses and hastening the revolutionary high tide cannot be as successfully achieved as you imagine. [14]

Mao's Kutien report, and its attendant 'rectification' of mistaken ideas, strengthened the Communist Party's hold over the Red Army. A wide expansion of the soviet districts followed the army's campaign of January to April 1930. All central and south Kiangsi was liberated, together with parts of western Fukien. These districts were soon expanded to include most of Kiangsi and Fukien provinces.

A further meeting on 7 February 1930 decided to hasten the formal organisation of the soviet districts and to set up over them the Kiangsi Provincial Soviet Government. The poor peasants received the new government's land redistribution policy with a warmth that stood the Kiangsi base in good stead during the hard times that were to follow the launching of the KMT's 'extermination' campaigns.

Agnes Smedley traced how the land policy was carried out in practice:

> Following the usual establishment of the Councils of People's Delegates (soviets) in the various cities, towns and villages, all old taxes were abolished . . . A single progressive tax on the grain crop was introduced instead. Since the army supplied itself by capture from the enemy, the tax revenue was devoted entirely to reconstruction. Usury and opium were forbidden, mortgages and papers of debt returned, primary schools and cooperatives of various kinds formed, and the first small Peasant Bank established.
>
> Before redistributing the land, Mao Tse-tung sent teams of political workers to survey land conditions. It was the first survey ever made in the region. It revealed that 70 percent of the land — including large estates, temple and ancestral lands — was owned or controlled by landlords who constituted 1–2 percent of the population. Of the remaining 30 percent of the land, about half was owned by rich peasants and the remaining 15 percent by middle and poor peasants.
>
> The survey classified 70 percent of the peasants as poor, 20 percent as middle peasants, and 10 percent as rich . . .
>
> With this survey as a guide, the land was redistributed among the landless peasants and the agricultural labourers. Middle peasants whose holdings were too small to support their families also shared in the distribution. [15]

Land redistribution was accompanied by a mass education programme designed to show the peasants that gaining knowledge and literacy were two keys to holding on to their new-found power successfully.

> The Cultural Department of the Soviets turned temples into free primary schools for poor children. At night,

when the children moved out, adult illiterates came in. Temples were also used for the training of mass organisers, or as headquarters for mass organisations of the army. There were few teachers, no textbooks, little paper, and not even blackboards . . . Kuomintang printing presses were confiscated and moved to the countryside. Only then could primers, small newspapers, and booklets for mass education be published. The first mass booklets consisted of a simple series entitled *Talks with Peasants*, *Talks with Workers*, *Talks with Soldiers*, and *Talks with Women*. Thus began . . . a movement reflected in slogans painted on walls, cliffs and even the trunks of trees: 'Learn, learn and learn again! . . . Study until the light fails! . . . Study as you plough! . . . Study by the reflected light of snow!' [16]

At the same time Mao offered some advice to the party's cadres about how to conduct their social investigations. In *Oppose Book Worship* of May 1930, he declared, 'No investigation, no right to speak.'

There are not a few comrades doing inspection work, as well as guerrilla leaders and cadres newly in office, who like to make political pronouncements the moment they arrive at a place and who strut about, criticising this and condemning that when they have only seen the surface of things or minor details. Such purely subjective nonsensical talk is indeed detestable. These people are bound to make a mess of things, lose the confidence of the masses and prove incapable of solving any problem at all.

When they come across difficult problems, quite a number of people in leading positions simply heave a sigh without being able to solve them. They lose patience and ask to be transferred, on the grounds that they 'have not the ability and cannot do the job'. These are cowards' words. Just get moving on your two legs, go the rounds at every section placed under your charge and 'inquire into everything' as Confucius did, and then you will be able to solve the problems, however little your ability; for although your head may be empty before you go out of doors, it will be empty no longer when you return but will contain all sorts of material necessary for the solution of the problems . . . Must you go out of doors? Not necessarily. You can call a fact-finding meeting . . .

Whatever is written in a book is right — such is still the mentality of culturally backward Chinese peasants. Strangely enough, within the Communist Party there are also people who always say in a discussion, 'Show me where it's written in the book' . . . Of course we should study Marxist books, but this study must be integrated with our country's actual conditions. We need books, but we must overcome book worship, which is divorced from actual situations.

Mao went on to place the role of investigation in the context of the revolution as a whole:

Our chief method of investigation must be to dissect the different social classes. The ultimate purpose of this is to understand their interrelations, to arrive at a correct appraisal of class forces and then to formulate the correct tactics for the struggle, so defining which classes constitute the main force in the revolutionary struggle, which classes are to be won over as allies and which classes are to be overthrown. [17]

He repeated a truism, but one which evidently needed repeating, that 'Victory in China's revolutionary struggle will depend on the Chinese comrades' understanding of Chinese conditions.' All 'investigation of the facts' should be undertaken to that end. Plan clear and simple outlines for your own investigation, said Mao, hold fact-finding meetings, discuss with all kinds of people, and do so in person instead of relying on reports, probe deeply and make your own notes.

A good example of a failure to investigate and understand

China's conditions came only a month later. The growth of the base areas in late 1929 and 1930 was evidence of the success of Mao's military policy. But in June 1930 a messenger arrived in Tingchow from the Central Committee of the CCP in Shanghai, bringing two resolution-orders, both signed by Li Li-san. The first was a plan for the re-organisation of the army under a single central command, with Mao as political commissar and Chu Teh as commander-in-chief. The second was an order for all forces, including the Chu—Mao forces, to leave the rural areas and capture the great industrial cities.

Li Li-san evidently wanted to use the strong Kiangsi base merely as a headquarters for adventurous forays against nearby cities. He ordered the Kiangsi Red Army, now more than 65,000 strong, to march out in July 1930 and attack Changsha, Nanchang and Wuhan to coordinate with strikes to be called within the cities. He wanted to generate a general strike and 'revolution now'. Mao's 'boxing tactics' he derided as too protracted.

Both Mao and Chu were sceptical of this 'adventurist' policy of onslaught against the cities. Their armies were still relatively small and armed only with light weapons. Their greatest strength was the solidity of the Red base, their closeness to the people in the soviet areas. The militarist armies were large, they had artillery and all the country's resources at their command to compensate for their weak social base. What is more, the KMT generals would wage positional warfare to defend the cities which, the Red armies had learnt, put the mobile guerrilla forces at a disadvantage — either they had to disengage or they had to fight on unequal terms.

Li Li-san's strategy was 'an attempt to leap over great difficulties and problems that had to be faced and solved before China could be emancipated,' said Chu Teh. 'Mao and I sensed this but lacked sufficient information to reject the plan; and we were practically alone in our misgivings.'

The attacks met disaster. Changsha was briefly occupied, its streets a mass of red flags and the city flooded with pamphlets and handbills denouncing capitalism and imperialism. While Mao and Chu approached Nanchang, Peng Teh-huai at Changsha proclaimed a Soviet government of three provinces, Hunan, Kiangsi and Hupeh. It was short-lived. The 'Red threat' stirred foreign gunboats into action. Ships of American, British, Italian and Japanese navies lay in the Hsiang River and bombarded Changsha for four days, starting great fires and killing thousands of troops and civilians. The forces of Ho Chien, the local warlord, moved up and the Red troops withdrew, taking the printing press, newsprint, rice, arms and money confiscated from the rich and from KMT and warlord forces, including $400,000 from the local Chamber of Commerce.

At Nanchang, Red soldiers were mown down by enemy fire. A second attack on Changsha was ordered, though Mao and Chu argued against it, saying the Red Army was neither equipped nor trained to fight positional warfare. After a week's battle Mao, Chu and Peng Teh-huai retired to the Kiangsi base against the orders of the Central Committee. Li's line was discredited, the attacks called off, and Chiang Kai-shek's government, thoroughly frightened by the scale of the Red Army's growth, intensified search-and-arrest operations of 'Red vermin' in the cities and launched the First Encirclement and Suppression Campaign against the Kiangsi base in December 1930.

Around the time of Chiang Kai-shek's first massive attack, the Red Army faced trouble from within. Under the influence of the KMT's Anti-Bolshevik League, whose agents had infiltrated the communist forces, 4,400 Red soldiers mutinied. The army command ordered their arrest. Their leaders, sons of landlords and gentry, were brought before tribunals at mass meetings of local peasants. Mao is said to have led the prosecution at these tribunals. He compared the false leaders of the Anti-Bolshevik League, who 'used words of revolution that stirred your hearts', with the leopard 'that cries in the forests at night in the deceptive voice of a human being until men go out in rescue groups, never to return!' This was an apt simile for men whose military policies were similar to those of Li Li-san and whose line in agrarian reform made sure the large estates belonging to their families or friends were excluded from confiscation and redistribution. Many of the mutineer soldiers were won over; the agents who had misled them, perhaps 400 in all, were shot; and the League's network was itself infiltrated and broken up.

Mutinies were by now more frequent on the KMT side, especially when Chiang's ill-paid, poor-peasant troops came into contact with the strong morale of the bulk of the Red Army and observed the fruits of the communists' land policy. A soldier of the KMT's Nineteenth Route Army told Agnes Smedley about the methods used by Chiang's troops to attack the 'Red bandits', and how the Red Army organised retaliation:

> Our officers made us burn everything to the ground in the Soviet territories. Everything within three hundred *li* of Hingkwo we burned down. Then they ordered us to kill every person we saw in the villages. They said it was an order from the highest command. So we did it. We took all the pigs and chickens and sheep and cows the peasants left behind and killed and ate them. We reaped their rice and ate it. The whole population hated us. When we came they would all take everything they could and retreat with the Reds. Nobody would help us. They would not even give us a drink of water, and they poisoned some of the wells and the rivers before they left. We had better guns and aeroplanes, and we even had poison gas, but we were afraid of them . . .
>
> They value their rifles more than their lives, so in the front ranks would come peasants with hoes, axes, spears, and only a few rifles. Then came men with more rifles. At last came men armed each with a rifle and pistol. By

the time the last ones had reached us we were tired of fighting and the armed men could capture our rifles and ammunition and machine guns, and we would have to retreat or be captured. We never did capture any of their guns, but they got a lot of ours. They have an ironic expression about the government troops: 'Our transport and munition supply troops are coming!' they would say of us.

Everybody in Kiangsi can fight. They have a very good organisation . . . Even though we occupied Hingkwo for a number of months, still they secretly controlled the government of the city. We were always afraid. Everybody who came and went from the city had to be examined and have a special certificate. We killed many of them, but still the communists knew everything we did . . .

In every village of even ten families they have primary schools. All the way to Hingkwo we found schools in huts . . . We would always tear down and burn their schools, for our officers said they were Red centres . . .

Sometimes we found some of their books of songs. I can remember a few lines of one of these songs. It was something like this: 'Chiang Kai-shek, you dirty traitor! You cheated workers and peasants when you were in Canton!' . . . One called *The International* . . . is about the poor of the whole world. Sometimes some of us tried to keep some of these books and songs in our coats, but if we were caught we would be shot.

Everywhere the Reds left large posters of propaganda amongst the White troops. They scattered leaflets and pamphlets all along the route we marched. I remember some of their posters:

'For whom are you fighting?'
'Soldiers should not fight soldiers!'
'The poor should not fight the poor!'
'Why are you fighting the toiling masses of workers and peasants?'
'You fight — your officers keep your money! You die — they live!'

In their leaflets they wrote all about their Soviet Government ... They said that every soldier in the Red Army is given land, and others cultivate it when he is away fighting ... They have boards with the name of the peasant or soldier and how much land the Soviet has allotted him. We saw these boards everywhere ...

They treated [our] common soldiers very well, but they killed our officers. When they capture a soldier they talk to him and ask him to join them. If the man agrees, he is given the same rights as everybody else. If he does not want to stay, they give him a passport to pass through Soviet territory and enough money for him to reach home. [18]

A foreign observer of the period quoted by H. F. MacNair in his book *China in Revolution*, wrote that Mao's and Chu's tactics were 'as simple as a schoolboy's primer. When they are strong enough to meet the foe, they meet him. When not, they drop out of the picture, dispersing like raindrops on the yellow surface of the Yangtze.' A leading physician in China, Ida Kahn, who appealed for foreign aid to fight the communists, commented, according to MacNair, 'Hence the famous slogan ... "If you come I will go, but if you go, then I will come." Can any troops run such elusive creatures to their covers? Never! No, never!'

Mao and the Red Army officers sometimes had difficulty restraining the violent revenge of the awakened peasants. Agnes Smedley told of the capture of the walled city of Shangpo in south Kiangsi in the autumn of 1931. Her story gives a vivid picture of the peasant upsurge at this time, its cruelty and its logic, and the arguments Mao used to channel it, encouraging the peasants to make the transition from destruction to construction, and after annihilating the old oppression to go on and build the new people's movement.

It was the peasants, spears and knives in hand, who dashed through [the gates of Shangpo] first and rushed upon the homes of the great landlords. Some of the landlords killed themselves, but most of them, with their entire families, fell into the hands of the peasants. When the Red Army tried to take the prisoners into their own hands, the peasants refused, claiming them as their own.

'As they have slaughtered our brothers, so will we slaughter them!' they cried. The Red Army protested, saying: 'Wait! Execute them only after they have been tried by the people.'

The storehouses of the great families remained bulging with rice and other food. When the peasants, taking charge of the fine homes, the ancestral temples, and the storehouses, saw this stored food, their hatred grew. These food stores were taken charge of by the Confiscation Committee of the Red Army, and thereto was added nearly two million dollars in gold and silver dug from the walls and tiled floors of the buildings . . .

These peasants began ripping from the walls every scroll, every picture, giving them to the flames lit on the meadows beyond the walls. They carried out all furniture, every strip of cloth, every dish, every pan from the kitchens. The old vases, the huge carved candlesticks, the ancient oil lamps, the old pottery and the carved ivory chop-sticks — all were piled on the leaping flames or smashed into dust . . .

They even carried out rifles from the buildings and were busily engaged in breaking or burning them, when Red Army men yelled and fought: 'Keep them, arm yourselves! Don't be fools like this!' And when peasants came rushing along, carrying the hated radio machines with which the landlords had talked to Nanking and Kanchow, the Red Army had to take them by force.

Then there were the great ancestral temples where ancestral tablets told a tale of generations of wealth and power . . . The peasants seized these tablets, and the scrolls, paintings, the carved tables and altars, and took them to the flames. Before the temples stood the stone monuments to the great mandarins. For hours they laboured, hammering them until nothing remained but piles of granite pieces on which an occasional lone character shone.

In the big houses . . . were found the chief stores of wealth of the great families — opium. Fully ten thousand *piculs* were found. The Confiscation Committee stood back and raised no voice of protest when men and women loaded themselves with it and ran with it to the leaping flames on the meadows . . .

When the buildings of the great landlords were almost gutted, [the Red Army] stepped in and took possession, to save what remained and to preserve the buildings for future use . . .

To the killing of the landlords the Red Army commanders agreed if the masses wanted it. But they made one request: they said that only the heads of the large families should be executed, that the women and children should be spared; nor should sons be killed just because they were sons. All day long the Red Army commanders talked like this. At first the peasants could not believe their own ears.

'What is this?' they exclaimed. 'It is the *family* that owns the land . . .'

'You say we shall kill only the heads of the family; that means we leave the roots to grow into a tree again . . .'

'Out there beyond are the White armies. If they come, they will give back the land to the big families . . .'

Some of the Red Army commanders went out and talked to the people. There came first . . . Mao Tse-tung. His name was a legend. But when he talked he also talked about communism and what it will do to the social system. He talked for a long time. His ideas were good. But about the families he was all wrong! From the audience men angrily accused him of trying to protect the landlords from the peasants. Nor could any of his replies silence them . . .

It was late in the day, when the sun was low in the west, that the eighteen great families were paraded through the streets and brought before the platforms where peasant men and women denounced them and demanded their death. Those who approved of their execution were asked to raise their hands . . . Up went the hands of every living soul except that of the landlords and their families and the Red Army commanders who remained silent observers in the background. The prisoners stood, the men with their hands tied behind them as once they had tied peasants . . . Then the prisoners were marched beyond into the meadows . . .

Once into their midst dashed a peasant woman . . . She ferociously fought her way to one of the kneeling landlords. He did not even see her, for he was bent in terror to the earth. But this woman knew him, and the watching peasants knew her. They recalled that she had borne eight children, but now she stood alone. Of her eight children, seven had died at the breast, and but one lived to work in the fields by the side of his father. The father and son had taken part in the harvest struggle two years before, and both had been captured by this land-lord and driven by him to Shangpo. Their heads had decorated the city gates. Afterward, this gaunt old woman had wandered from village to village and people treated her kindly because words of wisdom are said to come from the lips of the demented.

She had regained her senses, but insanity had been more merciful. Now she fought her way to the side of the landlord responsible for the killing of her son and husband. She passed him by and stood before his chief wife, who knelt, a baby clasped in her arms. The old peasant woman reached down and ferociously ripped the baby from the mother's arms, then lifted it above her and dashed it to the earth. Repeatedly she picked it up and hurled it to the earth until, exhausted, she turned and pushed her way through the crowd, screaming . . .

Then the peasant guards set to work with grim,

hate-laden determination. Time and again they plunged their spears, and the air was rent with screams of fearful terror and agony . . . The meadows became covered with the dead. There they lay through the night and on the dawn of the following morning were carried to the fields and buried in the raw earth, becoming fertiliser for the crops. There were those who said it was the only good they had ever done to any man . . .

In Shangpo in the days that followed there arose unions of peasants, apprentices, handworkers, arsenal workers, women, fishermen, transportation workers, and many others, and there sprang to life the Young Guards, the Communist Youth League, the Pioneers, and the Communist Party. Red peasant guards took the place of the *Min Tuan* [the landlords' militia], and were armed with their weapons. And from their delegates was elected the first Soviet government of Shangpo . . . Six weeks after the fall of Shangpo, delegates were elected to go to the first All-China Soviet Congress in Juichin. [19]

It was at that congress that the CCP set up a Central Soviet Government, or Soviet Republic of China, on 7 November 1931. Mao was elected chairman.

Chiang Kai-shek's three Encirclement Campaigns of 1930-1 were successfully resisted. After initial losses of some areas, the Red Army counter-attacked each time, regained the lost territory and even extended the soviets further.

The First Campaign was thwarted when troops under the warlord Chang Hui-tsan were lured into ambush. Ten thousand men were captured, along with General Chang himself and 6,000 rifles. Chang appealed to Mao to save him. Mao was lying on a rough bed in a peasant hut talking to some peasants. In these surroundings, which were strange to the general, Mao is said to have told him, 'I am not a White officer with the power to alter the decision of the masses. You are in a soviet country and only the soldiers can save you. Appeal to them!'

Chang was then taken to watch the defeat of the remainder of his troops. Then he was tried and executed by soldiers whose families his army had exterminated. His head was bound to a board with a red cloth. On the board were painted the words: 'This is the head of Chang Hui-tsan, commander of the Eighteenth White Division, enemy of the people!' The head on the board was thrown in the river where it floated into KMT territory. It was fished out and taken to Nanchang where Chiang Kai-shek arranged a great funeral for it.

Mao's poem, *Opposing the 'First Siege'*, celebrated the victory.

Beneath a frosty sky the woods blazed totally red,
The anger of Heaven's soldiers through the high clouds
    soared;
Round mist-filled Lungkang blurred a thousand peaks
    as
Together shouted all,
For away in front they had captured Chang Hui-tsan.

Two hundred thousand troops re-entered Kiangsi,
Great gusts of wind and dust choked half the world.
Workers and peasants in their millions were wakened
    up;
Acting with one mind
Red flags rioted round the foot of Puchoushan.

Chiang Kai-shek next sent 200,000 men against Mao's 30,000 in a Second Campaign in May—June 1931. They were defeated, with the loss of 10,000 KMT soldiers killed and 30,000 captured. Another poem imagines Chiang Kai-shek weeping over his failed strategy of 'a bastion at every step', that is, of consolidating his advance stage by stage.

On top of White Cloud Mountain clouds lingered
    to stay,
Below White Cloud Mountain the din of shouting
    quickened,

Even shrivelled wood and rotted branch took part.
A forest of rifles threatened,
Like the 'Flying General' zooming out of the blue.

Seven hundred miles forced march in fifteen days,
Through desolate Kan waters and green Fukien
    hills,
Like a broom sweeping up the thousands strong as
    folding a mat.
Someone is weeping now,
Whose strategy 'a bastion at every step', alas, of
    what use?

In the Third Campaign in June—September 1931 the Red Army defeated seventeen of Chiang's thirty-three divisions. The entire 50th Nanking Division and a part of the 14th Division, some 30,000 to 40,000 men, deserted to the communist side. More than 25,000 rifles, machine guns, cannon and ammunition were captured.

But despite their success, Mao's tactics had their critics. A dispute arose between Mao and Wang Ming and Po Ku (Central Committee members who had returned from Russia) over the military tactics to be adopted by the newly formed Central Soviet Government. Forced out of Shanghai by KMT repression, these and other members of the Central Committee had settled in Kiangsi, and, though they knew little about the situation in the base area apart from what they had read in reports, immediately ordered a modification of Mao's guerrilla principles.

Mao and Chu Teh had developed the fluid tactics of 'luring the enemy in deep', depending on concealment and deception in order to strike the enemy at his weakest. Their methods had become, according to Mao, 'a complete set of operational principles' by the summer of 1931. Now Mao's critics advocated the adoption of less flexible, 'forward and offensive' positional tactics, involving head-on clashes and great attacks. At a conference at Ningtu in August 1932 Mao was relieved of his control over the army, though he remained chairman of the Soviet Republic. The adoption of the new tactics in the next two years contributed to the reversals in 1934 which led in turn to the evacuation of the base area and the withdrawal, which became an advance, of the Long March.

The defence against the Fourth Encirclement Campaign of April—October 1933 thus went ahead under Mao's influence but outside his control. Meanwhile, in June 1933, Mao turned his attention to the 'land verification movement'.

The purpose of the verification movement was firstly the economic one of seeing that the Land Reform Law, passed by the Central Soviet Government in November 1931, had been carried out. According to this law, rich peasants were to receive inferior land and the landlords none. Middle peasants could keep their own land and need take no part in land reform unless they wished to. Mao saw the political aim of the verification movement as especially important, since it brought an upsurge of popular support, especially among the poorest, and helped to raise the peasants' consciousness by making a link between the economic and political struggles.

He listed three stages in rural transformation: land reform, the verification movement and agricultural development. In this, one can see the pattern of his thinking that political struggle leads to economic reform; economic reform to further political struggle in which the consciousness of the peasants rises in the course of defending their gains; and from that raised consciousness comes economic development. Development did not depend on machines or on officials. Mao was convinced that the masses of poor peasants must themselves effect the social and economic transformation, and not rely on 'a few Soviet functionaries' acting for them.

> Our class line in the agrarian revolution is to depend upon the hired farm hands and poor peasants, to ally with the middle peasants, to check the rich peasants, and to annihilate the landlords. The correct practice of

this line is the key to the success of the agrarian revolution and the foundation for all other policies of the Soviet government in the villages. Hence, the Soviet government should deal severely with all erroneous tendencies to infringe upon the middle peasants (mainly the well-to-do middle peasants) or to annihilate the rich peasants. At the same time, it should also not permit the error of making a compromise with the landlords and rich peasants. [20]

In the same speech at the Second All-China Congress of Soviets, held at Juichin in January 1934, Mao said that the living conditions of the peasantry had been much improved:

In the past, the peasants would live on tree-bark or grain husks for several months a year. This situation no longer prevails, and there is no more starvation in the Soviet districts. The life of the peasantry is improving year by year. They are no longer in rags. They now eat meat more regularly; it is no longer the luxury to them that it was in former times. [21]

At the end of the conference he chided the delegates for failing to stress the question of 'the well-being of the masses' during their debates. 'If we only mobilise the people to carry on the war and do nothing else, can we succeed in defeating the enemy? Of course not.' Besides redistributing land, they must, he said, increase agricultural production, establish co-operatives, develop trade and solve the everyday problems of the people, namely, 'food, shelter and clothing, fuel, rice, cooking oil and salt, sickness and hygiene, and marriage.'

Mao was beginning to see that the higher cooperative consciousness gained during class struggle, especially in the case of the poor peasants, would not only begin to transform social relationships but could also promote economic growth. Combining class struggle with the 'fight for production' later became a fundamental principle of Mao's, most clearly expressed in Yenan, the Great Leap Forward and the cultural revolution. Mao thus compensated for his enforced abdication from military matters in the period 1932-4 by these developments in his political and social thinking.

The social and economic achievements Mao summarised in his long report at the Second Juichin Congress made impressive reading: the spread of schools and adult education, the election of many women as deputies, the growth of marketing and food cooperatives and the beginning of production cooperatives, and the planning of irrigation and sanitation projects. Already news of the comparative, if limited, successes of the bases was spreading to other parts of the country. The picture in the Kiangsi base contrasted sharply with the realities in much of the rest of China:

> The cost of armies absorbed 60 to 80 percent of the [Nanking] government's income. Famines increased: that of 1927 affected 9 million people, that of 1928, 27 million, that of 1929, 57 million. The terrible flood, of 1931, aggravated by lack of proper upkeep of dykes, covered an area the size of Great Britain. Even the new roads, spectacular sign of China's progress, were to the poorer peasants an added burden. They were built by forced labour, sometimes without payment; the right-of-way was taken without recompense; and the local peasants were not allowed to use their sharp-wheeled carts upon them. [22]

Edgar Snow described the great north-west famine of 1929 in which between three and six million people died:

> Have you ever seen a man — a good honest man who has worked hard, a 'law-abiding citizen', doing no serious harm to anyone — when he has had no food for more than a month? It is a most agonising sight. His dying flesh hangs from him in wrinkled folds; you can clearly see every bone in his body; his eyes stare out unseeing; and even if he is a youth of twenty he moves like an ancient crone, dragging himself from spot to spot. If he has been lucky he has long ago sold his wife and daughters. He has sold everything he owns, the timber

of his house itself, and most of his clothes. Sometimes he has, indeed, even sold the last rag of decency, and he sways there in the scorching sun, his testicles dangling from him like withered olive seeds — the last grim jest to remind you that this was once a man.

Children are even more pitiable, with their little skeletons bent over and misshapen, their crooked bones, their little arms like twigs, and their purpling bellies, filled with bark and sawdust, protruding like tumours. Women lie slumped in corners, waiting for death, their black blade-like buttocks protruding, their breasts hanging like collapsed sacks. But there are, after all, not many women and girls. Most of them had died or been sold.

The shocking thing was that in many of those towns there were still rich men, rice hoarders, wheat hoarders, money-lenders, and landlords, with armed guards to defend them, while they profiteered enormously. The shocking thing was that in the cities — where officials danced or played with sing-song girls — there were grain and food, and had been for months. [23]

Seven years after the setting up of Chiang Kai-shek's Nanking government, a foreign oberver concluded:

Big landlords are consolidating their position at the expense of the poor peasantry . . . Through the connivance of corrupt military authorities, they acquire age-old state and community lands and entrench themselves at the expense of the poor and middle farmers . . . An army of refugees, driven from home by banditry, civil war, flood, drought, famine, has become the visible sign of China's plight . . . When the Nationalists became ascendant in 1927, a population greater than Holland was homeless. In 1933 that toll reached the population of post-war Germany, 65 million . . . The twin plagues of the rapacious landlord and the village usurer continue their seasonal triumph over the masses virtually unchecked. [24]

In 1933 the KMT crushed the 'People's Revolutionary Government', led by Tsai Ting-kai, in neighbouring Fukien province. It followed up this success with a Fifth Encirclement Campaign against the Kiangsi Soviet from October 1933 until October 1934.

The new blockade was effected by a ring of 2,900 blockhouses, concrete machine-gun nests, 150 bomber aeroplanes, barbed wire and over 900,000 troops, with the aid of vast funds including a loan from the United States and Britain. This time the blockade imposed an intolerable strain on the base area. The Soviet was reduced from seventy counties to six. Supplies were cut off, including salt; food prices rose. The Red Army lost 60,000 men. Chiang Kai-shek subjected the local population to mass executions and enforced migration. By the KMT's own estimate they killed or starved to death as many as a million peasants in the scorched earth campaign to 'recover' the Kiangsi Soviet.

Mao later said,

> In this period we made two important errors. The first was the failure to unite with Tsai Ting-kai's army in 1933 during the Fukien Rebellion. The second was the adoption of the erroneous strategy of simple defence, abandoning our former tactics of manoeuvre. It was a serious mistake to meet the vastly superior Nanking forces in positional warfare, at which the Red Army was neither technically nor spiritually at its best. [25]

In these deteriorating conditions Mao and Chu Teh announced in July 1934 that an anti-Japanese vanguard would go north 'to unite with all forces in China for a common struggle' against the Japanese, who had begun their occupation of China's north-eastern provinces in September 1931. The Red Army's offer was on condition that any such KMT allied force must stop attacking the soviet areas, grant democratic rights and arouse the masses for the war against Japan.

The vanguard managed to break through the encirclement but became isolated, and was destroyed. Another detachment reached Ho Lung's soviet base in Kweichow province and formed the Second Front Army under Ho and Jen Pi-shih.

During the Kiangsi years, Mao's life remained simple and unostentatious. According to Chen Chang-feng, a teenage boy who became his orderly in 1930 and later his bodyguard, Mao wore a grey uniform 'the same as ours . . . [except] that the pockets of his coat seemed to be especially large. His black hair contrasted sharply with his fair complexion. Maybe he was a bit too thin. His eyes seemed to be very big and keen.'

When Chen first met him, Mao was talking to a visitor. As he spoke 'he gesticulated; his voice was gentle. Although I didn't understand what he was talking about, I felt he was very sincere . . . He stood up. It was only then that I saw he was quite tall.' Mao asked him his name and age.

> 'Why did you join the Red Army?' Commissar Mao asked me like a schoolteacher questioning a pupil. 'The Red Army is good. It fights the local despots!' I was standing straight at attention. Commissar Mao made me sit down and asked with interest, 'Are there local despots in your home village?' 'Yes,' I said, 'I was driven away by them myself.' And I told him in detail how I had lived with my family and how I had run away and joined the Red Army. He listened to me attentively, sometimes nodding or smiling slightly. This put me at ease, and I felt I could get along with this man very well; so I talked on at great length. [26]

Chen Chang-feng 'soon got to know his habits'. He made Mao's meals and fetched his washing water. 'Because we didn't have a basin, he would soak the towel in the dipper and rub his face and sometimes his body to freshen himself up. Then he'd feel hungry, and I'd warm up the "rice sandwich" (two layers of rice with cooked vegetable in between) left in the bowl since the afternoon for him to eat.' Once Chen threw away the left-overs. When Mao found

out, he said 'There is a struggle for every grain of rice that
the people grow. In future you musn't throw away what I
leave. Keep it for the next meal.'

Often we captured a place and war booty came to us,
but Commissar Mao never kept anything. He would
always send what he got to his subordinates or the
hospital. In the winter of 1931, when we captured
Chian in Kiangsi, I found a thermos bottle there in the
house of a local despot who had run away ... On the
march I used to get someone else to carry it for me so
that he would not know about it. With that bottle I was
always able to keep some hot water ready for him, but
it was still difficult to prepare him a quick meal. His
small bowl could not hold very much rice ...

In November 1931, the Central (Soviet) Government
was founded in Juichin and he was elected chairman of
the Republic. That's when we began to call him Chairman instead of Commissar Mao. But he still used his
little bowl at meals. It was only in February 1934, when
we captured Changchow in Fukien, that I managed to
find a real three-decker enamel container for his food ...

We were constantly on the move. We'd seldom stay at
a place for more than a month ... His personal possessions included only two blankets, one cotton sheet, two
grey uniforms ... a worn overcoat, and one grey woollen
sweater. Then he had a broken umbrella, a bowl for
eating and a knapsack with nine compartments for his
maps, documents and books. When we were campaign-
ing or on the march, he carried the knapsack and
umbrella himself. I would carry the rest. When we came
to our camp site, I would find two wooden boards, put
them together and spread the blankets and sheet on
them, folding up his uniforms to make a pillow. This
was his bed. [27]

At the beginning of October 1934, Mao, recovering from a
severe two-month bout of malaria, joined the military council
set up to direct the evacuation of the Kiangsi base. But his

style of military preparation was still not restored. All he could do was to criticise the haste with which the evacuation was planned and the secrecy that kept the soldiers ignorant of the move and of the direction to be taken. Within a week the military council was ready to depart. On 16 October the Long March of 85,000 soldiers and 15,000 cadres began.

Chen Chang-feng recalled that 'Chairman Mao did not take his nine-compartment knapsack with him. His entire equipment consisted of two blankets, a cotton sheet, an oilcloth, a worn overcoat, a broken (oiled paper) umbrella and a bundle of books.' Mao was thin and emaciated from malaria. He told Chen they were 'going to the front to fight'. The enemy Mao had in mind was the Japanese, and it turned out that the 'front' was 6,000 miles to the north-west.

Mao's third wife, Ho Tzu-chen, whom he had met in 1928 when she was eighteen and who was now pregnant, went with them. Some 28,000 soldiers remained behind to fight rear-guard actions. Others were left to recover from their wounds and still others dispersed as small guerrilla groups to continue harassing the enemy for many years until their remnants joined the regular communist armies again in the Third Civil War of 1945-9.

Chen Chang-feng wrote:

> Around five o'clock in the evening, Mao and about twenty others left Yutu by the North Gate, and then turned to the left towards the river, which was all yellow, roaring and foaming, as though calling on the armies to advance. Soon the sun set and the gusts of bitter wind chilled us. The Chairman wore a grey cloth uniform and an eight-cornered military cap, with no overcoat. He walked with enormous strides along the riverbank. [28]

The Long March and a new phase of China's revolutionary struggle had begun.

4 A Manifesto, a Propaganda Force, a Seeding Machine

The Second Revolutionary Civil War:
The Long March, 1935

> Without the Long March, how could the broad masses
> have learned so quickly about the existence of the great
> truth which the Red Army embodies?
>
> Mao Tse-tung,
> *On Tactics against Japanese Imperialism*

In an epic tactical and strategic shift lasting 370 days, Mao's
First Front Army marched 6,000 miles, fighting enemy
pursuers and crossing fast rivers, snow-covered mountains and
boggy grasslands to reach the relative security of the North
Shensi Soviet.

Over the whole march, the main force of Mao's army
averaged nearly one skirmish a day and had fifteen whole
days of major pitched battle. They made 235 day marches
and 18 night marches. Their hundred days of halt included
days when they were fighting. Fifty-six of these 'rest' days
were taken all at one time while they were in north-west
Szechuan. The remaining forty-four days, spread over the
6,000-mile journey, averages out to one day's halt for every
114 miles. The average daily march was thus 17 miles. If the
halt in Szechuan is left out of the account, the average per
day was 26 miles.

Many diseases afflicted the marchers. The most common
were malaria, dysentery, typhoid, influenza and trachoma.
Many marchers suffered from severe ulceration of feet and
legs. All lost weight, became anaemic and showed signs of
nervous strain. It took many months and even years for
some of the Long Marchers to recover from their various

ordeals. Mao himself caught malaria again during the march and ended in Shensi in a very weak condition.

Each soldier set out carrying a pack containing a blanket, a winter uniform, cloth or straw shoes, a cup, a pair of chopsticks, a needle and thread, a bamboo hat against sun and rain, and a rifle. The men of the Supply Department took along the arsenal, the mint, printing presses, sewing machines and stretchers. Mao, still sick at the start, rode a white horse, captured from a KMT general in 1928, which served him throughout the march. The great line of marching soldiers often stretched for fifty miles without a break, coiling over the hills like a new Great Wall.

The chief engineer of the army's arsenal described the breakthrough from the Kiangsi base into enemy territory.

> The enemy knew nothing about our movements until we had broken through the second defence line and were in their rear. Once in enemy territory we often marched at night to avoid air-raids. Night marching is wonderful if there is a moon and a gentle wind blowing. When no enemy troops were near, whole companies would sing and others would answer. If it was a black night and the enemy far away, we made torches from pine branches or frayed bamboo, and then it was truly beautiful. At the foot of a mountain, we could look up and see a long column of lights coiling like a fiery dragon up the mountain side. From the summit we could look in both directions and see miles of torches moving forward like a wave of fire. A rosy glow hung over the whole route of the march.
>
> We marched through Kiangsi and along the mountain ranges of the Kwangtung, Hunan and Kwangsi borders. For weeks at a time we fought our way across plains, capturing cities and supplying ourselves from landlord warehouses and enemy ammunition dumps . . .
>
> The Kwangsi warlords . . . drove peasants from our route of march, then burned villages and told the people that we did it. We often saw villages burning far to the

south where we had never been, and we sometimes captured Kwangsi agents in the act of setting fire to villages. We shot them down . . .

We always confiscated the property of the landlords and militarist-officials, kept enough food for ourselves, and distributed the rest to poor peasants and the urban poor. When we captured great warehouses full of salt, every man in our ranks filled his pockets and ate it, like sugar.

Our medical workers searched everywhere for quinine and other drugs, but never found sufficient.

We also held great mass meetings. Our Dramatic Corps played and sang for the people, and our political workers wrote slogans and distributed copies of the Soviet Constitution and the Fundamental Laws of the Soviet Government. If we stayed in a place for even one night we taught the peasants to write at least six characters: 'Destroy the Tuhao' (feudal gentry and landlords) and 'Divide the land'.

When hard pressed by superior forces, we marched in the daytime, and at such times the bombers pounded us. We would scatter and lie down; get up and march, then scatter and lie down again, hour after hour. Our dead and wounded were many and our medical workers had a very hard time. The peasants always helped us and offered to take our sick, our wounded and exhausted. Each man left behind was given some money, ammunition and his rifle and told to organise and lead the peasants in partisan warfare as soon as he recovered. [1]

The fourth and last line of the KMT blockade, the Hsiang River, was crossed with the loss of as many as half the men. The river crossing showed Mao the unwise nature of the Red Army's marching tactics, which forced the non-combatants to pass down a narrow corridor formed by two columns who **were fighting what was in essence a covering operation against** the pursuing enemy. The possibilities for the combat troops to manoeuvre were thus limited. This went against the grain with Mao, whose inclination was always towards flexibility of movement and preserving the initiative in the Red Army's hands.

Once across the river the army found its path towards Ho Lung's North-west Hunan Soviet blocked by a massive KMT troop concentration. Faced with an army five or six times its size and the clear possibility of extermination in a head-on battle, the rank and file voiced doubts about the leadership of the CCP. Liu Po-cheng, a leading general on the march, recalled:

> It was at this critical stage that Mao Tse-tung came forward with a plan which saved the Red Army. He proposed to give up the attempt to join the Second and Sixth Army Groups, and proposed that the Central Red Army wheel towards Kweichow where the enemy was weak. This would give the Red Army the initiative, enable it to win several battles, gain a respite and get some necessary rest and consolidation. [2]

Mao's army, reduced to 30,000 men by enemy attacks, thus turned west and, crossing precipitous mountains and the swift Wu River, captured first Liping in December and then Tsunyi in January 1935. There they had their first rests, reviewed their position and reorganised, aiming to link up with Chang Kuo-tao's Fourth Front Army in Szechuan province.

Mao reasserted his strategy and tactics. At a conference at Tsunyi his principles of fluid warfare were re-adopted and his style of keeping soldiers well-informed and of developing comradely relations between leaders and soldiers and between soldiers and peasants was resumed. He was elected chairman of the political bureau and of the Revolutionary Military Council, giving him supreme leadership of the party's military affairs.

At the Tsunyi conference the destination of the march was re-affirmed. The slogan 'Go north to fight the Japanese' began to give political direction to the troops as well as identifying Shensi as the eventual base from which to fight the

Japanese. The army passed from being merely a passive force, whose retreat had to be covered in running combat, to a force that had recaptured the initiative and had begun to advance. The army also began to make its political and educational role among the peasants clearer. The programme of killing tyrants in the villages through which it passed, burning land deeds and titles, distributing grain, opening jails and calling mass meetings began to turn the army's passage through the countryside into a wider and more consciously implemented propaganda campaign against semi-feudal land ownership.

As if to cross the Yangtze River into central Szechuan, the First Front Army moved northward from Tsunyi, captured the Loushan Pass and pressed towards the river under attack from warlord and provincial KMT troops. They found the river defences too strong, so Mao's forces backtracked, recaptured the Loushan Pass, retook Tsunyi and inflicted a major defeat on the Kwangsi provincial forces, the first significant victory of the Long March. Mao directed this operation, encircling the enemy in a 100-square mile area of mountains, his troops cutting down the massed soldiers with broadswords. Twenty regiments were wiped out.

Mao celebrated the valour of the Red Army at this time in his poem *Loushan Pass*.

> Cold is the west wind;
> Far in the frosty air the wild geese call in the morning
>   moonlight.
> In the morning moonlight
> The clatter of horses' hooves rings sharp,
> And the bugle's note is muted.
>
> Do not say that the strong pass is guarded with iron.
> This very day in one step we shall pass its summit,
> We shall pass its summit!
> There the hills are blue like the sea,
> And the dying sun like blood.

Meanwhile Chang Kuo-tao's forces fled north-west towards the Tibetan border under warlord attack, making it more difficult for the First Front Army to join them. Mao decided to change route and strike out south and west into Yunnan, still aiming to swing north later towards his Shensi objective. A small force, sent to attack Kweiyang, succeeded in luring the main body of enemy troops out of Yunnan. 'The rest of the Red Army's main force', Liu Po-cheng recounted, 'thrust into Yunnan, marching in opposite direction to the Yunnan troops hurrying to the aid of Kweiyang. This time Mao Tse-tung again successfully applied the flexible tactic of making a feint in the east while actually attacking in the west. The enemy took our bait and thus enabled our army to turn to the west.'

Once in Yunnan, the main columns again made a feint. A division under Lin Piao appeared to threaten the provincial capital Kunming, while Liu Po-cheng led vanguard forces straight towards the Yangtze River, which in those reaches is called the Chinsha or Golden Sand River. Chiang Kai-shek, who had come to Kunming to direct operations only to flee at the noises made by Lin Piao's division on the road to the city, at last realised the drive on Kunming was a diversion of Mao's and ordered all the boats at the Chinsha river crossings to be burnt. The current was swift and navigation treacherous. It seemed impossible for an army the size of Mao's to cross safely.

> Nanking pilots reported that a Red vanguard had begun building a bamboo bridge. Chiang became more confident; this bridge-building would take weeks. But one evening, quite unobtrusively, a Red battalion suddenly reversed its direction. On a phenomenal forced march it covered eighty-five miles in one night and day, and in late afternoon descended upon the only other possible ferry crossing in the vicinity, at Chou Ping Fort. Dressed in captured Nanking uniforms, the battalion entered the town at dusk without arousing comment, and quietly disarmed the garrison. [3]

Meanwhile, Chiang started to move his troops to surround the Red Army and, pressing it up against the river, annihilate it in one final attack. Liu Po-cheng described how the Red Army 'slashed a way north across the river'.

> The broad, turbulent Chinsha River crashed its way through deep mountain valleys along the Szechuan—Yunnan border . . . Chiang Kai-shek's planes flew over the area every day trying to detect our movement. It was a race against time. The Red Army, marching by night, approached the Chinsha River . . .
>
> The cadres' regiment stole across . . . and sprang an attack on the enemy, destroying a whole platoon. The regiment immediately took control of both ends of the Chiaoche Ferry and seized seven ferry boats. The main force of the regiment sped on to the plateau thirty *li* away, traversing the yawning valley on the north bank of the river and routing the enemy reinforcements from Szechuan . . . The First and Third Army Groups moved to the Chiaoche Ferry to cross the river under protecting fire . . .
>
> Three days later, about six regiments of the enemy's 'dare-to-die' 13th Division reached Chiaoche Ferry in pursuit of the Red Army. But they were beaten back in a surprise attack by the Fifth Army Group, and were forced to retreat along the Chinsha River in utter confusion. Chiang Kai-shek discovered the change in the Red Army's tactics and called a meeting at Kweiyang at which our tactics were studied and plans made to try and outwit us, and so save his forces from annihilation by the Red Army. The enemy decided on a tactic of 'long pursuit, well-planned attack'. Now far away from its parent body and stunned by events, the Kuomintang's 13th Division dared not take action and dug itself in at Tuanchieh. By the aid of the seven ferry boats captured from the enemy our army crossed the Chinsha River at the Chiaoche Ferry in nine days and nine nights. When large reinforcements of the enemy arrived on the tenth

day, the Red Army was already far ahead, and all the
ferry boats were destroyed. [4]

The Red Army thus managed to extricate itself from the
several hundred thousand KMT troops pursuing and encircling it. The victory showed Mao again in full control of the
Red Army's movements, using fluid tactics to outwit, out-
march and outgeneral Chiang Kai-shek.

Once he had crossed to the northern bank of the Golden
Sand River, Mao supervised the passage of the remaining Red
Army forces. His bodyguard, the young Chen Chang-feng,
wrote that Mao had hardly landed when he was off with Liu
Po-cheng to plan the next stage of the march.

I set about looking for somewhere for him to use as a
temporary office and living quarters. It didn't look
hopeful. The river bank was nothing but bare rocks,
with a few holes in the cliffs, dripping with moisture,
hardly big enough to be called caves. I sought in vain for
planks or even straw to use for a bed. In the end I had
to lay out a piece of oilcloth on the ground and put the
blanket on it, feeling that that would at least give him
something to lie down on; he hadn't rested at all the
whole night. Come to that, he'd had no rest for the last
few days.

My next task was to lay out his documents, maps and
papers. Usually I did it with his secretary, Comrade
Huang Yu-feng, whenever we made camp. We used to
rig up some kind of a table or desk. But now there was
nothing at all to use even as a makeshift, and Comrade
Huang was still on the other side of the river. How could
the Chairman do his work? I tried pinning one map on
the wall of the cave, but it was no good — it was just
sand and wouldn't hold the nail, and there wasn't room
to spread the documents out. Already I had wasted
enough time; I was expecting Chairman Mao back from
his conference any minute, and I hadn't even got a drop
of boiled water ready . . . Chairman Mao came back and
sent for me . . .

'The work's the all-important thing at a moment like this. Food or drink are trifles. Twenty to thirty thousand of our comrades are still waiting to cross the river there. It's a matter of thirty thousand lives!'

I didn't know what to say, but stood there gazing at him. I could feel my heart pounding. He came right up to me. 'Go on,' he said. 'Find me a board or something to use as a desk before you do anything else.' I pulled myself together and ran off, and by hunting high and low found a small board which must have been used as a door for a cave mouth. Chairman Mao helped me to set it up, spreading out his maps and documents. Then I remembered the water; it must have boiled by now. I got up to fetch it, when the Chairman spoke to me again. 'Chen Chang-feng!' 'Yes?' 'Come back!' I went right back into the cave, standing before the 'desk'. 'I'll have to give you some punishment, you know,' he said. Although the tone of his voice was mild as usual, I felt the air very tense. I realised how I had failed in my job, and stood looking at him, very miserable. 'I want you to sit here and work with me the whole day without sleep.' I felt an uneasy smile come over my face and sat down opposite him. 'Right,' I said. He had got telegrams and documents all over his desk.

The field telephone was transmitting messages all the time, and he was absolutely immersed in work . . .

I was awfully drowsy, and had a habit of dropping off beside him when he was working . . . But that day when I saw him heart and soul in his work, I had not the least desire to sleep. From time to time he looked at me with a cheerful smile. I felt terribly uneasy. I got up and fetched the boiled water, and poured some out to cool.

Time enough to eat two meals passed before Chairman Mao stopped and stood up to stretch himself. 'You've been with me several years now,' he said. 'How is it that you still don't understand what comes first? The first thing you have to do when we make a stop is to find some place for me to work. Food and rest are quite secondary to that. You must realise that to us work is and will be the most important thing under all circumstances.' He stopped a minute and then rubbed his hand over my head. 'Now go and get some sleep,' he said. 'You can hardly keep your eyes open.'

For three days and nights while some 30,000 troops continued crossing the Golden Sand River, Chairman Mao never left his 'desk'. [5]

Mao's forces next struck north across Sikang, traversing the mountainous territory inhabited by the Yi peoples in May 1935. The Yis, long hostile to the Han Chinese, took some convincing that the Red Army, unlike the KMT, had not come to plunder and enslave. Liu Po-cheng remarked warily,

Adhering to the policy outlined by Mao Tse-tung, we entered into an alliance with the chieftains of the Kuchi tribe [an alliance cemented by Liu when he drank chicken's blood as an oath of brotherhood with the chief of a Black Lolo tribe] and succeeded in neutralising the Laowu tribe. We had some trouble with the Lohung tribe which constantly attacked us under promptings from the Chiang Kai-shek secret agents. To this tribe we repeatedly explained our policy was to help the minority nationalities achieve liberation. Thanks to this policy, the Red Army passed through the Yi areas unhindered and reached the ferry crossing of Anschunchang on the south bank of the Tatu River. [6]

Chen Chang-feng showed some of the apprehension the Red Army felt before entering the Yi area.

One day we were chatting with our host ... When the conversation turned to the Yi people he suddenly became very agitated and cried in alarm: 'That's the Lolos, eh? Ah, they're fierce they are!' 'How fierce?' we asked him, and he carried on in great excitement: 'They're savages and love to fight! They specially hate us Han people ... Once in there, you'll land yourselves in a trap. Suddenly you'll find a whole mountain full of their men, yelling and shouting, and sniping at you. It's said they're first-rate shots!'

We knew that the White Army oppressed them worse than it did the Hans, so we looked on them as our brothers. We'd not heard anything about them killing Hans, so I went and asked Chairman Mao. 'Chairman, it's said the Yis are fierce!' I began. 'Who told you that?' he rejoined. So I told him all that our host had said and asked him: 'Is it true?' Chairman Mao smiled and countered: 'What do you think?' I smiled in my turn and shook my head.

He then explained that the Yis in Szechuan and the Miaos in Kwangsi were cruelly oppressed by the White Army. This was why they hated the Whites. 'But to us', he said, 'they're different. We respect them and look on them as our brothers. We unite with them and fight together with them against oppression by the White Army. The Yis will be glad when they know that the Red Army has come to them. So what's there to be afraid of? . . .'

We reached the Yi region at noon. It was May. In my native Kiangsi, the fields would already be gay with the golden rice, but here the land was deserted and untilled. There were no rice fields, no farm houses, only some rough low shacks in the forests . . .

But soon . . . a group of men and women in strange clothes suddenly appeared before us . . . Five tall women came out from the group, each carrying a big red cock in her arms [to give to Mao]. They approached Chairman Mao and surrounded him. They said something that we could not understand. But Chairman Mao nodded his head and imitating their gestures, put his hands before his breast to show his gratitude. I, Tseng Hsien-chi [Mao's second bodyguard] and other comrades imitated him in turn to thank them.

Then Chairman Mao, closely followed by the women with the cocks, walked on. By this time there were Yi people everywhere, on the slopes, in the valley, and on the top of the mountain. Some of them raised their hands high in welcome, some bowed, others sang gaily. It was a strange and moving sight that brought tears to our eyes.

Chairman Mao turned to us: 'See! All that talk about fighting. They've come to welcome us! Just think why!' As we walked on, we discussed the matter. A while later Tseng asked: 'Chairman, although they are our good brothers, we can't understand what they say. It's as if we were in a foreign country!' 'It's not surprising,' Chairman Mao said. 'You know how big our country is. You, a Kiangsi man, can't even understand what I, a Hunan man, say. So how can you understand what the Yi people say?' This set all of us laughing. When the Yi people saw us laughing, they too laughed, uproariously. [7]

Not all the Red Army's encounters with the Yis turned out so amicably. The hostile tribes exacted a high price in rifles, cash and goods for permission to cross their land. The Red Army's policy of opening the prisons in the towns they occupied, however, won them new recruits, some of whom trekked north and fought hard with 'the poor peasants' army' for many years. One of them, later a colonel in the Red Army, told the story of how the Red soldiers opened the prison in the town of Yuehsi, illustrating the way Mao's policy was calculated to win the respect of those suffering from the KMT repression.

Tense with excitement, I edged my way through the crowd towards the prison. It was frightfully dark inside. From the gloom came a revolting, stomach-turning smell. The Red fighters, with torches and hammers, went in imperturbably, calling out as they entered: 'Fellow-countrymen, how you have suffered! We are the Red Army, we've come to save you.'

I followed them in. What a heart-rending sight it was! Thin as withered vines, with long dishevelled hair, they lay, stark naked or at best with a piece of rag around their loins, on a mixture of mud, excrement and foul water. They were chained together, handcuffed and fettered. Some were dead. The Red fighters carefully knocked off their chains and carried them out into the fresh air. I and many others helped. Altogether we brought out about two hundred. They were heads of the various tribes of Yuehsi and of Puhsiungngole, Ahou and Kuochi. They had been in prison for as long as a dozen years. Countless numbers had been tortured to death in various ways. And all because of what? Because they did not carry out the Kuomintang policy of 'pitting the Yis against the Yis'; because they did not have the heart to kill their brothers from other tribes; because they did not provide young girls for the Kuomintang officials according to the 'regulations'; or because they could not afford the endless exorbitant taxes . . .

The pitiable sight of those who survived and the dreadful sight of those who had died evoked outbursts of wailing and suppressed sobbing from their family members who were present, then from sympathisers around. I, too, could not suppress my tears. The living and their families gave their thanks to the Red Army; the families of the dead, crying, supplicated them to avenge their loved ones. The Red fighters, with tears in their eyes, soothed them. 'Fellow-countrymen, we shall remember your trust and wipe out the Kuomintang to avenge all who have suffered at their blood-stained hands.'

I felt a wave of bitter indignation and cried impulsively: 'I'll join you to fight the Kuomintang!' The sombre atmosphere was broken by my sudden cry. For a moment everybody looked at me with a blank expression. Then many of them followed my example: 'I too, will join to fight the Kuomintang!' was the cry. [8]

Having escaped the KMT trap at the Golden Sand River, the Red Army· found itself in a natural trap, an area of Sikang boxed in by three great rivers, the Chinsha, the Min and the Tatu. It was imperative to break out of this natural encirclement before Chiang Kai-shek could use it to hem them in. Pressing north, Mao's troops faced the savage Tatu River. This barrier proved the most difficult to overcome of the whole Long March.

The current was so swift navigation was impossible and ferries crossed at their peril. The few roads over the river were on bridges made of iron chains or ropes. The main ferry crossing at Anshunchang, related Liu Po-cheng,

> ... was where Shih Ta-kai of the Taiping Heavenly Kingdom suffered a final defeat when his army failed to cross the Tatu River and march north. The river cut its way through gaping valleys banked by towering mountains which extended for a distance of fifty *li*. The terrain afforded little room for an army to manoeuvre or deploy its forces, and we were exposed to the danger of being ambushed and destroyed by the enemy. The Szechuan warlords had once boasted that they would make a second Shih Ta-kai there and bring about the final defeat of the Red Army. A Szechuan warlord had a battalion stationed at Anshunchang. It had only one small boat, the other two having been hauled to the north shore. We surrounded the Szechuan troops at Anshunchang, commandeered the small boat and organised a shock force to cross the Tatu River.
>
> As soon as our eighteen volunteers got to the other side, they crushed the enemy and took the ferry. They were followed by the First Division which, after crossing, cleared the north bank of enemy troops and routed a brigade of the Szechuan warlord, Liu Wen-hui. Then, marching abreast of the Second Division under Lin Piao on the south bank, it swept onwards along the river towards the Luting Bridge. Lin Piao's unit was the first to reach the iron-chain bridge and, giving the enemy no time to destroy the structure, crossed the Tatu and joined the First Division. This was in June 1935. [9]

This modest account of the crossing of the Luting Bridge does not bring out the heroic nature of an exploit that is still commemorated today in poetry, paintings, drama and film. Agnes Smedley's description gives some details:

> Platoon Commander Ma Ta-chiu stepped out, grasped one of the chains, and began swinging, hand over hand, toward the north bank. The platoon political director followed, and after him the men. As they swung along, Red Army machine guns laid down a protecting screen of fire and the Engineering Corps began bringing up tree trunks and laying the bridge flooring.
>
> The army watched breathlessly as the men swung along the bridge chains. Ma Ta-chiu was the first to be shot into the wild torrent below. Then another man and another. The others pushed along, but just before they reached the flooring at the north bridgehead they saw enemy soldiers dumping cans of kerosene on the planks and setting them on fire. Watching the sheet of flame spread, some men hesitated, but the platoon political director at last sprang down on the flooring before the flames reached his feet, calling to the others to follow. They came and crouched on the planks releasing their hand grenades and unbuckling their swords.
>
> They ran through the flames and threw their hand grenades in the midst of the enemy. More and more men followed, the flames lapping at their clothing. Behind them sounded the roar of their comrades, and, beneath the roar, the heavy THUD, THUD, THUD of the last tree trunks falling into place. The bridge became a mass of running men with rifles ready, tramping out the flames as they ran. The enemy retreated to their second line of defences, but Lin Piao's division appeared suddenly in their rear and the battle ended.
>
> The battle of Lutingchiao lasted just one hour. Seventeen men were killed, many scorched and wounded, and a few severely burned. [10]

With the bridge captured, Chen Chang-feng went with Mao to survey the scene:

I walked up and looked at those cables, each as thick as a bowl, at the charred planks and the seething river below. I felt nervous. The Chairman noticed this. He pointed his finger at me and asked, 'Scared?' 'No.' He started across, with all of us right behind. I watched him carefully . . .

He looked up at the cliffs towering into the clouds on either shore. The roaring of the water was unable to disrupt his thoughts. Because there were so many people on the bridge, when we reached the middle it began to sway. I grabbed the chain railing and stopped. The Chairman turned his head and said something to me. But I couldn't hear a thing. The thunder of the river obliterated all other sound. Obviously he was asking whether I was having trouble. I shook my head. He halted and took my hand. Then we walked on together.

I stared downward for a moment. Huge boiling waves seemed to thrust up like long swords stabbing at the bridge. It made me dizzy. I raised my eyes and looked at my comrades on the bridge. Some were advancing cautiously step by step, some were crawling prone along the steel cables. Others were walking in a line, hand in hand, chatting and laughing.

Still leading me by the hand, the Chairman kept looking back at the men following. Sometimes he stopped and waved at them, or said a few words. At last we left the bridge behind us. 'Chairman,' I said when we reached the shore, 'with one squad we could hold a bridge like that indefinitely. But the enemy . . .' The Chairman laughed. 'The enemy are the enemy. We can't compare them with an army led by our Communist Party. Right?' 'Right!' we chorused. [11]

Thus the Red Army escaped encirclement and Mao was not made 'a second Shih Ta-kai' by the Szechuan warlords.

With the Tatu crossed, the Red Army was less than a hundred miles from Chang Kuo-tao's Fourth Front Army in north-east Szechuan. In between them, however, lay part of the Great

Snow Mountains, a huge range stretching to the Tibetan border and rising to over 4,000 metres. On the march from Hualingping to Shuitseti, soon after crossing the Tatu, Mao's men found themselves attacked by enemy planes. The incident was recalled by Chen Chang-feng:

It was the usual early start. Chairman Mao was held up by some business or another and went with the medical corps instead of the Central Committee staff. The squad leader of the bodyguards and I went with him. We were crossing an open valley, a dozen *li* long, when we were suddenly dive-bombed by three enemy planes. The bombs fell really near and we rushed to shield Chairman Mao. He was up at once, though, bending over the squad leader, who had been hit. He lay there, clutching his abdomen, quite silent. Chairman Mao touched him gently, and turned to the medical corps officer. 'Can you do anything?' he asked urgently. My squad leader struggled to wave help aside. 'No!' he said, 'go on.'

He could hardly speak. He was terribly pale, as though all his blood was draining away from him. Chairman Mao sat down by him and lifted his head. 'You'll be all right, Comrade Hu Chang-pao,' he said gently. 'Just keep quiet, and we'll carry you to Shuitseti, where we can get a doctor, who'll see to you.'

My squad leader moved his head as it lay on Chairman Mao's arm. 'I can't let you carry me,' he said. 'Don't trouble yourself. I can feel I'm bleeding inside. It doesn't matter about me, I'm quite content. But will you tell my parents? They live in Kian, in Kiangsi. I'm only sorry that I can't go on with you to Shensi, and see our base there.'

He stopped and breathed hard for a minute. Then he looked at me. 'Chen Chang-feng,' he said, 'take good care of our Chairman Mao and the other leaders.' His voice died away, and we couldn't hear what else he said. He tried to speak again; we could see his lips move. Suddenly, with a great effort, he spoke loudly. 'Victory to the Revolution!' he cried. His head fell over and his eyes fixed and closed. 'Squad leader, squad leader,' I cried, but he was dead.

Chairman Mao slid his arm out from under him and stood up. 'Give me the quilt,' he said. I gave him a quilt from the bedding-roll, and Chairman Mao laid it over the body. [12]

Many years later, talking to Edgar Snow, Mao dwelt on the question of death. It had often seemed to come so close. His second wife, Yang Kai-hui, had been murdered by the KMT. Many other members of his family had been killed. But death, he said, just didn't seem to want him. Several times he had thought he might die. His bodyguard, he said, had been killed while standing right beside him (on the occasion just described). Once he was splashed all over with the blood of another soldier but the bomb had not touched him. It was odd, Mao said, that death had passed him by.

The Red Army next climbed the pass over the Chiachin Mountain. The peak, part of the Great Snow Mountains, was nearly 5,000 metres high and covered in snow. Mao's remaining bodyguard, Chen Chang-feng, related:

We paused for a day at its foot. Chairman Mao had advised us to collect ginger and chilli to fortify ourselves against the bitter cold ... We started the climb in the early morning of the next day ...

At the start the snow was not so deep and we could walk on it fairly easily. But after twenty minutes or so the drifts became deeper and deeper. A single careless step could throw you into a crevasse and then it might take hours to extricate you. If you walked where the mantle of snow was lighter, it was slippery; for every step you took, you slid back three! Chairman Mao was walking ahead of us, his shoulders hunched, climbing with difficulty. Sometimes he would slip back several steps. Then we gave him a hand; but we too had difficulty in keeping our foothold and then it was he who caught our arms in a firm grip and pulled us up. He wore no padded clothes. Soon his thin grey trousers were wet through and his black cotton shoes were shiny with frost.

The climb was taking it out of us. I clambered up to him and said: 'Chairman! It's hard for you, better let us support you!' I stood firm beside him. But he only answered shortly: 'No, you're just as tired as I am!' and went on.

Half way up the mountain a sudden, sharp wind blew up. Thick, dark clouds drifted along the top of the range. The gusts blew up the snow which swirled around us viciously. I hurried a few steps forward and pulled at his jacket. 'Snow's coming, Chairman!' I yelled. He looked ahead against the wind. 'Yes, it'll be on us almost at once. Let's get ready!' No sooner had he spoken than hailstones, as large as small eggs, whistled and splashed down on us. Umbrellas were useless against this gusty sea of snow and ice. We held an oilskin sheet up and huddled together under it with Chairman Mao in the centre. The storm raged around us as if the very sky were falling. All we could hear were the confused shouts of people, neighing of horses and deafening thunder claps. Then came a hoarse voice from above us. 'Comrades! Hold on! Don't give up! Persistence means victory!' I lifted my head and looked up. Red flags were flying from the top of the pass. I looked enquiringly at Chairman Mao. 'Who's that shouting there?' The Chairman replied, 'Comrades from the propaganda team. We must learn from them. They've got a stubborn spirit!'

The snowstorm dropped as suddenly as it had started, and the warm, red sun came out again. Chairman Mao left the oilskin shelter and stood up on the snowy mountainside. The last snowflakes still whirled around him. 'Well, how did we come out of that battle?'' he asked. 'Anyone wounded? . . .'

As we went up higher, the going grew more difficult. When we were still at the foot of the mountain, the local people had told us: 'When you get to the top of the mountain, don't talk nor laugh, otherwise the god of the mountain will choke you to death.' We weren't superstitious, but there was some harsh truth in what they said. Now I could hardly breathe. It seemed as if my chest was being pressed between two millstones . . .

Finally we gained the summit of the mountain pass. White snow blanketed everything. People sat in groups of three or five. Some were so exhausted that they lay down. When they saw Chairman Mao, several comrades came up calling: 'Chairman, come and take a rest!' When Chairman Mao saw all this he immediately went up to them and said gently: 'Comrades, we can't rest here! The air is too rarefied. Make another effort and we'll meet the Fourth Front Army on the other side.'

With this, our spirits rose again, and we began to scramble down the slope . . . Suddenly I grew dizzy. It seemed that the mountain shook beneath my feet. I lost control of my limbs and began to shiver violently. I stumbled up to Chairman Mao, cried out: 'Chairman . . .!' and collapsed. But I was not wholly unconscious. I felt Chairman Mao supporting me with his arm and calling me by name. It was as if I was swimming in air . . . I heard Chairman Mao asking me: 'What's wrong? Are you all right now?' I struggled to my feet and on we went . . .

Going down was easier than going up, but since there was no sunshine on this side of the mountain it was colder. We were all wearing the same thin cotton clothes, and we shivered with cold. I tied a blanket round my waist and so went walking, slipping and rolling down the snowy slopes.

Not long afterwards, we met comrades of the Fourth Front Army carrying banners with the words: 'Expand the revolutionary base in north-western Szechuan!' We felt new strength come into our limbs. We felt for them as we would for brothers we had parted from long ago. As we came down the last slopes, I turned and looked upwards. The red flags were still fluttering on the top of the snow-covered mountain. The untiring voice of the propaganda comrades was still ringing in my ears.
[13]

In fact many soldiers died of exposure and Mao himself caught a fever and was carried by stretcher over part of the mountain. A few months later Mao summarised his feelings about these great snow mountains in a poem. Describing the high peak called Kunlun, he wrote: 'On a summer's day ascending Minshan and looking afield, the distant mountains could be seen dancing, filling the eyes with a sense of whiteness.'

Rising straight in the air above this earth,
Great Kunlun, you have witnessed all that was fairest in the
    world of men.
Your three million white jade dragons in their flight,
Freeze the sky with penetrating cold;
In summer days your melting torrents
Fill the streams and rivers over the brim,
Changing men into fish and turtles.
What man can pass judgement,
On all the good and evil you have done these thousand
    autumns?
But now today I say to you, Kunlun,
You don't need this height, don't need all this snow!
If I could lean on the sky, I would draw my sword,
And with it cut you into three pieces.
One I would send to Europe,
One to America,
One we would keep in China here,
So should a great peace reign in the world,
For all the world would share in your warmth and cold.

When the First and Fourth Front Armies at last met near Moukung on 12 June 1935, Chang Kuo-tao maintained that Mao's men were weak almost to the point of defeat and should rather remain in Sikang and north-west Szechuan. He thought they should help build a soviet there, making contact with Russia through the border province of Sinkiang. Mao disputed this; it made no strategic sense to him. His eyes were still on the Japanese and building a strong base in Shensi from which there would be access to north and central China.

As for the Long March being a defeat, Mao answered this criticism in a speech in December when he claimed that the First Front Army had merely shifted from its old Red base in Kiangsi, a temporary and partial defeat, and had on the contrary won victory by evading first encirclement and then pursuit. But by December Mao was already home and dry; in Moukung, there were more mountains, the Great Grasslands and hostile tribal and KMT troops still to face before the Long March could be said to have been successfully concluded.

At a further conference at Maoerhkai, a hundred miles north of Moukung, in July 1935, the political bureau of the CCP adopted the *Appeal to Fellow Countrymen Concerning Resistance to Japan and National Salvation*. The appeal called for a united front against Japan and represented a victory for Mao's long-term national anti-Japanese strategy and a blow to Chang Kuo-tao's regionalism. Two columns of the Red Army then resolved to cross the Great Grasslands into Kansu and towards Shensi, the eastern column headed by Mao and the western by Chu Teh and Liu Po-cheng.

On the Great Grasslands, a rainy upland swamp of strong winds and cold nights, the Red Army soldiers slept standing in pairs or groups of four back to back. Many died of fever or hunger or were sucked under the surface of the marsh. Chen Chang-feng again shows his practical affection for Mao:

> We spent about a month at Maoerhkai. Then finally in mid-August of 1935, we started out for the Great Grasslands that had never before been crossed by human beings. We hadn't gone forty *li* before we came to a huge primeval forest. Its trees, with immensely thick trunks, towered above us. When we stopped for the night we would sling Chairman Mao's hammock between two trees, but he would rarely rest in it. He would be off at meetings or visiting the men. So Chung Fu-chang, the medical orderly, let me rest in it.
>
> I was lying there one night when it was already dark. The troops had lit many bonfires. Neither birds nor

animals had probably ever seen fire before in this ancient forest. They were scared, made strange noises and flew or prowled around in panic. My comrades were sleeping around a nearby fire. I had Chairman Mao's blanket over me and wore a new suit that he had given to me at Maoerhkai, but suddenly I felt a bout of uncontrollable shivering coming on. As I shivered violently, I told myself not to groan so as not to wake the others. I was specially afraid of disturbing Chung Fu-chang, because if he knew I had a malarial attack he would immediately tell Chairman Mao who would then refuse to use his own hammock. I held my breath, doubled my knees up to my chin and kept silent. Suddenly I noticed a tall shadow in front of me. Chairman Mao had come back! ... 'What's wrong, Chen Chang-feng?' He put his hand on me and cried out, 'Chung Fu-chang! Chen Chang-feng is sick again!' He didn't speak very loud, but everyone around the fire woke up and they all crowded round me. When I saw Chairman Mao and the other comrades around me looking at me with such concern, strength seemed to return to my body and I was able to sit up. 'You lie down,' ordered the Chairman gently and used his two hands to press me back into the hammock ... When he saw that I was quiet again he told Chung Fu-chang to give me some medicine. Then he and the other comrades went back to the fireside to sleep.

The ancient forest was left behind and we entered the **grasslands**. A vast stretch of desolate marsh confronted us. Not a single human being lived there. There were no houses. Wild grasses grew in profusion in the stagnant water. There seemed to be no end to it. The sodden earth squelched monotonously *pu-chi*, *pu-chi*, as we laboured over it. A careless step could send you to a fearful death in its muddy depths, trap your feet in a morass. Once caught it was difficult to pull your legs out of the quagmire without the help of your comrades. More than once the Chairman helped some of us with his strong hands.

The weather was cold and changeable. Now it rained, now it snowed. Sometimes it hailed. Every step was an effort. Chairman Mao was walking ahead of us. He would stop for a moment now and again, look back with great concern and call our names until we all answered him. Then he would go on. Sometimes when he saw we were tired he would tell us stories and jokes and make us burst out laughing. And we forgot our tiredness . . .

The troops too had entered the grasslands. They wore a motley set of uniforms. Some were in field grey, others wore greatcoats made of various pelts, some had flung blankets over themselves as capes. Some wore large round hats of plaited bamboo, others carried battered umbrellas. But this tatterdemalion throng brought life to these dead marshes. They marched linked together hand in hand in long lines, advancing slowly but steadily.

One day we suddenly noticed a black spot on the otherwise desolate horizon . . . It was Panyu. I can't describe our feelings. When we finally reached it, Chairman Mao and we bodyguards took up billets in a house belonging to a Tibetan family. Our men were elated. We lit fires of cowdung to dry our wet and mildewed clothes.

Soon afterwards we arrived in Pahsi, and here we witnessed a strange scene: some men of the Fourth Front Army were marching slowly and dejectedly in the opposite direction to us, towards the grasslands! We couldn't understand this and asked Chairman Mao the reason. He didn't reply immediately, but from the expression on his face we could see that he was deeply stirred. Then he told us. This was the result of the intrigue of the renegade Chang Kuo-tao to split the party. It was he, like a slave driver, who was forcing these innocent comrades to take this road to destruction.

After a while Chairman Mao asked us: 'Do you want to turn back and recross the grasslands?' We replied with one voice, 'Never, we'd rather face death.' The Chairman stood up and looked back at those shabby, tired figures marching back to where we had come from. 'They'll come back! We must open a way ahead for them so that they can come to us!' he said in a low, but confident voice. [14]

Mao's section went on to win the battle of Latsekou Pass and to cross the Liupan Mountains. According to Chen Chang-feng,

> At dusk in the middle of September, we arrived at a village close to Latsekou. I spread the Chairman's pallet so that he could get some rest. But when I went into the next room, he was already in conference with Lin Piao, Nieh Jung-chen, Liu Ya-lou and Lo Jui-ching. The table was spread with maps.
>
> Latsekou, known as a strategic pass, connects the provinces of Szechuan and Kansu, and was one of the major passes we had to get through to reach northern Shensi. I was sure this was what the Chairman and the others were discussing, so I withdrew without a word. The Chairman didn't get to sleep until very late that night. We attacked the pass the next morning at dawn. After taking it we didn't linger, but pushed on. At the end of September, we crossed the Weishu River blockade line and headed for Mount Liupan.
>
> Mount Liupan, a spur of the Lungshan Range, is the highest peak in western Kansu. It was also the last great mountain we had to cross to get to northern Shensi . . .
>
> The sky was cloudy and a cold wind blew the day we set out to climb it. Soon it started to rain. But although we were soaked by the time we reached the foothills nothing could dampen our determination . . . The trail twisted and turned. At the start of the climb there were small trees we could grab. But as we neared the summit, there was nothing, only clumps of withered grass. It was very tough going.
>
> I was still weak from the malaria. The trail was about thirty *li* to the top and very uneven. By the time we were halfway up, I was gasping for breath. My heart was

pumping hard and I was drenched with sweat. Chairman Mao quickly noticed the shape I was in ... 'It's not malaria, Chairman,' I cried. 'It's just that I have no strength. I'm afraid I'll never get to northern Shensi.' 'You will, definitely. Don't worry,' the Chairman said encouragingly. 'There's nothing frightening about difficulties. The only thing to worry about is being afraid of them.' He and Tseng carried me and continued on ... 'Are you cold?' the Chairman asked. I was chilled to the bone. 'Here, put this coat on and drink some more hot water. You'll feel better when you warm up a bit.' The Chairman took off his overcoat ... I pushed it back. 'I don't need it. I can march.' I refused to put it on, and struggled to walk. But I was too weak. I took one step and collapsed in a faint. When I opened my eyes again, I was wearing the Chairman's coat. The Chairman stood in the rain, the autumn wind ruffling his thin grey army tunic ...

By dusk we finally crossed Mount Liupan and reached the foot of the other side. I looked back up. 'You see, you made it,' said the Chairman. 'That's the way to deal with difficulties.' [15]

Mao's poem *Mount Liupan* gives his version of the ascent.

The sky is high, the clouds are pale,
We watch the wild geese flying south till they vanish;
We count the myriad leagues we have come already;
If we reach not the Great Wall, we are no true men!

High on the crest of Liupan Mountain
Our banners idly wave in the west wind.
Today we hold the long cord in our hands;
When shall we bind fast the Grey Dragon?

With the initiative to seek out and oppose the Grey Dragon (the Japanese) thus coming to their hands, Mao and his column reached Wuchi in Shensi on 20 October 1935, concluding their part of the Long March. Chen described the scene as they came to the ridge dividing Kansu and Shensi.

On the top of the ridge stood a large tablet with bold characters 'Dividing Ridge', marking the border . . . We sat down for a rest under a chestnut tree near the tablet. The Chairman was reading the characters on the back of the tablet. 'We have crossed ten provinces already,' he told us elatedly. 'When we go down this mountain, we'll be in the eleventh — Shensi. That's our base area, our home!'

A day and a half's march from the dividing ridge brought us to Wuchi Town where we stayed in the cave rooms cut in the side of the loess hills. It was the first time in our lives we had seen such caves. We were now in the Soviet area. The Chairman got busy conferring with leading comrades on how to dispose of [KMT warlord] Ma Hung-kuei's cavalry . . .

We stood with the Chairman on a mountain top which was bare of all vegetation. As the battle began, our machine-guns rattled. The frightened horses bolted in all directions neighing and attempting to escape the hail of bullets, throwing their riders and rolling down the slopes with them. Those who survived ran for their lives. It was a real treat to watch the battle from the 'grand stand'. 'Chairman!' we exclaimed. 'We've only got two legs and they've got four, but we've made them run all over the mountain!' He joined in our general burst of laughter.

While the troops were taking a rest in Wuchi Town, we accompanied the Chairman to Hsiashihwan, the seat of the Shensi–Kansu Provincial Party Committee and the Provincial Soviet. Large snowflakes were falling when we set out. Although we weren't wearing too many clothes, nobody felt the cold as we trudged over the rough mountain paths. It was dusk when we reached Hsiashihwan. We heard the beating of gongs and drums and the noise of a crowd of people. From a distance we could see a large gathering on a spacious ground at the entrance to the village. The people were waiting to welcome the Chairman. As soon as they caught sight of him, they cheered madly. Amidst a tremendous din of gongs and drums, the crowd rushed up, waving small red and green banners bearing the words:

Welcome Chairman Mao!

Welcome the Central Red Army!

Expand the Shensi—Kansu—Ningsia Soviet Area!

Smash the enemy's third encirclement campaign!

Long live the Chinese Communist Party!

In the worn overcoat which he had brought along from Kiangsi, and his old cap, Chairman Mao nodded and waved at the crowd again and again. Then the people cleared a way for a score of leading comrades to come and shake hands with the Chairman. They included Comrades Liu Chih-tan [the local guerrilla leader] and Hsu Hai-tung, commander of the twenty-fifth Red Army. Standing with Chairman Mao to receive the welcomers were Comrades Chou En-lai, Tung Pi-wu, Hsu Teh-li, Lin Po-chu and Hsieh Chueh-tsai. They shook hands all around and introduced one another. 'Welcome to Chairman Mao!' the crowd cheered. Shouts rose from every corner, shaking the very earth. 'We've won through! We've won through!' Tseng Hsien-chi and I also shouted. [16]

Another account of the meeting has Mao proudly yet modestly disclaiming the rigours of his march and humorously implying that if there had been hardships they had been suffered by Hsu Hai-tung's twenty-fifth Red Army on its own march up country from the Anhwei soviet base to join Mao in Shensi. 'Is this Comrade Hai-tung?' Mao asked. 'Thank you for taking so much trouble to come here to meet us.'

Mao had arrived. But Chang Kuo-tao had called back the western column and for six months he wandered westwards under KMT attack, trying to set up his own party leadership. Finally, urged by Ho Lung and Jen Pi-shih, whose army had broken out of Hunan to join him, he recrossed the Great Grasslands and met the First Front Army under Nieh Jung-chen at Huining in October 1936. Ho Lung continued his march into Shensi, whereas Chang turned even further north-west, only returning to Shensi at the end of the year to answer the Central Committee's criticisms of his wayward- ness. His influence was eradicated at a conference in Yenan in April 1937 and in 1938 he defected to the KMT.

Some 100,000 started on the Long March. Between 25,000 and 30,000 finished it, despite recruitments en route. In his report of 27 December 1935, Mao said:

> In one respect the Red Army has failed (*ie* failed to maintain its original positions), but in another respect it has won a victory (*ie* in executing the plan of the Long March). In one respect the enemy won a victory (*ie* in occupying our original positions), but in another respect he has failed (*ie* failed to execute his plan of 'encircle- ment and suppression' and of 'pursuit and suppression'). That is the only appropriate formulation, for we have completed the Long March.
>
> Speaking of the Long March, one may ask, 'What is its significance?' We answer that the Long March is the first of its kind in the annals of history, that it is a mani- festo, a propaganda force, a seeding-machine. Since Pan Ku divided the heavens from the earth and the Three Sovereigns and Five Emperors reigned, has history ever witnessed a long march such as ours? For twelve months we were under daily reconnaissance and bombing from the skies by scores of planes, while on land we were encircled and pursued, obstructed and intercepted by a huge force of several hundred thousand men, and we encountered untold difficulties and dangers on the way; yet by using our two legs we swept across a distance of more than twenty thousand *li* through the length and breadth of eleven provinces. Let us ask, has history ever known a long march to equal ours? No, never. [17]

A manifesto, proclaiming to the world that 'the Red Army is an army of heroes'; a propaganda force, announcing 'to some 200 million people in eleven provinces that the road of the Red Army is their only road to liberation'; a seeding-machine, 'it has sown many seeds which will sprout, leaf, blossom, and bear fruit, and will yield a harvest in the future'. These seeds, sown at mass meetings, and at agitational drama performances, and through struggles against landlords, officials and tax collectors in the villages and towns the march passed through, yielded indeed a rich harvest of political consciousness and class struggle in the following years.

In more romantic and ebullient mood, Mao made light of the agonies of the march in a poem.

> The Red Army fears not the trials of a distant march;
> To them a thousand mountains, ten thousand rivers are
>   nothing;
> To them the Five Ridges ripple like little waves,
> And the mountain peaks of Wumeng roll by like mud
>   balls.
> Warm are the cloud-topped cliffs washed by the River
>   of Golden Sand,
> Cold are the iron chains that span the Tatu River.
> The myriad snows of Minshan only make them happier,
> And when the Army has crossed, each face is smiling.

This epic exploit certainly created a legend of indestructability around the Red Army which was useful to them in later periods when they were similarly under pressure. Beneath the heroic poetry, however, lay the mundane requirements of strategy. The area of northern Shensi the Red Army had now entered was remote and backward, but geographically it was a very well-chosen base from which to develop a national anti-Japanese movement and from which, when war came, to fight. And beyond its usefulness in the anti-Japanese war, it proved a deciding factor in the final revolutionary war against the KMT, for, perched in their mountain stronghold, the communists had access to the great plains of northern and central China and the industrial areas of the north-east, the heart of the country, where the great battles were at last fought and won.

With this great shift of base from Kiangsi to Shensi success-fully concluded, Mao turned to building a strategy for the next decade.

5 Save the Country: Save the Revolution

The War of Resistance Against Japan:
The Yenan Base and the United Front, 1936–1938

> In terms of relative political importance the development
> of the national contradiction between China and Japan
> has demoted the domestic contradictions between classes
> and between political groupings to a secondary and
> subordinate place. But they still exist and have by no
> means diminished or disappeared.
>
> Mao Tse-tung, *The Tasks of the Chinese Communist*
> *Party in the Period of Resistance to Japan*

Mao laid the political groundwork for the war against the
Japanese invaders in a speech given to a conference of party
activists at Wayaopao, north of Yenan, in December 1935 –
On Tactics against Japanese Imperialism – the same speech
in which he summed up the Long March. He judged that in
the new situation, one in which Japan wanted to monopolise
the colonisation of China, only an alliance between the
national bourgeoisie and the workers and peasants would
provide forces strong enough to counter the threat. He called
for a united front with the KMT in which the CCP and the
Red Army would play the leading political role.

United front tactics would mean, he said, the recruitment
of large forces to divide, surround and annihilate the invader;
without a united front, limited forces could only fight single-
handed in desperate combat against a formidable enemy. He
reminded the party of the reasons for the betrayal of the first
united front, when, because of weak CCP leadership, the
leadership of the front passed into the hands of the KMT.
That need not recur, so long as the CCP preserved its class
and organisational independence within the alliance. The new

base in Shensi was a good strategic position from which to defend the CCP's political independence, while developing the national anti-Japanese war.

Mao also observed in his Wayaopao speech that world-wide preparation to resist fascism and nazism had changed the situation in China to the communists' advantage. In the past, Chiang Kai-shek had succeeded in isolating them, but from then on the communists were a necessary part of the common struggle. 'Because the rice bowl of the Chinese capitalists is being broken by the Japanese, they can join the broader united front,' Mao told Nym Wales in 1937. Mao also judged that, although the development of revolution would accelerate during the Japanese occupation, China's revolutionary war would remain a protracted one and it would pass through the stage of bourgeois-democratic revolution before emerging into a socialist revolution.

The decisions in 1935 at Wayaopao and earlier in the year at Tsunyi and Maoerhkai marked the period when the CCP began to transform itself under Mao's leadership from a largely defensive and reactive military and political body engaged in revolutionary experiments at a local level, to a main political force in the nation as a whole.

The main forces in the united front which Mao and the CCP now proposed were thus the CCP and the KMT. But Mao knew that in the remote and backward areas in China and also in some cities there existed other groups and societies who wished to defend China against the invaders. Some of them were also seeking social reform and revolution. Mao appealed to the peoples of Inner Mongolia and to the Muslim minorities of north-west China to unite in common struggle against the Japanese imperialists and for social revolution. The founder of the Shensi soviet, where Mao arrived after the Long March, was Liu Chih-tan, a leader not only of the Red Army but also an 'exemplary member of the Elder Brothers Society', who died of his wounds in March 1936. Mao's appeal to the members of this secret society was to their patriotism and sense of social justice.

> In the past, you supported the restoration of the Han and the extermination of the Manchus; today, we support resistance to Japan and the saving of the country. You support striking at the rich and helping the poor; we support striking at the local bullies and dividing up the land. You despise wealth and defend justice, and you gather together all the heroes and brave fellows in the world; we do not spare ourselves to save China and the world; we unite the exploited and oppressed peoples and groups of the whole world. Our views and positions are therefore quite close; there is even more complete correspondence as regards our enemies and the road towards salvation. [1]

The spirit of pride in the people which Mao was seeking to arouse is shown in *Snow*, perhaps his best-known poem and one which he probably wrote in February 1936 as the movement towards the united front was beginning to build up. His call to patriotism was not only directed towards the KMT and the secret societies; it was heard clearly by increasingly broad sections of society and, in particular, and for the first time, by the progressive bourgeoisie.

> This is the scene in that northern land;
> A hundred leagues are sealed with ice,
> A thousand leagues of whirling snow.
> On either side of the Great Wall
> One vastness is all you see.
> From end to end of the great river
> The rushing torrent is frozen and lost.
> The mountains dance like silver snakes,
> The highlands roll like waxen elephants,
> As if they sought to vie with heaven in their height;
>   And on a sunny day
> You will see a red dress thrown over the white,
>   Enchantingly lovely!

> Such great beauty like this in all our landscape
> Has caused unnumbered heroes to bow in homage.
> But alas these heroes! – Chin Shih Huang and Han Wu Ti
> Were rather lacking in culture;
> Rather lacking in literary talent
> Were the emperors Tang Tai Tsung and Sung Tai Tsu;
>   And Genghis Khan,
> Beloved Son of Heaven for a day;
> Only knew how to bend his bow at the golden eagle.
>   Now they are all past and gone:
> To find men truly great and noble-hearted
> We must look here in the present.

The new heroes, the 'men truly great and noble-hearted' were hardly Chiang Kai-shek and Mao himself, as has been suggested by some western scholars. Rather they were all those willing to fight to defend China, and most of all the masses of the people who were to Mao 'the real heroes' who 'made history'.

So far as his estimate of Chiang Kai-shek was concerned, Mao played a waiting game throughout 1936, working to manoeuvre national pressures to build up against Chiang so he would be obliged to turn to a united front as the best way for China to deal with the main enemy. By May 1936, Mao said, the CCP had abandoned its anti-Chiang Kai-shek slogan and called instead for his 'awakening', tempting him, in a telegram from the Red Army to the Military Council of the Nanking National Government, to play the part of 'the butcher who lays down his knife [and] at once becomes a Buddha'.

> The Revolutionary Military Commission of the Red Army hereby solemnly advises the gentlemen of the Nanking government at this critical juncture, when our country and people are threatened with imminent destruction, to make a determined effort to atone for past misdeeds and end the civil war in the whole country, to join forces against attacks from without in the spirit

of brothers quarrelling at home, and first of all end the civil war in Shensi, Kansu and Shansi, whereupon both sides should appoint delegates to discuss specific measures for resisting Japan and saving the nation. [2]

If Chiang refused to do this, the telegram said, 'your rule will surely collapse in the end and you will be spurned and over-thrown by the whole nation. The old saying runs "a thousand pointing fingers accuse, and a man dies even without a sickness." '

The Red Army's 'anti-Japanese' campaign into Shansi province in January and February 1936, although having no chance of actually engaging the Japanese, showed the communists' enthusiasm to do so. It was an 'exemplary' campaign to demonstrate to the people and to Chiang that the Red Army was in earnest. Chiang, ignoring the communists' May appeal for an end to the civil war, made a counter-sweep against the base area which was defeated on 21 November 1936.

The united front which the CCP proposed made a clear distinction between forming an alliance *with* Chiang Kai-shek, and forming a united front with him and the KMT *against* the Japanese invaders. The aim was the *against*; the method was the *with*.

The reason for requesting the united front was simple. As Mao said to Edgar Snow at Pao An in the summer of 1936, 'For a people being deprived of its national freedom, the revolutionary task is not immediate socialism but to struggle for independence. We cannot even discuss communism if we are robbed of a country in which to practice it.' In 1938 he was to define the relationship, as he saw it, between patriotism and internationalism: 'Can a communist, who is an internationalist, at the same time be a patriot? We hold that he not only can be but must be . . . Only by achieving national liberation will it be possible for the proletariat and other working people to achieve their own emancipation . . . In wars of national liberation patriotism is applied internationalism.'

The year 1936 was thus a period of transition from the politics and strategy of the Second Revolutionary Civil War to the new politics and broader strategy demanded by the War of Resistance against Japan that was about to begin. In the autumn of that year of manoeuvring, propagandising and waiting, Mao lectured at the Red Army College in northern Shensi, summing up the experience of the Second Revolutionary Civil War. Five chapters of those lectures were put together under the heading *Problems of Strategy in China's Revolutionary War* in the *Selected Works*. The remaining chapters on the strategic offensive, political work and other problems were left undone, according to a note in the *Selected Works*, 'because he was too busy in consequence of the Sian Incident' in December 1936.

Problems of Strategy is a manual of considerable importance for practitioners of guerrilla warfare. In it Mao sketched the laws of war most relevant to China's revolutionary situation, and in doing so provided a lesson for others in similar situations. He said that the laws of war in general must certainly be studied, but if the Red Army copied the manuals of war published by reactionaries at home and abroad, and even those of the Soviet Union, without the slightest change in form or content 'we shall be "cutting the feet to fit the shoes" and be defeated.'

The Chinese Red Army, he said, must study the 'specific laws of revolutionary war in China'. Neither were the laws for directing a specific war ever static: 'All the laws for directing war develop as history develops and as war develops; nothing is changeless.' War, 'this monster of mutual slaughter among men', can only be eliminated by opposing war with war, by opposing 'counter-revolutionary war with revolutionary war' and opposing 'national counter-revolutionary war with national revolutionary war' and opposing 'counter-revolutionary class war with revolutionary class war'. These three types of legitimate revolutionary war prepare the way, he thought, for a future period 'when human society advances to the point where classes and states are eliminated, [and] there will be no more wars ... that will be the era of perpetual peace for mankind. Our study of the laws of revolutionary war springs from the desire to eliminate all wars; therein lies the distinction between us communists and all exploiting classes.'

Mao then listed some guidelines for the successful waging of revolutionary war. He weighed up the relationship of strategy to campaigns. 'The situation as a whole cannot be detached from its parts ... "the careless move loses the whole game" ... As in chess, so in war.' Defeats or victories in a single battle or in a series of battles only take on meaning in a whole situation, governed by decisions at the strategic level. The science of tactics deals with the laws that govern battles and is applied in directing battles. Tactics should accord with concrete circumstances — the situation of the enemy, the terrain, the strength of the contending forces — but 'the principle is to centre our attention on the important links that have a bearing on the situation as a whole'.

> Many people appear impressive when discoursing on military science in classrooms or in books, but when it comes to actual fighting, some win battles and others lose them ... In real life we cannot expect 'ever-victorious generals' ... What we can ask for is generals who are brave and sagacious and who normally win their battles ... One must acquire a method ... to familiarise ourselves with all aspects of the enemy situation and our own, to discover the laws governing the actions of both sides and to make use of these laws in our operations ... Reading is learning, but applying is also learning and the more important kind of learning at that. Our chief method is to learn warfare through warfare ... [3]

In his section on strategic defence and strategic retreat, Mao quotes an account by the Chou Dynasty historian, Tsochiu Ming, where a weak state successfully resisted a strong one. With a superior strategy, Mao argued, a people can always defeat an invader, the weaker defeat the stronger. There is a sense in which Mao's whole thinking is premised in this understanding, that weakness can be overcome by an understanding of the laws of development and by a correct strategy based on those laws. History might be on the people's side, according to Mao, but much is weighted against the masses. To remove this weight and release the people's initiative is the duty of the Communist Party leadership, as Mao saw it; the military art of the Red Army must be shaped to that purpose.

Mao borrowed from the ancient military scientist, Sun Tzu, such ideas as 'Know the enemy and know yourself, and you can fight a hundred battles with no danger of defeat'; 'Avoid the enemy when he is full of vigour, strike when he is fatigued and withdraws'; and 'Counterfeit an appearance,' that is, make feints. Warlords also studied Sun Tzu. The difference between them and Mao is contained in the question: 'For whom?' The principle that the Red Army existed solely to help propel forward the programme of a party seeking revolutionary justice for the masses of the people is what distinguishes Mao's military science from that of the ancients and the warlords and those of western military academies. This principle runs like a red thread through *Problems of Strategy* and through all Mao's military writings.

Chiang Kai-shek arrived in Sian in southern Shensi on 7 December 1936 to plan another attack on the north Shensi base area which would be, he said, 'the last five minutes' of 'the bandit-suppression campaign'. Instead, he found himself arrested in Sian by one of his own generals, Chang Hsueh-liang, whose troops preferred fighting the invaders to attacking their communist compatriots.

However surprising this may have been to Chiang, it was not unexpected to Mao. He had reckoned that Chiang's generals were 'not all ready to become the slaves of Japan', and that they and the growing anti-Japanese mass movement would compel Chiang to 'realise his mistakes', stop the civil war, begin to fight Japan and co-operate with the CCP. But Mao criticised the arrest of Chiang as rash. With Chiang overthrown an even more reactionary leader might install himself in Nanking and sue for peace with the invaders.

The Communist Party resisted leftist pressure to try Chiang at a people's court and instead worked to preserve him as the man most able to unite all patriotic forces against the foreign enemy. The 'Sian Incident', as the kidnapping came to be known, ended when Chou En-lai secured Chiang's release on condition he stopped the civil war and formed a united front.

At the same time, the CCP gave Chiang four promises: they would not overthrow the Nanking government by force; they would reorganise the Shensi soviet as the government of a Special Region of the Republic under Nanking, and reconstitute the Red Army as a unit of the national army under the KMT Military Council, though retaining its own political-educational system; they would set up in the Special Region an all-party system based on universal suffrage; and they would stop confiscating landlords' land.

In return, they demanded that the KMT end the civil war, start democratic reforms, including freedom from KMT censorship and release of political prisoners, set up an all-party conference to discuss saving the country, improve the people's livelihood and prepare at once to resist Japan.

Agreement on this basis was made on 15 July 1937 but it was not announced until 22 September, ten weeks after the Japanese struck at Lukouchiao (Marco Polo Bridge) near Peking and embarked on a full-scale invasion of the main part of China.

In this changed situation the CCP set about instructing the Red Army in the principles of the united front and the tactics of the new war. This was not easy. As Chu Teh put it,

> Our troops are workers and peasants. They are not intellectual, cultured men. Their ideology is Red Army

ideology. As peasants and workers they have hated land-lords and militarists all their lives. They knew how to work before, but it is now very difficult for them to be called upon to work with every person willing to fight Japanese imperialism. To restrain them, we have called hundreds of cadres to Yenan to pass through special training courses in Kangta [the Resistance University] on the principles and tactics of the united front. After completing their courses, they will return to the army and others will be trained. Our army must be a model in carrying out the united front.

Until now our chief Red Army discipline has said: 'We are the sons of the workers and peasants, and the interests of the workers and peasants are ours.' We must now say: 'We are the sons of the Chinese nation and the interests of the nation are our interests.' We must teach our troops to realise that if China becomes a Japanese colony there will be neither a Kuomintang nor a Kungchantang [Communist Party], but only a nation of slaves. We must keep our eyes on the goal and not be diverted by intrigues or hostility from the right, or from the infantile left. [4]

As well as organising the Kangta training courses, the army sent political workers into the villages and urged the people to form anti-Japanese associations of peasants, workers, merchants, students, women and children.

Writing on 29 August 1937 in Yenan, Nym Wales noted the more superficial, but still significant, changes demanded by the united front policy.

Through a small hole in the paper window . . . I can see my bodyguard . . . fingering his new Kuomintang cap in gingerly fashion, rubbing the bourgeois blue-and-white enamel symbol. No doubt he is thinking of the tattered old cloth Red Star that he wore from Kiangsi on the Long March and resewed with his own loving fingers when it became unrecognisable. But the Red Star is no longer visible on the once-Soviet horizon. Even Chu Teh wears a Kuomintang cap. The whole Chinese Red Army is now clothed in regulation Kuomintang uniforms supplied by Nanking. It has not even a name, but only a number like all other armies under the Central Government; it is the Eighth Route Army of the National Revolutionary Armies of China.

A few days ago I asked Mao Tse-tung . . . if the Red Army would carry the Red flag as well as the national flag in fighting the Japanese. 'No. When we change the uniforms of course we must change our flag also,' he replied. [5]

Comments on these changes came from non-revolutionary democrats and from opponents on both right and 'infantile left' of the CCP. Both right and left had begun to maintain that the communists had abandoned their revolutionary aims by joining in a second united front with the KMT. Much of the party's work in 1936-7 was devoted to explaining to its activists and to the poor peasants, who had benefited most from the agrarian reforms the CCP had carried out, that this was not the case.

Mao argued that nine years of war, in which well over a million peasants, workers and intellectuals had been killed, and whole families and even clans of communists and their supporters had been tortured and murdered by the secret police, had in fact enabled the revolutionary forces to grow strong enough to establish a peace with the KMT in which they could develop the next stage along the uneven revolutionary path, which was the anti-Japanese war. When that stage had been passed, however, and the Japanese defeated, the contradiction between feudalism and the masses of the people would re-emerge and the revolutionary struggle resume. Meanwhile the CCP must keep the initiative in its hands in its organisational and military relations with the KMT. Mao thus measured what was possible in the present against what was desirable in the long run and recommended the course which would most effectively achieve the long-term objective.

Speaking to Nym Wales in the summer of 1937, Mao described the first stage of the revolution as 'the bourgeois-democratic revolution of the proletariat, the peasantry and the petty bourgeoisie' which 'will conclude its victory by transforming into a socialist revolution. We communists believe that such a possibility exists.' Looking forward to the founding of the People's Republic, he went on, 'During its transformation it will pass through the Democratic Dictatorship of the Peasants and Workers.'

Impressed by Mao's patriotic statements, as well as by the good sense of the CCP's policy towards the KMT and the reality of the communists' opposition to the Japanese, students from bourgeois families, especially from the cities on the coast, flocked to Yenan where the party centre had settled after its move from Pao An in December 1936. The students brought with them from the cities, according to Mao, the impetuous wish that the revolutionary path should be 'straight, absolutely straight'. They had gained experience mainly in urban demonstrations. Following the demonstration in Peking on 9 December 1935, the patriotic movement in the cities had pierced the terror of the KMT censorship and police rule to win the people's support for 'a movement of national salvation' in the face of Japanese aggression. This strong current of patriotic feeling was accelerated by the CCP's criticism of the KMT's deference to Japan and caused many of the most articulate and talented intellectuals to look to Yenan.

Those who went received training in political and military work. A department was set up especially for them in the Resistance University. Some students graduated to become cadres, helping replace the many lost in the civil war and on the Long March. Many found difficulty in adjusting to the rigour of party debate and party line. The method of intra-party democracy, of exposing and dividing the contending views during the formulation of policy, must have seemed strange, and rather punctilious. The party's insistence on strict accordance to party decisions once they were made must have been equally unfamiliar to the free-thinking students.

Again, in contrast to what many of them were accustomed to at home, living conditions in Yenan were hard and simple. But the honesty of the cadres and party leaders impressed the students who, under KMT rule, had come to assume that all authority meant corruption. Part of the problem of training the young people was to demonstrate that authority consituted to change social conditions was qualitatively different from authority concerned to preserve them. This was a lesson that a later generation of Chinese students were in turn to teach the party.

The students that revolted against KMT rule did not find in Yenan simply an 'alternative' authority, one with the same ideals as the KMT but who practised them more effectively: they found instead a wholly opposed authority with a communist set of values. The Yenan cadres, whom Mao in his philosphical and political lectures helped to educate, were new men, their authority arising slowly from the demonstrated usefulness of their acts. The bourgeois students learnt that individuality, expressed in talent directed along a certain path of social usefulness, was needed in Yenan, whereas individualism, acting for onself alone, was criticised, isolated and struggled against.

To draw the outline of the genuine revolutionary more clearly for the students and for other potential fighters, Mao hit out at 'half-hearted revolutionaries' who fought at first but 'as soon as pressure came, changed and presented their comrades [to the enemy] as a gift'. He praised his old 'teacher' and friend from Changsha days, Hsu Teh-li, for his modesty: 'For you, it is "revolution first", "work first", and "other people first", whereas for some others it is "limelight first", "rest first", and "oneself first".'

In *Combat Liberalism* (7 September 1937), Mao listed

eleven weaknesses ('we could name more') arising from a less-than-positive attitude to revolutionary struggle. Among them were refraining from principled argument for fear of hurting old friends; criticising in private and not in public; pursuing personal vendettas; working half-heartedly with no plan or direction; living on one's laurels as a revolutionary veteran; and knowing one's failings but not correcting them.

He praised Lu Hsun, the revolutionary writer who died in 1936 and who, though not a Communist Party member, epitomised for Mao certain of the characteristics of the man of vision, combining militancy with self-sacrifice. According to Mao, Lu Hsun was a vanguard and

> ... we need ... a large number of vanguards to find the path. Vanguards must be frank, positive and upright people. They seek no self-interest, only national and social emancipation. They fear no hardships; instead, in the face of hardships they are determined and forever moving forward. Neither undisciplined nor fond of lime-light, they have their feet firmly on the ground and are realistic. [6]

Mao, grown thin during the Long March, gathered strength. His style of life remained frugal and moderate, though hardly severe. In Pao An, the party's centre during 1936, Mao lived in two rooms, his only luxury a mosquito net. Edgar Snow, who visited him there, wrote, 'After ten years of leadership of the Reds, after hundreds of confiscations of property of landlords, officials, and tax collectors, he owned only his blankets and a few personal belongings, including two cotton uniforms.'

At Yenan Mao worked in his office in simple cave houses, often at night, at first in the hillside above the town itself and then in a series of settlements in the surrounding valleys. He had a squad of bodyguards who lived in his compound with him. At the Date Garden, three miles north of the town, which he did not leave until 1945, his three cave rooms held few possessions. In his office were a table, a chair, a cup, a lamp, an ink box, a pot to hold pens, a map on the wall, books of political theory on the shelves. In his bedroom, a washstand, a soap tray, a wooden bed. Next door, in a reception room for talking to cadres setting out for, or returning from, the anti-Japanese front, were a few canvas folding chairs. Outside in the courtyard a stone seat stood beneath a locust tree where he sat smoking and chatting. These made his home. In adjacent cave houses, when they were home, lived his nearest associates, including at different times, Chou En-lai, Lin Piao, Jen Pi-shih and Liu Shao-chi.

Mao saw no purpose in ostentation or in possessing anything unrelated to the needs of the struggle. He ate and dressed simply because it suited his nature but also because it accorded with his principles. Seeing his guards always eating millet, he asked for it to replace his rice. He said the clinic at the Date Garden must be open twenty-four hours a day for the peasants because they were always busy, whereas cadres, who could regulate their hours, should visit it only during normal opening. If there were to be privileges, it should be the peasants who had them, not the cadres.

Principle dominated him. 'He was as stubborn as a mule, and a steel rod of pride and determination ran through his nature,' wrote Agnes Smedley, who stayed nine months in Yenan in 1937. The principles of Marxism were the guide, the reference, the record of the laws of material and historical development; but in his lectures at the Resistance University and in his down-to-earth speeches before mass meetings (as in his conversation) he spoke of China, its people, history and literature. Students from the cities arriving in Yenan well-versed in the Marxist classics of Germany and Russia came face to face with a Chinese reality.

Snow described his impressions of Mao, who was then forty-three years old, when he met him at Pao An in 1936. He was 'a gaunt, rather Lincolnesque figure, above average height for a Chinese, somewhat stooped, with a head of thick black hair grown very long, and with large, searching eyes, a high-bridged nose and prominent cheekbones'. He transmitted a feeling of 'a certain force of destiny' which seemed to come from 'a kind of solid elemental vitality'. He had a peasant sense of humour and he could turn his laughter on himself and on the shortcomings of the soviets. Snow called it 'a boyish sort of laughter which never in the least shook his inner faith in his purpose'. But Agnes Smedley found his humour 'often sardonic and grim, as if it sprang from deep caverns of spiritual seclusion'.

Snow thought that some might have found him 'rather coarse and vulgar', yet remarked that 'he combined curious qualities of naivety with incisive wit and worldly sophistication'. He was 'an accomplished scholar of Classical Chinese, an omnivorous reader', and possessed an unusual memory and extraordinary powers of concentration. He seemed 'careless in his personal habits and appearance but astonishingly meticulous about details of duty'. He had 'a deep sense of personal dignity', appeared 'quite free from symptoms of megalomania', yet

> something about him suggested a power of ruthless decision when he deemed it necessary. I never saw him angry, but I heard from others that on occasions he had been roused to an intense and withering fury. At such times his command of irony and invective was said to be classical and lethal . . . I thought he had probably on the whole been a moderating influence in the communist movement where life and death were concerned. [7]

Six months later Agnes Smedley met Mao at Yenan and wrote this impression:

> Calling on him at midnight, I pushed back a padded cotton drape across a door in a mountain cave, and stepped into a dark cavern. Directly in the centre of this darkness stood a tall candle on a rough-hewn table. Its

glow fell on piles of books and papers and touched the low earthen ceiling above. A man's figure was standing with one hand on the table; his face, turned towards the door, was in shadow. I saw a mass of dark clothing covered by a loose padded greatcoat . . . The tall, forbidding figure lumbered towards us and a high-pitched voice greeted us. Then two hands grasped mine; they were as long and sensitive as a woman's . . . Whatever else he might be, he was an aesthete. I was in fact repelled by the feminine in him and by the gloom of the setting . . . What I now remember of Mao Tse-tung was the following months of precious friendship; they both confirmed and contradicted his inscrutability. The sinister quality I had at first felt so strongly in him proved to be a spiritual isolation. As Chu Teh was loved, Mao Tse-tung was respected. The few who came to know him best had affection for him, but his spirit dwelt within itself, isolating him . . . I had the impression he would wait and watch for years, but eventually have his way . . . [8]

Nym Wales told how she was received by Mao on 11 August 1937. She found him by that time 'an Olympian figure indeed' in the gregarious world of Yenan, his personality was 'dramatically aloof' and 'when you went to call on him at night, the affair seemed as ceremonial as keeping a tryst with an oracle'.

Although a misty rain was falling, I found Mao . . . sitting in his garden in a foreign-style canvas chair smoking cigarettes . . . He preferred not to see people at all, but to have them send him a list of short, concise questions, consecutively numbered, on which he could scribble brief 'yes' or 'no' answers . . . He had got into the habit of working at night when he was a journalist, and this habit had been confirmed by night marches when leading the Red Army . . . You sit in the candlelight, and he concentrates two bright intense eyes upon you from the outer darkness . . . Mao speaks in quiet decisive syllables like someone reading from a familiar book. He never shakes the shaggy black mane away from his eyes. He never plays with a pen or pencil. His large, shapely hands are as quiet as his voice. Ho Tzu-chen, his gentle little wife, brings in cocoa and cakes and sits unobtrusively on the *kang* [bed], lined with dozens of books on philosophy and political science. [9]

Agnes Smedley recalled that during one of her meetings with him, 'he asked me if I had ever loved any man, and why, and what love meant to me.' It was in 1937 that Mao and his third wife Ho Tzu-chen were divorced.

Ho Tzu-chen was the daughter of a Kiangsi landlord and had been both a 'farm girl' and a schoolteacher. Nym Wales described her as 'a small, delicate woman with a pretty face and a shy, modest manner, who devoted most of her time to caring for her husband — whom she worshipped — and bearing children'. Anna Louise Strong, the American journalist who also visited Yenan at this period, said she was 'fragile and dainty' but painted a rather different picture of her character. Preferring to use the name 'Commander Ho Tzu-chen', this determined fighter had for ten years worn the uniform of the Red Army, 'fought at the front, organised groups of women fighters, nursed the sick, and carried full-grown men to field hospitals. She started on the Long March with twenty recent wounds from shrapnel in her body, eight of which were serious; she was also pregnant at the time and bore a child on the way. She was forced to leave her child behind with a peasant family, and has never since been able to find it. Yet all these bitter experiences have not dimmed her spirit or the youth of her twenty-eight years.'

She married Mao in 1930 after the execution of Yang Kai-hui. She bore five children in those difficult years. In 1937, reports Edgar Snow, Ho Tzu-chen 'formally charged Wu Kuang-wei (Lily Wu), an interpreter in Yenan, with having alienated Mao's affections. Mao denied the charges in the same year and then sought a divorce, which was granted by a special court set up by the CCP Central Committee. Both Miss Wu and Ho Tzu-chen were exiled from Yenan.' By 1939 Ho had gone to the Soviet Union, apparently for medical treatment, but in 1970 she was reported to be living obscurely in a Kiangsi commune.

In late 1938 or early 1939 Mao married Chiang Ching, an actress who had been divorced from her actor husband more than a year before and had come to Yenan. There she enrolled at the Lu Hsun Art Academy which trained propaganda troupes for the front, and attended lectures given by Mao at the party school. Snow said she was 'slender, vivacious and rather tall for a Chinese'. She could play bridge and 'cooked a simple excellent meal for us, done to Mao's taste for hot foods'. She left Yenan with Mao in 1947, and travelled with him during a year of fighting in northern Shensi. She took little known part in political life until 1964, when she supervised some of the initial moves of the cultural revolution, especially in the field of revolutionising Peking Opera.

In its deep valleys between ancient loess hills which 'roll like waxen elephants', Yenan possessed two jeeps, a few printing presses and a radio transmitter powered by a pedal; yet in social relationships it was the most modern town in China. The rule of feudalism was being uprooted. Associated aspects of the material lives of the people — opium, beggary, foot binding, infanticide, child slavery, prostitution, polyandry and polygamy — had gone. Spiritual aspects, superstition and witch-doctoring, had been countered with confidence in man and medicine. Political and social aspects had been challenged, in 1936 before the united front put a brake on the reform, by the overthrow of the large landlords and the confiscation and the redistribution of their estates to the peasants.

These reforms accorded with Sun Yat-sen's slogan, 'Land to those who till it'. As Mao said, this was not a socialist revolution. The power of the small landlords and the rich and middle peasants was left largely unchanged, though the poorest peasants gained most from the redistribution. But co-operative movements were set up, with some animals and implements owned collectively. Prototypes of the mutual-aid teams enabled public and Red Army lands, much of it land of absentee landlords that had gone to waste, to be reclaimed, worked, sown and harvested collectively. 'Saturday Brigades' of children, women, soldiers and all levels of cadres, worked at least one day a week at agricultural tasks in busy seasons. These mobilisations of collective effort, together with primary education set up in the schools, taught peasants the elements of the social method.

In September 1937, two months after the Japanese attack at Lukouchiao, elements of the Red Army, redesignated the Eighth Route Army, left the soviet base, the new 'Border Region', and crossed the Yellow River to engage the invaders. Their own small numbers, originally limited by the KMT to 45,000 men, and the Japanese strength, made them adopt guerrilla tactics. In a countryside so vast that the invaders could never hope to occupy it all, the Eighth Route Army split up into units of 1,000 to 2,000 men, difficult for the Japanese to take on and impossible for the KMT to control. The number of their units grew as young men fleeing from the invaders flocked to join them.

A system of three-in-one local government was set up in the guerrilla areas, composed of one-third communists, one-third from other anti-Japanese organisations and one-third officials belonging to no party. These local authorities provided honest government, lowered taxes and limited rents, but made no moves to confiscate land. The director of the political department of the Eighth Route Army, Jen Pi-shih, explained, 'We soften rather than emphasise class struggle. In places where we have driven out the Japanese and are called upon to form local governments, we no longer do this by calling a meeting of poor farmers and excluding the rich. We form local governments representing all classes. We do, however, demand that rents, taxes and interest rates be lowered, since otherwise the common people will not be able to endure the strain of the war.' Jen said that even blood feuds between tenants and landlords must not be pursued. 'Chinese must not fight Chinese while we are all faced with a greater danger of slavery to Japan'.

This danger was indeed extreme. As the Japanese pushed west into northern Shansi, Agnes Smedley reported, 'One glimmer of light penetrated the darkness of north China. This was the battle of Pinghsingkuan.' At this battle Lin Piao led part of one division against the invaders at the Pinghsingkuan pass near the Great Wall in the Wutai Mountains, where the Japanese were attempting a breakthrough. After a forced march to the pass of two days and nights, Lin's Eighth Route Army units had a few hours' sleep and then divided into two flying columns, one going far to the rear and the other against the flanks of the advancing enemy, while one regiment was held back at Pinghsingkuan to meet the Japanese head on. The enemy, accustomed to weak resistance, had no airplanes or tanks to protect them. Neither could they cope with the difficult roads cut in the loess soil as deep as ravines. According to Smedley's account, Lin Piao's units placed machine-gun nests

> along these tunnel-like roads, while troops lay in wait on the cliffs above. They would let an enemy column advance, then open up on it with hand-grenades from above and machine-guns from below. When the battle ended on 26 September, one brigade of the old Samurai 5th Japanese Division had been annihilated. The Eighth Route had wiped out brigade headquarters and captured military maps, documents, diaries, and great quantities of clothing, money and provisions. In one of the captured Japanese diaries I read the lines: 'The Red Army gives me a headache.'

The battle of Pinghsingkuan was important because it was the first time the Chinese combined mobile and guerrilla warfare against the Japanese, because the civilian population had been drawn into the fight, and because it proved that by using the techniques of a 'people's war' even a poorly equipped Chinese force could defeat a fully equipped army. [10]

In the words of General Li Tien-yu, a commander under Lin Piao at this first encounter, the Japanese 'had got what they richly deserved. Scanning the battlefields, you could see that the gully stretching for about ten *li* in length was littered with "Imperial Army" bodies, dead horses, carts and lorries. The road was spattered with blood and several thousand disfigured Japanese bodies were lying about . . . When I trod on the battered rifles and the torn flags with the "rising sun" and stepped over Japanese corpses strewn about the fields, I thought: "So this is the so-called invincible 'Imperial Army'!" ' General Li remarked that 'The Japanese aggressors experienced the might of the Chinese people for the first time,' though, he added scathingly, the victory was won with no thanks to the KMT. 'We succeeded in exhausting the enemy by our persistent attacks. They rushed here and there, trying to break through our encirclement to get away, but the Kuomintang troops, whom we could see clearly, were still not in action. They didn't lift a finger.'

The Japanese were a new kind of enemy even for the seasoned fighters of the Eighth Route Army. The same general recalled,

They were a batch of beasts who had been trained in the code of the Bushido . . . I remember a telephone operator of the First Battalion who was going along the highway examining the telephone lines when he saw a dying Japanese soldier lying beside a lorry. He ran up to him and said: 'Give up your weapon; we won't kill you. We give magnanimous treatment to prisoners of . . .' Before he had finished, the Japanese raised his hand and thrust the bayonet into his chest. One comrade carrying back a seriously wounded Japanese soldier had his ear bitten off. Some comrades were killed or wounded while trying to bandage wounded Japanese soldiers. [11]

Anna Louise Strong spent some months in the winter of 1937-8 in north Shansi and learnt about the new type of war which Mao was developing, 'people's war', which employed 'the methods of keeping an army close to the people for whom it fights'.

I would mention first the simplicity and directness of its leaders, their absence of concern for 'face' ... Next I would note sincerity and incorruptibility as illustrated by the fact that both commanders and men cut down their salaries and rations in order to enlarge the size of their army ... Divison commanders like Ho Lung got a monthly wage of five Chinese dollars; Chu Teh got six [Mao received seven]. In English money this is less than eight shillings a month, a laughable fraction of the usual pay in China for commanders ... I noted also the comradeship ... The characteristic of these leaders which most impressed my Hankow interpreter, who had had a wide experience with Chinese generals, was the total absence of bureaucracy, the friendship among all ranks and the development of initiative from the lowest to the highest ... This development of initiative is essential in mobile warfare where men must act in small groups and yet must be able to correlate their action over a wide area. [12]

Chu Teh described to Agnes Smedley the tactics and general plan of the Eighth Route Army which he and Mao had worked out with the Central Committee for the first and later stages of the war.

Strategically, we aim at sustained, protracted warfare and attrition of the enemy's fighting power and supplies. Tactically we fight quick battles of annihilation ...

Our plan is to establish many regional mountain strongholds in the enemy rear throughout north and north-west China, such as this one in the Wutai Mountains where the enemy's mechanised forces cannot operate. Our regulars can return to such bases for rest, replenishment, and re-training; guerrilla forces and the masses can be trained in them, and small arsenals, schools, hospitals, co-operative and regional administrative organs can be centred there. From these strongholds we can emerge to attack Japanese garrisons, forts, strategic points, ammunition dumps, communication lines, railways. After destroying such objectives, our troops can disappear and strike elsewhere. We will consolidate and use these strongholds to enlarge our field of operation until our defensive strategy can be turned into a strategic offensive. Chiang Kai-shek has agreed to this plan and the Wutai Regional Base is being organised with his permission. [13]

'I saw the programme of daily training,' wrote Anna Strong from the same headquarters in the Wutai Mountains, 'which developed the initiative and fighting ability of the soldiers'.

Military training was only part of the programme; general and political education were included as well. Most of the new recruits, like most Chinese peasants, were illiterate but they were immediately taught to read and write. The day's programme included rising at six-thirty, morning exercises at seven-thirty, breakfast at nine-thirty, political training at ten, military training at twelve, general education at two, dinner at four-thirty, then games, social gatherings and singing until nine or ten, when they went to bed. A two-hour period was allowed for each type of education, the first hour usually being given to lectures and the second either to discussion, study, or rest. The rather long time allowed for sleeping made up to some extent for the very scanty ration of millet or steamed bread with some vegetable, served but twice a day . . .

Even on a march and before a battle some type of educational training goes on. 'If we march only ten or fifteen miles we can still have a short class,' said the director of the Education Section. 'If we march twenty or thirty miles we have no formal class on that day, but the political leader in each company uses the halts and the lunch period to lead songs and discuss current events. Before a battle the commander and political director call together the officers and explain the purpose and importance of the coming fight; then the officers and lower political workers explain it at meetings of the men. The plan of the great battle at Pinghsing Pass was explained to all the soldiers by Lin Piao on the day before. In most armies soldiers are not told where or why they are going. In our army some details are concealed for reasons of military secrecy, but every soldier knows the meaning and general plan of the coming action and must be prepared to act on his own initiative in emergencies.' [14]

Training and education were only the basic requisites of the Eighth Route Army soldier. 'Our army,' said Jen Pi-shih, 'gives great attention to arousing the masses.'

Only if the people take part against Japan can we win. The old forces cannot beat Japan, we must release new forces. The Japanese, of course, have also their propaganda. Some of them say, 'We also are Chinese who have come back to our old home to save you from your evil government, and especially from the Eighth Route Army.' They preach defeatism through Chinese agents, who say, 'We are too weak to fight Japan', or who penetrate into various religious organisations with the cry, 'Let us submit and call upon god to save us.' They pour heroin and morphine into north China to debauch the people . . .

However, wherever we have enough organisers to explain the situation it is easy to get the people on our side . . . The savagery of the Japanese is our best argument. In Kohsien they slaughtered over 2,000 Chinese civilians; in Ningwu over 1,000; in Naiwen they burned the county officials alive and killed over 600 people. They massacred the entire population of seven villages near Pinghsing Pass, accusing them all of being Soviet agents. Throughout north Shansi they burn nearly half the houses in the places they occupy . . . [15]

Once the people are aroused,' wrote Anna Strong, 'they are next organised either into civilian organisations or fighting groups. This work is done by the political department of the army . . . It contacts the local officials, both civil and military, and also organises farmers' unions, workers' unions, student unions, teachers' organisations, self-defence corps, and farmer fighting groups . . . Through all these organisations, the people agitate against traitors, furnish emergency help to the army and also try to improve their own conditions of living.'

After the battle of Pinghsingkuan, the soldiers were taught how to shout, 'Give us your arms and we won't kill you!' in Japanese. 'Since that time,' remarked Anna Strong, 'it has been easier to take prisoners. They are not only well treated but are given better food than the Chinese soldiers, because they are accustomed to it. After a period of explanation they are often sent back into the Japanese lines. It is considered that even if they again fight, the knowledge that they were well treated will weaken the firmness of the enemy. If they are killed by Japanese officers for having been with the Eighth Route Army, as often happens, this will also injure Japanese morale.'

Anna Strong summed up her view of the outcome of such a people's war. In the mountain stronghold she met a professor of philosophy recently from Peking, now dressed in a soldier's uniform of cheap grey cotton.

I challenged him, asking, 'What can you do with your philosophy here? The job here is to teach patriotism to peasants and reading and writing to soldiers . . .' He answered, 'There is philosophy of war and revolution. There are progressive wars and retrogressive wars . . . This war for China is a progressive war. It will smash the thousand-year-old social forms, for they cannot sustain

the shock of it. It will release the new. The freeing of
China will be good for the whole world also.' [16]

But at first, as Chu Teh had said, the war would be a war of
attrition. The invaders had to be 'let in' to areas where they
would later be tactically at a disadvantage, the mountain
areas. The Japanese invasion spread elsewhere, too. Shanghai
and Taiyuan fell in November 1937. The enemy advance
towards Nanking forced the KMT government to retreat to
Wuhan, and a year later to Chungking. Nanking was occupied
and sacked with extreme savagery in December 1937. The
main coastal cities fell by the summer of 1938 and Wuhan in
October.

In Nanking 300,000 people were murdered by the Japanese
occupiers in a four-week massacre. Hundreds of wounded
soldiers, left there after the evacuation, were slaughtered,
along with their doctors and nurses. Unarmed soldiers were
machine-gunned or burned alive. Rape, often followed by
mutilation and murder, became common. Wherever the
Japanese went they looted vehicles, livestock, food, clothes,
money, furniture — even doors and window-frames. Countless houses were burnt. The dark night of occupation had
begun. It was a war to subjugate a people and break their will
to resist.

The communist-led guerrilla units operating within
Japanese-held territory became the main political force in
those areas, and guerrilla warfare the most effective instrument of resistance.

In his Yenan stronghold, Mao developed the basis of his
thinking on military, political and theoretical questions. His
methods of relating these three aspects of his thinking
matured in a series of writings of far-reaching significance for
China's next three decades.

Of the 158 articles in Mao's four-volume *Selected Works*,
92 were written in Yenan and 112 in the north-east areas as a
whole. All of volumes two and three were written in Yenan.

The method of his thinking was shown in two lectures — *On Practice* and *On Contradiction* — in July and August 1937, later revised for the *Selected Works*. He discussed military affairs in three important works during the first half of 1938, *Basic Tactics*, *Problems of Strategy in Guerrilla Warfare against Japan* and *On Protracted War*. These two groups of writings related tactics to strategy. He also wrote shorter, more specific directives, reports and messages which linked his thinking to the day-to-day struggle.

On Practice and *On Contradiction* laid a foundation of method in the thinking of the party. Both lectures attacked the blindness of channelling reality into preconceptions. Marxism, said Mao, demanded that concept grow from observation of reality. He placed the Marxist approach to investigation and study in a clear relationship to practice, the knowing to the doing, the perceptual to the actual. *On Practice* attacked empiricism in the forms Mao judged it had affected some party activists, restricting their outlook to their own fragmentary experience without contemplating the revolution as a whole.

The lectures paved the way to the reform in the party's methods of work which took place from 1942 to 1944. Their elaboration of the meaning of Marxism applied to Chinese conditions also expressed the party's principled independence of the KMT under the united front. All Mao's writings of the period reveal that although national warfare was his overriding preoccupation, his thinking was constantly directed to the re-emergence of open class warfare.

Mao's directives of 1937-9 reminded the KMT of its obligations under the united front agreement and exposed its failures in the eyes of the Chinese people. His call to mobilise the whole nation to fight Japan and not to rely solely on a government and army inhibited by corruption and treason, defined the differences in approach between the two parties.

The government, said Mao in August and September 1937, was still a one-party dictatorship of the KMT and not a government of the national-democratic united front. The KMT army still worked by the old system: it denied 'the principles of unity between officers and men and unity between the army and the people'. Because much of the warfare, in order to be effective, had to be guerrilla warfare, which depended on the active co-operation of the population, Mao maintained that the KMT units were ill-suited to the task of defeating the invaders.

Summing up the political working style of the Eighth Route Army in the early part of the War of Resistance, Mao said that the feudal practices of beating and abuse of men by officers were forbidden and a spirit of comradeship, of 'sharing weal and woe', marked relations between the ranks. The army expressed its unity with the people by good conduct and by giving aid to the villagers, the opposite of the looting and destruction that attended KMT operations in the countryside. It spurned coercion and instead explained the situation to the people to win them over to fight, organising them and arming them. It reduced rents and suppressed traitors, collaborators and despots. Its lenient treatment of prisoners of war added to the demoralisation and disintegration of the enemy. Unlike the KMT units, who obeyed (or did not obey) purely military orders, the communist units were politically conscious forces, able to carry out positive social action in the areas where they moved.

When Mao characterised the situation in November 1937 as one of 'transition from a war of partial resistance to a war of total resistance', criticism within the party came from the right, led by Wang Ming, who had returned to China after six years in Moscow. The right's pressure to capitulate to the KMT lasted nearly a year, during the worst period of Japanese inroads and the fall of major cities. Capitulation would have meant relinquishing leadership of the struggle to the KMT, or, in Mao's words, sinking 'to the level of the KMT dictatorship of the landlords and bourgeoisie, to the level of partial resistance', whereas Mao's aim was to convert the CCP's military strategy into one that would decide the struggle in the nation as a whole.

Mao's writings of 1938, especially *On Protracted War*, formulated a national military strategy divided into three phases. During the first, which was nearly complete, the Japanese offensive would run its course, while the Chinese troops stayed on the defensive, conducting small-scale operations to take advantage of enemy weaknesses. The second phase would see the planning and development of guerrilla warfare at the enemy's rear, and in its bases. The third phase would use combined guerrilla units in larger scale actions culminating in mass offensives of armies in conventional mobile warfare, including the seizure of cities.

Mao's national military strategy was part of his long-term national revolutionary strategy, which continued to require clear tactics for the party in its relations with the KMT. In his speeches of 5 and 6 November 1938, concluding the Sixth Plenary Session of the Sixth Central Committee, Mao again emphasised the need for the CCP to preserve its independence and initiative in the united front. Wang Ming's policy of all-out unification with Chiang Kai-shek was finally rejected at this conference. Mao taught that speedy victories, which Wang hoped for, were impossible. Protracted guerrilla warfare was unavoidable. This was the message which at last won the bitter debate inside the party.

While capitulation to the KMT was therefore discredited, capitulation to Japan by the KMT continued to be a serious danger as long as China's military successes were confined to undramatic, piecemeal assaults on the inrushing Japanese, the first stage in the long war of attrition. It was only with the start of the second stage and the widespread development of guerrilla warfare, involving the masses of the people, that the capitulationist wing of the KMT was itself eventually discredited. Meanwhile, with the KMT government remaining in Chungking, a Japanese puppet government had been set up at

Nanking by March 1939 under Wang Ching-wei, the KMT's former premier.

If capitulation was easy, the cost of defence was high. In the first year of war, 1937-8, the Eighth Route Army suffered some 25,000 casualties, a third of which were killed.

In his speech of 6 November 1938, Mao compared the situation of the revolutionary movement in the bourgeois democratic countries with the prospects facing the Communist Party in China. He began by saying that everywhere in the world 'the seizure of power by armed force, the settlement of the issue by war, is the central task and highest form of revolution'. But the internal conditions in different countries required communist parties to find various ways of evolving a long-term strategy.

> Internally, capitalist countries practice bourgeois democracy (not feudalism) when they are not fascist or not at war; in their external relations, they are not oppressed by, but themselves oppress, other nations. Because of these characteristics, it is the task of the party of the proletariat in the capitalist countries to educate the workers and build up strength through a long period of legal struggle, and thus prepare for the final overthrow of capitalism. In these countries, the question is one of a long legal struggle, of utilising parliament as a platform, of economic and political strikes, of organising trade unions and educating the workers. There the form of organisation is legal and the form of struggle bloodless (non-military) ... The one war [the communist parties of the capitalist countries] want to fight is the civil war for which they are preparing ... [In] this insurrection the first step will be to seize the cities, and then advance into the countryside, and not the other way about ...
>
> China is different however. The characteristics of China are that she is not independent and democratic but semi-colonial and semi-feudal, that internally she

has no democracy but is under feudal oppression, and in her external relations she has no national independence but is oppressed by imperialism. It follows that we have no parliament to make use of and no legal right to organise the workers to strike. Basically, the task of the Communist Party here is not to go through a long period of legal struggle before launching insurrection and war, and not to seize the big cities first and then occupy the countryside, but the reverse. [17]

'China is different', and the anti-Japanese war was a war to liberate China. But it was intended by Mao to lead naturally into a war of liberation against her internal, as well as external, exploiters. The Chinese communist armies continued, throughout the anti-Japanese war, to carry into the country-side the message of social liberation as well as national liberation. That was their force and their attraction. Their military effectiveness grew out of their social usefulness. Without the gun, they would have been helpless; no political power could have grown without it. This was the lesson Mao learnt in 1927 and which he acted on in the Chingkang Mountains and the Kiangsi base. But with the gun, they became effective because of the social action that accompanied their military action. Mao was fusing China's national destiny with her revolutionary destiny. His military strategy in the war against Japan was not a strategy merely to win a war; it was designed to create conditions for the people to win their revolution.

6 To Serve the People

The War of Resistance Against Japan:
The Yenan Base and Towards New Democracy, 1938–1945

Not only do we want to change a China that is politically oppressed and economically exploited into a China that is politically free and economically prosperous, we also want to change the China which is being kept ignorant and backward under the sway of the old culture into an enlightened and progressive China under the sway of a new culture. In short, we want to build a new China.

Mao Tse-tung, *On New Democracy*

In December 1939 and January 1940 Mao wrote two important articles in Yenan. The first, *The Chinese Revolution and the Chinese Communist Party*, was part of an unfinished textbook which sought to place the party's role in the context of the wider national movement. Mao developed his argument further in the second piece, *On New Democracy*, written for the first issue of the Yenan magazine *Chinese Culture*.

Mao's main claim in these articles was that the 'ultimate perspective' of socialism and communism could be reached in China through the stage of a 'bourgeois-democratic' revolution of a new type, a 'new-democratic revolution', led by the Communist Party, in which 'a certain degree of capitalist development would be inevitable' alongside the development of socialist forces.

This 'new-democratic revolution' would give rise to a transitional state system, which would be a dictatorship of 'all the revolutionary classes' with a democratic-centralist system of government extending 'from a national people's congress down to provincial, county, district and township people's congresses, with all levels electing their respective governmental bodies'. State enterprises would regulate capital so that it was not 'privately owned by a few'. 'Equalisation of landownership' would confiscate the land of the feudal landlords and hand it over to the ownership of peasants having little or no land, though co-operative enterprises would also exist which would 'contain elements of socialism'.

On New Democracy was published widely over the next few years and its message found its way in print or by hearsay to many intellectuals. It was especially through this article that the communists' appeal began to be received warmly even by middle-of-the-roaders and by some previously apolitical people whose patriotism had been stirred by their country's sufferings. Its clear vision of where China should go, its evident patriotism and constructive proposals for government was what many desperate men and women had been waiting for. In the darkest days it contained a fundamental call to action; 'What is to be done? Whither China?' Whereas it was the CCP's deeds — especially the tax reforms — that won over the peasants in the border region and base areas, it was Mao Tse-tung's practical optimism, his measured and determined spirit which caught the mood of the intellectuals in *On New Democracy*.

For many of these intellectuals, two things in the article stood out. Firstly, China's 'new democratic culture is national . . . It bears the stamp of our national characteristics.' Secondly, new democracy supported and advanced the cause of modernising Chinese society politically, economically and culturally, which had been the unrealised aim of the May 4th Movement.

This combination of cultural change and national revival was irresistible to many previously pessimistic intellectuals. As a result, more of them made their way to Yenan, bringing with them problems of adaptation to the new life in the border region similar to those that faced the students of two or three years before. The big intake of bourgeois intellectuals into the party in the years after the Long March created an imbalance of bourgeois leading cadres against peasant and worker leading cadres and presented Mao with the need to start adjusting their thinking. This need was one of the reasons for the rectification campaign of 1942-4.

On New Democracy was not aimed exclusively at intellectuals, however. It was studied and lectured upon at all levels of the party. It was even used to win back soldiers who were collaborating with the Japanese. In one incident on the western Hopei plain in 1941, Eighth Route Army political instructors

> climbed up on mounds or other high points and shouted through megaphones to the puppet soldiers in the strongholds, blockhouses and the battlements ... 'Hello!' they shouted. 'Listen! Get together! Today we'll give you a lecture on Chairman Mao's article, *On New Democracy*. Don't move about. Listen attentively!' The puppet soldiers dared not shoot. In fact they did not want to. They listened attentively to our political instructors' lectures. Twenty minutes ... thirty minutes ... until their officers interfered. Actually these puppet officers had been listening to our lectures too.
>
> During the night our soldiers sneaked into the enemy strongholds. The day's lectures had produced results. The puppet soldiers sent the following messages to our troops: 'We'll withdraw immediately. You'll find white flour in the warehouse on the west side and ammunition in the cellar on the south side. Be careful not to damage them.' The next day this stronghold was in our hands. [1]

The CCP's resistance policies were having the effect of separating out those non-party people — leaders, intellectuals, and the masses — who were genuinely interested in fighting the invaders and in social reform, and those who sided with KMT reaction and even with the Japanese. Generals and officials began to come down clearly in favour of one or the other course of action, resistance and revolution or collaboration. This division tended to isolate Chiang Kai-shek in the political middle. On the right, Wang Ching-wei's puppet 'Central Chinese Government' in Nanking openly proclaimed its intention to exterminate all communists. Chiang himself began again to drift in the same direction. He was never against permitting his generals the occasional onslaught on the New Fourth or Eighth Route Armies. Intermittently in 1939-40 KMT and CCP units clashed.

Chiang grew disturbed at the communists' military successes. The most impressive of these, whose tactics and aims it is not at all certain Mao approved, was planned by Chu Teh and Peng Teh-huai. Known as the Hundred Regiments' Offensive, it inflicted severe damage on the Japanese in five northern provinces from August to December 1940.

> Enemy-held coal mines and power stations, railways, bridges, highways, trains and telecommunications were destroyed . . . Great stretches of northern railways were ripped out, the ties carried away, and the rails carried to small arsenals in the guerrilla mountain strongholds . . . Thousands of liberated railway workers and miners joined the Eighth Route Army.
>
> By the time the offensive ended in late December, 2,933 Japanese forts had been destroyed; 20,645 Japanese, including eighteen officers, killed or wounded; and 281 Japanese taken prisoner. Over 51,000 Chinese puppet troops had been killed or wounded and 18,407 taken prisoner, about half of them former Kuomintang soldiers. Vast quantities of arms and ammunition and other supplies had been captured and put to immediate use. [2]

Chiang's government in Chungking interpreted this victory as a threat to them as much as to the Japanese. In December 1940 the KMT High Command ordered the communist-led New Fourth Army to evacuate the zone in the Yangtze valley where it had been operating for nearly two years. It was told to cross the Yangtze and march north to join parts of the Eighth Route Army, whose activities had penetrated all northern China.

General Yeh Ting, commander of the New Fourth, at first refused, claiming his troops would be decimated by the Japanese and puppet troops if they marched along the routes designated by the KMT. Finally, he agreed so long as the New Fourth Army could cross the river at points chosen by themselves. By 7 January 1941 all but 9,000 had done so. The remaining men were members of the headquarters force and two rear base hospitals. When these 9,000 began to move towards the river they were surrounded and attacked by some 50,000 KMT troops. About 4,000 were killed in the ten-day battle. One thousand escaped across the river to join the other troops. Yeh Ting was wounded and captured. About 4,000, most of them wounded, were taken prisoner and died in KMT concentration camps, nearly 2,000 of them succumbing to torture or neglect at the infamous Shangchiao camp in Chekiang province. During the battle, wrote Agnes Smedley, 'The wounded and sick in the hospital column were simply put to the sword. As men fell dying or dead, women political workers and nurses took up their guns and fought until their ammunition was finished. Then they hanged themselves in the forest.'

The New Fourth Army incident went far to convince Mao that the communists would have to rely much more on their own forces than on the KMT in their opposition to the Japanese under the terms of the united front. Two months after the slaughter two of Chiang's generals crossed to the Japanese side with 50,000 KMT troops. Chiang neither reprimanded them, nor deprived them of their rank in the KMT army, nor sent a punitive force against them.

The Yenan government issued directives, guiding all the liberated areas, to pay attention to their defences and establish bases to withstand the pressure of both Japanese and KMT units. Further divisions were sent to the rear of the Japanese to set up pockets of resistance that could grow into bases.

For two years intensive efforts had been made to spread

the nuclei of future stable base areas. One cavalry regiment of the 129th Division of the Eighth Route Army, facing Japanese encirclement of its base in the Taihang Mountains in South Shansi, was ordered to cross the plains to Shantung province to open up a base there. Their passage was hard. They left the mountains just as the rainy season set in.

> Low-hanging clouds pressed upon the shadowy mountains and torrential rain lashed us. Our clothing was never dry, not for a single day. Rivulets of yellowish water coming down the mountain converged to form a roaring, rolling deluge, reverberating through the valley. On the way, we had only millet mixed with grit and wild roots to eat. Many of our men went down with dysentery and malaria. But even more serious was the problem of our horses. Their shoes wore out from walking on the sharp cobble-stones, then their hooves wore thin. Their soles gradually turned red and swollen, and festered. The fighters took off their own shoes and tied them on the horses, but in a day they too were worn out. The horses raised their heads and neighed in pain. It made our hearts break to hear them. The soldiers, standing on bare feet, stared at their horses with tears rolling down their cheeks. [3]

The Japanese Army found the tactics of encirclement and massive thrusts unrewarding. Their enemy divided and disappeared. In a move that recalled the KMT's extermination campaigns against the Kiangsi base, they tried to separate the population from the guerrillas, who moved among the people, in the celebrated phrase, 'like fish in water'. The Japanese 'three-all' measures — burn all, kill all, loot all — was an attempt to establish no-man's-lands of destruction between them and the liberated areas. They herded villagers into settlements or 'safe' areas, a tactic also used unsuccessfully by the United States in Vietnam. Further, they constructed blockhouses, earthworks and barbed wire fences to isolate the communists. At the same time the KMT began to impose an economic blockade on the communist areas, and ceased to pay or supply the Eighth Route Army.

As a result of these blockades, inflation broke out in Yenan. In 1942 grain prices increased fourteen-fold. Other prices soared as trade with the rest of China became impossible. The Yenan government imposed a severe tax of 200,000 *piculs* of millet in 1941. Grain tax collection work teams were sent to each district; they increased the number of families on the tax roll in 1941 from 20 percent to 80 percent of all families. In 1941-2 the major burden of taxation fell on the formerly exempt or little taxed poor and middle peasants. The hardest hit were the poor, only the poorest being exempt. These were the communist government's closest allies.

Mao's answer to the economic difficulties caused by the blockades was to organise a drive for production in the border region and the liberated areas, beginning in the first months of 1941. Soldiers took the lead in opening waste areas to agriculture and participated in farm work and small-scale industry, while the peasants developed their mutual-aid teams. In the Yenan base Mao continued to encourage party members to adopt the 'proletarian working style'; cadres were to work alongside the people to help with production and army leaders were to keep close links with the masses when, in their wasteland operations, they became a productive as well as a military and political force.

The production movement has given rise to numerous legends of soldier heroes who, inspired by Mao's call and armed with picks and hoes as well as guns, went out and cultivated the virgin land in the service of the poor. One of the most intensely selfless heroes, still held up in school textbooks in present-day China as a model of how to follow Mao's principles, was Chang Tzu-teh from Szechuan province. Chang Tzu-teh was a squad leader in the Guards' Battalion of the party's Central Committee. His short life was recorded by Chen Yao, a soldier in Chang's squad.

Chang Tzu-teh was born in a poor peasant family without a single room or plot of land to call its own. His father and elder brother were hired hands, and at twelve Chang too started to work for a landlord, cutting fodder, herding cattle, fetching water and sweeping the courtyard. He was treated worse than a dog. In 1933, at the age of seventeen, he joined the Red Army . . .

Chang lived a very simple and thrifty life. His padded tunic was almost too ragged to be patched again . . . But he patched it again and made it do for another two years.

The dirt roads and mountain tracks in Yenan were so stony that our shoes wore out very quickly. Every time new shoes were issued, Chang refused to take them, saying, 'I can make sandals myself. If I take one pair less, that will mean one pair less for the villagers to make.' Actually his cloth shoes were a mass of patches, with straw or bark stuffed in the holes. When they could no longer be worn, he undid them instead of throwing them away and, having washed the material, found some more scraps of cloth with which to make a new pair. To save shoes he often went barefoot. Often he unravelled the thread from his own worn out socks and those cast off by others, washed the thread and knitted more socks with it. Sometimes he gave these to other comrades to wear.

Chang had an enamel bowl which he had used during the Long March. Now most of the enamel had peeled off and the bowl was badly dented, but still he would not throw it away. When new bowls were issued, he gave his to somebody else and stuck to his old one. Chang also had an old fountain pen, the nib of which was so blunt after much use that the words written with it looked as if written with a brush. But he used it all the same. When the nib became too blunt he sharpened it. He treasured this pen so much that he made a small cloth pouch for it.

When Chen Yao asked why he was so thrifty, Chang Tzu-teh

pointed out how much better off he was then, compared with his childhood. Tens of thousands in China, he said, were poorer than he. 'We should think of their sufferings. If everybody economises it will be a great help to the revolution . . . We should do what Chairman Mao teaches us . . . work for the people, be the first to put up with hardships and the last to enjoy comforts.' These were the qualities Mao sought in the soldiers and leaders and Chen Yao showed how necessary was Chang Tzu-teh's spirit in backward Shensi.

The years 1941 and 1942 were the most difficult period for the anti-Japanese bases in the enemy rear. We were short of grain, even of millet . . . In the late autumn of 1941 our guards battalion arrived at Nanniwan, over ninety *li* from Yenan. In response to Chairman Mao's call to provide ourselves with ample food and clothing by our own efforts, we set to work to wrest grain from the barren mountains . . . Only a few households lived at Nanniwan. When we first arrived there we had nowhere to live. Chang got us to build a shed with branches and cut grass to spread on the ground. At night we slept huddled together in this shed. We could see the stars as we lay there. The food was bad. We had no vegetables at all and not enough salt . . .

Our commanders instructed every company to move into caves before winter. An expert at digging caves, Chang acted as our technical adviser. After selecting our sites we started to dig. Except for the picks which we had brought from Yenan, we made all our own tools including wheelbarrows and baskets. The red clay of the Nanniwan hills was very hard. Our picks clanged as they struck it, jarring and hurting our hands. Chang swung away at the clay even when his hands were covered in blisters. If someone took his pick away, he immediately started to push a wheelbarrow. Some chunks of clay were too big for the barrow, and he would ask us to put them on his back for him to carry off and throw into a ditch. When the mouth of the cave was made he was the first to go inside to work. It was growing colder every day but Chang, though stripped to the waist, was sweating all over. The clay, mixed with his sweat, clung to his body. By the time we knocked off Chang looked like a clay figure.

Chang's attitude of 'serve the people', which Mao promoted, was not cultivated for effect but for solid reasons of survival: hard work had to be done to save the people. The Eighth Route Army's principles could only be carried out in unity with the people and would collapse in isolation from them. Such a spirit as Chang's elicited a naive and sincere response from the poorest peasants.

> One day in Nanniwan, Chang and I went to borrow a hoe from a villager. We found the old man and his wife chopping up fodder in the courtyard. Chang urged them to rest and took over the chopper while I fetched straw for him. The old woman smiled at us and asked, 'Have you ever seen Chairman Mao in Yenan?' We replied that we had. 'Chairman Mao is our great saviour,' she said with feeling. 'If the Eighth Route Army led by Chairman Mao weren't in Yenan, we could never enjoy such peace here. Nanniwan used to be overrun by Kuomintang troops and bandits. But since Chairman Mao came we've had a peaceful life.' Chang said at once, 'That's true. It's at Chairman Mao's order that we've come to reclaim the wasteland. We shall make Nanniwan look like the fertile provinces south of the Yangtse. We shall thoroughly smash the blockade ... Guided by Chairman Mao, we shall liberate the people of our whole country, so that they will be free from exploitation and oppression like our people in the Shensi—Kansu—Ningsia Border Region.' The old woman cried out happily, 'How good that will be!'
>
> Back in the squad Chang told the comrades what the old woman had said. 'We are the soldiers of the people,' he said. 'We must integrate ourselves with the people no matter where we are. When we carry guns we are soldiers. When we put down our guns we are peasants.

We must bear in mind Chairman Mao's teaching: 'The people's army is as inseparable from the people as fish from the water.'

The people's army, as Mao conceived it, was to be an educational force, too. Its propagandist duties made it necessary that the soldiers should be able to read and write. Yet the people had almost no written culture.

Chang often advised us, 'Look further, look to the future . . .' Whether burning charcoal in the mountains, opening up wasteland, working at some construction site or on regular duty, and no matter how tired he was, he always found time to study. He learned new characters, read newspapers and studied political textbooks. During breaks when we were working in the open, he would practise writing on the ground with a stick. Back at base after supper, he would write new characters on a sand tray he had made. We could hardly get paper or pencils, not only during the most difficult period but even after the big production movement had started. People counted themselves very lucky to get old books or newspapers to write on. A notebook or a pencil was a rare treasure. Chang was once awarded several notebooks and pencils, which he kept carefully in his pack . . . While we were making charcoal at Tuhuangkou he made notebooks out of birch bark. He cut a nib out of an old tin and tied it to a stick to make a pen. Later on he made a fountain-pen out of an old cartridge . . . As we were allowed very little oil for our lamp, it was almost impossible to study at night. Chang cut some cypress branches to serve as torches. After we picked castor oil beans, he collected those left on the ground and strung them together to be burned as candles. Sometimes he studied by the light of the moon . . .

At first I was not very enthusiastic about learning. He said to me, 'Fancy not even being able to write your own name! You know, you must learn so that you can read the newspaper and understand more about revolution.' He guided my hand and taught me stroke by stroke how to write my name. To give me more time for study he often carried out assignments for me. He also got those in the squad with more education to help the rest of us. So eventually we took study more seriously and in twos or threes would read newspapers, write new characters or study our political textbooks together. I wiped out my own illiteracy with the bark notebook, half a pencil and a wooden pen presented to me by Chang.

In all these respects Chang was an outstanding example of Mao's model soldier. Chen Yao described the sorrow felt at Chang's death and the extraordinary passion of his memories of him.

On 5 September 1944, Comrade Chang Tzu-teh was killed by the sudden collapse of a kiln when making charcoal in the mountains of Ansai County. This sad news cut me to the heart. Chang Tzu-teh had been such a fine comrade! He worked entirely in the people's interests, never giving a single thought to his own. He loved and helped his comrades, showing concern for them in every way. He was always the first to bear hardships, the last to enjoy comforts, always worked hard and set an example by his conduct. He lived simply, studied hard, was modest and prudent, and always set a high demand on himself. He had been a model for me in every respect and given me great help. Now this fine comrade-in-arms, who had been so dear to me, had left me for ever! I could not help weeping as past events rushed to my mind. For the first few days after I learned of his death I was overwhelmed with sadness. The mere mention of his name brought tears to my eyes.

On the afternoon of 8 September, we held a memorial meeting for Comrade Chang Tzu-teh in the Date Garden at the foot of the West Hill in Yenan. The rostrum was filled with garlands of flowers presented by various organisations. And there was an inscription written by Chairman Mao: 'All honour to Comrade Chang Tzu-teh who has given his life for the interests of the people.' It was at that meeting, attended by over a thousand people, that Chairman Mao delivered his famous speech *Serve the People*. Chairman Mao's words showed me the direction to take. I determined to turn my grief into strength. [4]

In his speech of tribute to this ordinary peasant who 'has done some useful work', Mao said,

> The Chinese people are suffering; it is our duty to save them and we must exert ourselves in struggle. Wherever there is struggle there is sacrifice, and death is a common occurrence. But we have the interests of the people and the sufferings of the great majority at heart, and when we die for the people it is a worthy death. Nevertheless, we should do our best to avoid unnecessary sacrifices. Our cadres must show concern for every soldier, and all people in the revolutionary ranks must care for each other, must love and help each other. [5]

The 'Yenan Spirit', the spirit of selflessness, hard work and collective self-reliance, continued as a model into the cultural revolution of 1966-9. Then, too, with China at a much higher stage of economic development, Mao insisted that the strength of the revolution lay in its identity with the people and its cadres must continually correct any tendency to become separate from those they served and led.

The party conducted intensive self-criticism and study in its base areas from 1942 to 1944. The object was to convert its organisation into a national, broad-based body capable of carrying out the new-democratic programme for the whole of China.

Previous campaigns to correct the party's methods of work had been limited to sections of the party or to aspects of the party line. The rectification campaign of 1942, however, involved a thorough inspection and reinvigoration of the whole range of the party's principles and affected all party members. It was a 'three-style rectification', that is, it was supposed to correct the party members' styles of study, work and writing.

In a broader sense it aimed at remoulding the thinking of the party member, and hence at correcting his conduct. The individual party member had to be adjusted to the conditions in which he had to work — blockade, shortage and rural backwardness. It was obvious that those who had to change more than the rural-born cadres and local party members were the new and often younger revolutionary recruits from the cities and the bourgeoisie. Such recruits often arrived with deeply-felt but high-flown ideas on what could be done. Others had learnt a lot of communist theory which they tended to impose indiscriminately in practice.

The rectification movement combated the habit of dogmatically taking Russian models and parroting Marxist–Leninist phrases while doing nothing to analyse Chinese conditions. Mao tried to make the best use of talented cadres by turning the 'subjective enthusiasm' of those who merely theorised into objective study and practical application. He advised the Party School 'to grade students . . . according to how they look at China's problems after they have studied Marxism–Leninism'. Students should 'analyse every problem concretely on the basis of detailed material and then draw theoretical conclusions'. Book-learning must be supplemented by learning from practice, while the reverse process must be taken up by those experienced in work, who should study theory to systematise and synthesise their experience.

To increase party unity, Mao attacked the tendency to assert 'independence', to see 'only the interests of the part and not the whole'. Party propaganda must express materialism in understandable and vital forms. He derided the empty verbiage, the striking of poses to intimidate readers, lack of aim, drab language, the formal listing of points, lack of preparation and forethought, all of which were to be found in stereotyped party writing.

Mao attacked the dogmatism of some party writers with biting sarcasm.

> Our comrades must understand that we do not study Marxism–Leninism because it is pleasing to the eye, or because it has some mystical value, like the doctrines of the Taoist priests who ascend Mao Shan to learn how to subdue devils and evil spirits. Marxism–Leninism has no beauty, nor has it any mystical value. It is only extremely useful. It seems that right up to the present quite a few have regarded Marxism–Leninism as a ready-made panacea: once you have it, you can cure all your ills with little effort. This is a type of childish blindness and we must start a movement to enlighten these people. Those who regard Marxism–Leninism as religious dogma show this type of blind ignorance. We must tell them openly, 'Your dogma is of no use,' or to use an impolite phrase, 'Your dogma is less useful than excrement.' We see that dog excrement can fertilise the fields and man's can feed the dog. And dogmas? They can't fertilise the fields, nor can they feed a dog. Of what use are they? [6]

Marxist–Leninist doctrine, he reminded the party, was 'a guide to action'.

Mao also attempted to draw up the principles under which literature and art could be brought within the compass of the party line on the development of classes. At a forum (in Chinese, literally a 'sit and talk meeting') held in Yenan in May 1942, at first eighty and, by the third session on 23 May, as many as 200 intellectuals and 'art-workers' met to discuss the way ahead for the party's cultural expression. Great concepts such as 'people's art' and 'freedom of expression' were wrestled with. In his talks which opened and concluded the forum, Mao asked the question: 'For whom?' Do writers write for themselves? Or do they write for the people? If for the people, then for which people, the bourgeoisie or the working people? And shouldn't writers who write for the working people live as the working people do and learn from them? Mao concluded that 'the duty of learning from the workers and peasants precedes the task of educating them . . . [We must not] raise the workers, peasants and soldiers to the level of the feudal class, the bourgeoisie or the petty-bourgeois intelligentsia but . . . along their own line of ascent, along the line of ascent of the proletariat.'

In the actual period of rectification most artists were silent and concentrated on study, investigation and analysis. The creative fruits of Mao's line on literature and art began to show in the New Year of 1944 when the Party School organised the writing of *yangko* plays, a type of new-style folk opera, such as *Brother and Sister Tilling Virgin Soil* and *The White-haired Girl*, the latter still popular today in the form of a ballet with a revised story and updated political relevance.

The Yenan Forum, and especially Mao's speeches, encouraged a variety of popular arts, including woodcuts which were developed at the Lu Hsun Art Academy in Yenan led by the artist Ku Yuan. Influenced initially by the German artists Kollwitz and Grosz, Ku Yuan learnt from the Yenan Forum that there was a positive as well as a negative side to the horrors of the Japanese occupation.

> My peasants were always starving or being beaten to death . . . Now most of my drawings are not about the miseries but about their strenuous efforts to make a new world. [7]

The novelist Ting Ling, who helped organise *yangko* drama groups, described how after the Yenan Forum she listened to the songs of the people and studied them.

> In northern Shensi, everyone . . . without exception could sing these songs. There were love-songs and labourers' songs and there were songs cursing the officials and scholars, and they were mostly anonymous songs. Also, there were story-tellers, who are also singers, and I

think most of us learned more from these old blind story-tellers than we learned from anything we ever read. [8]

Novels in the traditional style of story-telling, such as Chao Shu-li's *Rhymes of Li Yu-tsai*, began to flourish and professional poets learnt to imitate the rhythms and idioms of folk song. The poet Ai Ching summed up the attitude of many creative artists to the revolution in the Yenan period.

We subordinated everything — our lives, our customs, our traditions — to winning the war. It had to be. We had everything to gain from organisation. No-one starved and no-one was without weapons. We relied on our selves, and we knew that China would have to rely on herself for victory. And gradually, over all those long years, we built up in the north a system of democracy which can never fail, because it represents so intimately the demands of the peasants. [9]

If it was a primary purpose of the rectification campaign to change the individual party worker's attitudes (especially those of bourgeois intellectuals), towards the people they were serving, it must not be forgotten that Mao himself had had to change, and had to continue to change, in exactly the same way as he was recommending others to remould themselves. In his talks at the Yenan Forum, he spoke of his own struggle to change the bourgeois feelings towards the 'unclean' masses which he said had been implanted in him by his education. He underlined the fact that it was only after long experience of working alongside workers and peasants that he himself had come to share their attitudes.

I began life as a student and at school acquired the ways of a student; I then used to feel it undignified to do even a little manual labour, such as carrying my own luggage in the presence of my fellow students, who were incapable of carrying anything, either on their shoulders or in their hands. At that time I felt that intellectuals were the only clean people in the world, while in comparison workers and peasants were dirty. I did not mind wearing the clothes of other intellectuals, believing them clean, but I would not put on clothes belonging to a worker or peasant, believing them dirty. But after I became a revolutionary and lived with workers and peasants and with soldiers of the revolutionary army, I gradually came to know them well, and they gradually came to know me well too . . . I came to feel that compared with the workers and peasants the unremoulded intellectuals were not clean and that, in the last analysis, the workers and peasants were the cleanest people and, even though their hands were soiled and their feet smeared with cow-dung, they were really cleaner than the bourgeois and petty-bourgeois intellectuals. That is what is meant by a change in feelings, a change from one class to another. If our writers and artists who come from the intelligentsia want their works to be well received by the masses, they must change and remould their thinking and their feelings. [10]

After liberation, in 1957, Mao referred again to the need for him to continue remoulding his thinking.

Many of us make some progress each year; that is to say, we are being remoulded each year. For myself, I had all sorts of non-Marxist ideas before, and it was only later that I embraced Marxism. I learned a little Marxism from books and so made an initial remoulding of my ideas, but it was mainly through taking part in the class struggle over the years that I came to be remoulded. And I must continue to learn if I am to make further progress, otherwise I shall lag behind. [11]

The most outstanding result of the rectification campaign and the concurrent study of the history of the Kiangsi Soviet and the Shensi border region was a new concept of party leadership, the mass line. This concept was at once Mao's summarisation and distillation of the party's experience up until then and a bold initiative by Mao against the rigidity, dogmatism and bureaucracy that accompanied the party's growth and widening influence.

> In all the practical work of our party, all correct leadership is necessarily 'from the masses to the masses'. This means: take the ideas of the masses (scattered and unsystematic ideas) and concentrate them (through study turn them into concentrated and systematic ideas), then go to the masses to propagate and explain these ideas until the masses embrace them as their own, hold fast to them and translate them into action, and test the correctness of these ideas in such action. Then once again concentrate ideas from the masses and once again go to the masses so that the ideas are carried through. And so on, over and over again in an endless spiral, with the ideas becoming more correct, more vital and richer each time. [12]

Mao decisively rejected the manipulative, bureaucractic approach to mobilisation, which, from a protected position at the centre, directed masses of men in the localities according to a prearranged blueprint. His organic view of leadership, reflecting a dialectical relationship between leaders and led, placed a proper balance between the democratic and the centralist aspects of the party's democratic-centralist work methods. This showed itself in relations between party members. Liu Shao-chi in his *Training of the Communist Party Member*, which was also used as a text during the rectification campaign, emphasised party loyalty as a virtue above all other virtues, the test of which was the party member's 'ability, regardless of the situation, to subordinate his individual interests unconditionally and absolutely to those of the party'. For Mao, obedience was not desirable in itself: it was a Marxist—Leninist principle, he reminded the party as recently as 1970, 'to go against the tide'. For Mao it was political consciousness that marked the good cadre, his level of understanding of the people's needs and his concern to serve them.

Mao's emphasis was born of a more accurate analysis of class struggle within the party. It demonstrated, too, his deeper confidence in the people's constructive capacities: while the line of policy must be decided at the centre as a result of mass line investigations, the initiative of party members and cadres at lower levels must be given full play.

Mao also showed this confidence in his policy of self-reliance which developed further at Yenan, especially in the border region's efforts to meet its food and other basic needs. 'What you need to do, do with your own hands' was his advice to the army units going to open up wasteland during the Yenan production drive. Several times, while speaking to visitors at Yenan, Mao held up his hands and said it was with 'our own hands' that the revolution would succeed and China would be liberated. The idea of collective self-reliance ran very deep in Mao in those years and remained at the core of his thinking. Both before and after that period, he urged the people to depend mainly on their own efforts in war, in political struggle and in agricultural and industrial development, and not to rely entirely on military and party leaders or, later, on foreign aid.

In the Great Leap Forward in 1958 and especially in the cultural revolution, Mao was to stress again the mass line as the correct method of mobilising the people's productive energy. Marx's saying that 'Social being determines social consciousness' is only the passive aspect of class realities. The active side is that once the consciousness of the masses (in Mao's words, 'the correct ideas characteristic of the advanced class') has been released it becomes 'a material force which changes society and changes the world'.

The rectification campaign brought about a political renovation of the party. It gave it a stronger base in the community. It enabled the production campaign to succeed at the village level and the economic situation improved. It also gave rise to the education movement of 1944 in the border region and liberated areas. The education movement went under the slogan of 'develop production, expand the schools'. The stress was laid on spreading literacy and elementary economic and medical skills quickly in the villages. School management was 'by the people with the assistance of government' and the role of the teacher changed from all-knowing arbiter to an instructor whose usefulness was judged by his articulation of the people's needs. Mao's insistence that study be related to society, and in particular to the productive needs of a backward society, found expression at this time and was renewed twenty years later in the cultural revolution.

Yenan's growing strength, born of a rectification campaign which was carried out in the midst of the vicissitudes of blockade, brought the CCP increasing respect and a new following. By 1944 the party's organisation had been built up to a high enough level for the Chinese nation as a whole to begin to see in the CCP the possibility that it was the one mass party capable of putting democracy into practice. They also began to see in its chairman a leader of far profounder qualities than any the KMT could put forward. To show its promise as the major national party of the future, it remained for the CCP to develop the basis of a national, revolutionary foreign policy. The publication of Chiang Kai-shek's *China's Destiny* late in 1945 revealed a man retiring into Confucian righteousness, ranking western bourgeois democracy lower than Chinese tradition. Mao, on the other hand, was known to value the tradition of Washington, Jefferson and Lincoln and to appraise the historical role of the English, French and American revolutions. Mao's appeal as a leader therefore extended even to the 'third party' democrats who had lost all hope in the KMT and who had at first been suspicious of the CCP. Mao's attitude to democracy and especially to America at that time did much to attract the third party intellectuals to his side. In 1944 Mao was still hopeful that bourgeois-democratic America would find it more in its interest to develop relations with the new democracy of the Chinese communists than with reactionary, semi-feudal and paternalist KMT nationalism. It would take a generation before this hope began to be fulfilled.

The attraction of Yenan as 'the beacon of the future' became still more compelling when the success of its production drive was compared with conditions in many other parts of China, a comparison many made at the time. The destitution of the mountain villages, such as those of south Shensi, only 200 miles outside the Yenan base area, was created not by one or two natural disasters or local misgovernment but by generations of peasant ignorance and merchant and landlord avarice and oppression. Plunder and expropriation, taxation and eviction had plunged the rural population of huge areas into a poverty which affected even the rocks. Peasants, forced to cut down and use or sell all timber, had released forces of erosion that, once begun, they could not reverse, and the rain pouring off the deforested watershed between the Yellow and Yangtze rivers in south Shensi, cut deep into the land, washing away the very soil that brought them a living. Graham Peck travelled in that area in the early 1940s.

The land was dying and its people with it. The first Westerners who travelled through Shuangshihpu and wrote about it, early in the nineteenth century, had reported that this was wild empty country, heavily wooded with pines, holding only a few farmhouses along the torrential mountain stream. Now there were wretched little farms right up to the summit of the mountains. Except for the cherished domestic trees around the farmhouses, only a scruff of secondary growth was left on the most inaccessible steps. Already, the thin red and yellow soil of the hilly fields was clutched on every flank by jagged erosion gulleys ... The few acres of good farmland in the flatter valleys were slowly being covered by dry deltas of gravel and boulders, tumbled out of the ravines by the fierce, brief rains which came in the summer when they could also harm the mountain fields, washing out the new crops . . .

The final stages in the slow murder of the country proceeded inexorably all the time I was there . . . Every day farmers would stumble past, weighted down with huge stacks of kindling and brushwood to sell in the village. Sometimes soldiers from the garrison climbed up with laughter and axes, and returned with great logs which showed they had 'confiscated' another farm-yard tree as firewood. Sometimes the farmers themselves carried fine big logs down to the fuel market, tokens that they had been forced to sacrifice one more guardian of their fields. Because of the decreasing fertility of their land, they could not afford not to cut and sell their trees, even though they were dimly aware that it meant bad luck — worse crops . . .

The newer farmhouses, higher in the hills, were little more than kennels of mud and straw . . . On the mountains, the homes of the living were outnumbered by the mounds which housed the dead and the shrines to appease local spirits. Each new grave, always placed in a good field, took more farmland from the survivors . . .

Apart from the grinding poverty which kept them in rags, unwashed except at birth, marriage, and death, they suffered an unknown multitude of ills. None could afford the refugee doctor in the village and there had never been a public medical service here. Some limped, some walked sidewise, some winced at every step, many had peculiarities that approached lunacy. [13]

In 1943 the normal terror of famine again stalked the land. The Honan famine that year, which in the end killed two or three million peasants, followed the customary pattern of starvation and emigration to the cities for the many, grain-hoarding by the rich and food enough for those with money. Travelling near Chengchow in the bitter north China winter,

Theodore H. White and Annalee Jacoby witnessed the flight of the peasants from their starving villages.

> Across the flat plain were strung beads of bunched figures. The endless procession rose beyond the horizon, wound across the paths between the fields, passed silently into the greyness behind . . .
>
> Some father pushed a wheelbarrow past, the mother hauling at it in front with a rope, the baby on the padding sometimes silent, sometimes crying; or the woman of the family sat sidesaddle on her mule with her baby in her arms . . . Old women hobbled along on bound feet, stumbled and fell; no one picked them up. Other old women rode pickaback on the strong shoulders of their sons, staring through coal-black eyes at the hostile sky. Young men, walking alone, strode at a quicker pace, with all their possessions in a kerchief over their shoulder. Small mounds of rags by the roadside marked where the weak had collapsed; sometimes a few members of a family stood staring at a body in silent perplexity. The children leaned on their staffs like old men; some carried bundles as large as themselves . . . Behind them all, from the land of famine a cold wind blew, sending the dust chasing them over the yellow plain. The march had been going on for weeks; it was to continue for weeks more . . .
>
> The peasants, as we saw them, were dying . . . And as they died, the government continued to wring from them the last possible ounce of tax. The money tax the peasant had to pay on his land was a trivial matter; the basic tax exacted from him was the food tax, a percentage of all grain he raised . . . The government in county after county was demanding of the peasants more actual poundage of grain than he had raised on his acres. No excuses were allowed; peasants who were eating elm bark and dried leaves had to haul their last sack of seed grain to the tax collector's office. Peasants who were so weak they could barely walk had to collect fodder for the army's horses, fodder that was more nourishing than the

filth they were cramming into their own mouths. Peasants who could not pay were forced to the wall; they sold their cattle, their furniture, and even their land to raise money to buy grain to meet the tax quotas ... Merchants from Sian and Chengchow, small government officials, army officers, and rich landlords who still had food were engaged in purchasing the peasants' ancestral acres at criminally low figures. [14]

After famine, the Japanese. In 1944 the invaders moved through Honan 'clearing up' the stricken land. The Japanese army's 'three-all' scorched earth policy topped desolation with eradication. But by 1944 the mopping-up operations were taking on the appearance of greater desperation. The guerrilla areas were again expanding. The communists in a grim way gained from the fact that there was hardly a village in Hopei and Shansi that had not been burned or partly burned. According to Chalmers Johnson,

The revolution spread and became irreversible in the years 1941-2. Instead of breaking the tie between the Eighth Route Army and the peasantry, the Japanese policy drove the two together into closer alliance ... By the spring of 1943, the Eighth Route Army was again moving in the plains of Hopei and operating throughout Shantung. The army's strength and the size of the guerrilla areas very soon surpassed those of 1940. [15]

On 30 September 1944 Yenan Radio broadcast a warning to the Eighth Route Army and the Shantung peasants that the Japanese were trying to seize the autumn harvest. Eighth Route Army soldiers intercepted the marauders and turned the tide further in the communists' favour, liberating new areas that had been under puppet, KMT or Japanese control. Large numbers of puppet troops deserted to the communists in northern China in the last months of the anti-Japanese war.

Looking beyond the end of the war, Mao gave a number of

interviews to western journalists visiting Yenan in the summer of 1944. He gave the impression that a communist future in China was far distant, while the new-democratic programme, on the other hand, provided a common basis around which all shades of Chinese democratic opinion could unite within a short time. He told Gunther Stein that there was a distinction between 'the communist method of observing, studying, and solving social problems on the one hand, and the practical policies of our new democracy on the other'. The latter were the CCP's immediate aims; the former would eventually lead to 'the communist system of social organisation' after 'a long period'.

> What China needs now is democracy and not socialism. To be more precise, China's needs at present are three: (1) to drive the Japanese out; (2) to realise democracy on a nationwide scale by giving the people all the forms of modern liberty, and a system of national and local governments elected by them in genuinely free and general elections, which we have already done in the areas under our control; and (3) to solve the agrarian question, so that capitalism of a progressive character can develop in China and improve the standard of living of the people through the introduction of modern methods of production ... To speak of the realisation of socialism before these tasks are accomplished would merely be empty talk. This is what I told our party members in 1940 in my book *On New Democracy*. I said already then that this first democratic phase of our revolution would by no means be short ... It is quite possible that China may reach the stages of socialism and communism considerably later than your countries in the west which are so much more highly developed economically.

Mao was not consistent in holding this last view. Seven years before he had told Nym Wales, 'In the world revolution the backward countries will be victorious first. America will probably be the last.'

Mao went on to tell Stein the principle foundations of the new democracy.

> The central economic feature ... is the agrarian revolution ... Our peasantry is the chief object of exploitation — not only of Chinese reactionaries but also of the Japanese imperialists in the occupied territories. Only the introduction of the new democracy in our war regions had enabled us from the beginning to resist the Japanese as successfully as we do, because of its reforms in the interest of the peasant masses who constitute the very basis of our war effort.
>
> The present unreformed agrarian system in the rest of China, with its scattered, individual peasant economy — in which the farmers are not free but bound to the land, in which they have little contact even with one another and live a stagnant cultural life — has been the foundation of our ancient feudalism and despotism. The new democracy of the future cannot rest on such a foundation. For the progress of Chinese society will mainly depend upon the development of industry.
>
> Industry must therefore be the main economic foundation of the new democracy. Only an industrial society can be a fully democratic society. But to develop industry, the land problem must first be solved. Without a revolution against the feudal landlord system it is impossible to develop capitalism, as the course of events in western countries many years ago has shown quite clearly.
>
> Our agrarian revolution until 1937, during the period of the civil war, was fundamentally of the same social character as the great agrarian revolutions which took place in the past in all progressive countries of the West and cleared away the feudal obstacles to the growth of the capitalistic democratic system ...
>
> In certain periods there have been a few individuals in our party who believed that communism is feasible in China at this time. But the party as such has never held that view. Even the existence within our party of a

group advocating the immediate practice of a communist social system is impossible on account of the concrete conditions in China which make communism unfeasible for a very long time to come . . .

We are firmly convinced that private capital, Chinese as well as foreign, must be given liberal opportunities for broad development in postwar China; for China needs industrial growth . . .

It is conceivable that even the gradual transfer to the tillers of all the land now under feudal exploitation may be brought about peacefully all over China if a genuinely democratic system of government is introduced everywhere. The way of bringing about such a gradual transfer of all land to the tillers would be to encourage the investment of the landlords' capital in industrial enterprises and to devise other measures of economic and fiscal policy that would be beneficial to the landlords, the tenants, and the development of Chinese economy as a whole.

But such a solution depends upon genuine internal peace and genuine democracy in China. The possible need in the future for outright confiscation and distribution of land to the tenants can therefore not be ruled out entirely. For in the postwar period there may again be civil war if the Kuomintang insists on attacking us. [16]

In these statements can be seen Mao's clear signals to the United States to support a coalition government of the CCP and KMT, hold the KMT to their promises of continuing the united front and of peace with the communists, and let new democracy develop.

Indeed the agreement signed in 1944 by Mao and the representative of the US government, Patrick Hurley, gave the communists representation in the proposed coalition government with the KMT. In its military council it obliged the coalition to institute democratic freedoms and provide for equal distribution of aid to the two parties. But the draft

was rejected by Chiang Kai-shek, and on 24 Decen,
Mao told Hurley he saw no point in negotiating furth
the KMT showed no sincerity. In January 1945 M,
Chou En-lai approached President Roosevelt to try to est. ush
relations with the United States to avoid becoming too
dependent on the Soviet Union when the CCP took power.
But Hurley began to advocate a US–Chiang alliance and the
first cautious approaches of 1944 turned from June 1945
into a cold isolation of the communists by the United States.

For nearly thirty years after that Mao and the Chinese
Communists were driven to defend their party and the revolution first against KMT attack, then against US blockade.
Mao's fear that the KMT would not let a coalition work and
that civil war would be renewed became a reality in 1946.
The politics of the new democracy period have not been
repeated openly in China since. They remain, however, as an
undercurrent. Many of the adherents who were first attracted
to the Communist Party in its new democracy period, still
administer in China and Mao has had to rebut some of the
liberal policies he was earlier advocating in order to put a
brake on the power of the new 'capitalist-roaders' of post-
liberation China.

Mao's life in Yenan continued simply. He was paid the salary
of the equivalent of three American dollars a month. He cultivated a patch of tobacco plants to provide himself and
other leaders with cigarettes which Mao chain-smoked.
Harrison Forman visited Yenan in 1944 and in his book
Report from Red China gave a picture of Mao as 'tall for a
Chinese, broad-shouldered and loose-boned. About fifty
years of age, he seemed less than forty. His full face, with an
unusually high brow topped by a shock of bushy black hair,
is enlivened by wonderfully expressive eyes. He smiles easily,
speaks softly, and is almost boyish in his enthusiasms.'

In the same summer Gunther Stein described him as a man
'in a baggy tunic, tall, massive, good-natured, and somewhat

awkward in his speech and movements, with whom the people in headquarters seem to be on warm and affectionate terms . . . Easygoing and simple, thoughtful and precise. His unusually powerful forehead, his penetrating eyes with their air of deep concentration, and the calm and clarity of mind which his mellow personality seems to express mark him as a mature statesman of ability and a popular leader. He is poles apart from the stern, rigid, and care-burdened military figure of Generalissimo Chiang Kai-shek in Chungking.'

This difference between the two leaders was not lost on the people. When Robert Payne attended the performance of a play at Yenan in June 1946 based on the classical novel *Water Margin*, a favourite of Mao's, the audience evidently took the leader of the peasant forces to represent Mao and the white-faced old landlord with the long grey beard, Chiang Kai-shek. Mao himself attended this performance. At one point, according to Payne, when the landlord was reviling the peasant leader, Mao 'became lost in a horrible fit of giggles . . . and seemed in danger of sliding under his seat'.

Yet even to his closest and oldest friends Mao remained an enigma. 'Mao is the most complex person we have,' said Hsiao San the same summer. 'None of us have really understood him. I have known him longer than anyone else but I have never got to the root of him.'

Hsiao San recalled,

> Three or four times he nearly died of weakness during the Long March . . . He was strong . . . but he looked ill when it was over. He still looks after his health carefully . . . His speaking voice is not good, but when he makes speeches he has all the air of an old peasant, *un sage paysan*, and he is loved by the peasants because he says (only more forcibly than they can say them) the things that are on their minds. He is not an actor. He has no dramatic appeal. He talks simply. He delights in being as scientifically accurate as possible, but at the same time he is a dreamer and a poet . . .

He is 53 now and he has been many things in his time
... but it was only this year [1946] that he assumed for
the first time the acknowledged leadership of the Communist Party. There have been many changes within the
party, many quarrels. But what he likes to remember
most are the days when he wandered round the districts
of Hunan in great poverty, wearing a sun-helmet, a
white shirt, white trousers and sandals, and organised
the peasants. [17]

Mao confirmed to Gunther Stein that 'from time to time
there may be certain differences of opinion within our ranks'.
Less euphemistic was Mao's description of how democracy
within the party worked. The disagreements, he said, were
resolved

... by discussion and analysis of the problems in question. If a minority is still not convinced of the correctness of a majority decision, it submits to it after thorough
debates in party meetings. The decisive factor in our
work is that we always find out which of our policies
the masses of the people accept and which they criticise
or reject. Only policies which prove popular with the
masses become and remain the policies of our party.

At the time of the introduction of a new measure
there may be people inside and outside the party who
do not quite understand it. But in the course of the
execution of any measure a united opinion of an over-
whelming majority inside and outside the party is
invariably formed, because our party organisations are
all the time watching out for popular reaction, and
because we modify our measures continuously according to the actual needs and opinions of the people. All
party organisations from the top down are held to
observe our vital principle of not separating ourselves
from the masses of the people but of being in closest
harmony with their needs and wishes.

The correctness of any of our policies has always
been tested and is always being tested by the masses
themselves.

Stein noticed that Mao here began to speak with special enthusiasm. Evidently this was his favourite topic. He went on,

> We listen to the people. Through the media of popular meetings in villages, towns, districts, regions, and everywhere in our territories; through individual conversations between party members and men and women of all strata of the population; through special conferences, newspapers, and the telegrams and letters we receive from the people; through all this we can, and do, always find out the real, undisguised opinion of the masses.

Mao next introduced the subject of how the party used models of advanced types of work to hold up as examples to the party and people.

> Our method is to find typical samples both of satisfactory and unsatisfactory work in every field of activity. We study those samples thoroughly, learn from them, and sum up our experiences on the subject in order to draw concrete conclusions for the necessary improvements. The period of such observation of reality and of studying samples of good and bad work may in one case be a few weeks, in another several months, and sometimes even a few years. But in this way we always keep in close touch with actual developments, discover what the people want and need, and learn from those among the people inside and outside the party who do the best work.
>
> Some of our cadres may sometimes fail to understand our policies thoroughly and make mistakes in their execution, so that such comrades have to be criticised and taught. For this purpose, too, the thorough study and analysis of a specimen of good work is of great importance.
>
> Take the example in tonight's newspaper. Here is a long article covering a whole page which describes in detail the ways in which one of the companies of the Eighth Route Army got rid of its shortcomings and

became one of the best units. The cadres and fighters of every company in our armies will read and study and discuss this article. This is the simple way in which the positive experiences of one company will be taught as policy to five thousand companies. On other days you may find similar articles about a co-operative, a school, a hospital, or a local administrative unit. [18]

Returning to the question of party unity, Mao said that in applying the party's policies to concrete conditions 'certain deviations are liable to appear from time to time, deviations partly to the left and partly to the right. They are, however, not deviations of the party as a whole or of groups in the party, but of certain people in our ranks. From all these mistakes the party as a whole has learned . . . I have been in the minority myself. The only thing for me to do at such times was to wait. But there have been very few examples of that in recent years.'

Indeed the Yenan period was the first in which Mao could demonstrate the effectiveness of his ideas over a relatively large area and a relatively long time in conditions suitable for experiment, indeed in conditions where his style of experiment was essential for survival. Mao always found the easiest debates to win were those in which he could translate his ideas immediately into practice. His ideas were best seen, and most convincing when opened out for the people, so that they no longer remained the prerogative of disputing intellectuals. Mao's ideas, without a mass movement in which they could grow and bear fruit, were incomplete. His writings primarily existed as a manual for action. The Yenan mass movements were just such fertile ground for his style of thinking.

The transformation of rural society which was begun in 1942 made Yenan a laboratory for the greater work of agricultural co-operation after liberation. In October 1943 Mao explained two stages in this early transformation.

In the past, feudal exploitative relations restricted the border region's productive power and prevented its development. Half of the region, through land revolution, has destroyed these feudal bonds, and half, through reduction of rent and interest, has weakened the feudal bonds. Taken together, the great majority of feudal relations in the border region have been destroyed. This is the first revolution.

However, if we cannot change the methods of production from individual to collective labour, then productive power still cannot develop. For this reason, it is essential to create labour mutual-aid organisations on the basis of the individual economy (do not destroy the individual private base), that is, the peasants' agricultural production co-operatives. Only thus can productive power be greatly raised.

Earlier co-operatives had made mistakes.

Before 1939, co-operatives everywhere were based on government share-capital, in addition to assessing the masses for shares. At this time they came increasingly under the management of the district and subdistrict government. Co-operative enterprise was not concerned with the masses but primarily with government, acting for government to solve problems of finance. All decisions were made by government. This was the first stage. After 1939, the slogan 'Popularise the co-operatives' was proposed; but everywhere the old method of going among the masses and exacting shares was increased in carrying out so-called 'popularisation'. For this reason the masses still viewed the co-operatives as burdensome, and did not recognise them as their own. Co-operative personnel still seemed like officials who wanted the masses to do substitute cultivation. The masses saw the co-operatives not as serving their own interests but, on the contrary, as increasing their labour burden. [19]

By 1940 the co-operative movement was abandoned except for one area, the South District co-operative which persisted and which by 1943 had become a model in a new co-operative drive, launched in January that year. Mark Selden has summed up Mao's vision of the co-operatives.

> The vision of a co-operative economy rested on the spirited participation of the entire population, with each man, woman, and child contributing to the limit of his ability and resources. The goal was national salvation through strengthening the economy, but now there was an important element of self-interest involved for every peasant participant. For if co-operative efforts proved successful, members could anticipate substantial improvement in their meagre livelihoods. Here again was Mao's principle: 'Those who have labour give labour; those who have much give much; those who have little give little; human and animal power are put together. Thus one can avoid violating the seasons, and is able to plough in time, sow in time, hoe in time, and harvest in time . . .'
> In Mao's vision, the co-operatives served as an intermediary between the state and the family. Rather than the government directly taxing the peasantry, co-operatives would eventually contribute assessments for their members; when funds were required locally for schools or the militia, the government would avoid direct imposition on the people inasmuch as funds could be channelled from the co-operatives' surplus. The potential of the co-operatives — eventually developed and embodied in China's communes — lay in providing effective popular channels for directing the economic, social, political, and military life of the community. The focus of power and the key to rural development lay neither in the individual family farm nor in state management but in the co-operative community. From the small mutual-aid units of 1943 to the communes, this fundamental principle has distinguished China's distinctive path to development. [20]

The success of collective self-reliance during the Yenan

production drive gave a boost to co-operative efforts. Mao concentrated together the essentials of the spirit that under-lay 'serving the people' when he spoke to cadres of the famous 359th Brigade of the Eighth Route Army which spent three years opening the Nanniwan wasteland to culti-vation. Mao held up this brigade as a model of self-reliance. He urged its cadres to continue to cultivate two strengths in serving the people well — the stability of the pine and the flexibility of the willow. The pine, he said, is evergreen: it withstands the elements. Willows will live wherever you plant them; when spring comes and the branches grow, their leaves flow in the wind.

In the spring of 1945 the 359th Brigade received orders to go south to expand the anti-Japanese bases. Mao went to see them off. 'Little Devil' Hsieh Kuang-chih, a young soldier in the brigade, described a meeting held at Yenan airport prior to the brigade's departure.

> The meeting was presided over by General Ho Lung. He gave us very specific instructions. He wanted us to take good care of our equipment and uniforms, because it was very difficult to get supplies in the enemy's rear. He went on to say, 'You are tigers with unbounded energy. When tigers come out of the mountains, they fight battles to prove their worth.'
>
> The next speaker was Chairman Mao. He praised our accomplishments in protecting the Central Committee of the Party and in our task of production. He also made a detailed analysis of the current situation. Finally he said with humour, 'You are the backbone of the revolution. You are just like hens; when you get to the enemy's rear, each of you is expected to lay thirty eggs and to hatch thirty "chicks". Incidentally, tell the people of the places through which you will be passing on your march that you are bringing with you the best compliments to them from a man who lives in Yenan and whose name is Mao.' [21]

Thus the Eighth Route Army marched to open new bases in

1945, bearing with them, in Hsieh Kuang-chih's words, 'the hope of the people of the entire country'.

On 24 April 1945, as allied offensives were ending the Second World War in western Europe, Mao made a speech to the Seventh Congress of the CCP, held in Yenan, in which he posed the choice that would face the Chinese people after the defeat of Japan. Either there would be a coalition government of the CCP and the KMT, leading to 'a national assembly on a broad democratic basis . . . which will lead the liberated people of the whole country in building an independent, free, democratic, united, prosperous and powerful new China'; or there would be a continuation of the KMT's 'fascist dictatorship', its generals plunging China 'once again into the maelstrom of civil war'. In his concluding speech to the congress on 11 June, he warned that 'two big mountains lie like a dead weight on the Chinese people . . . imperialism [and] feudalism'. The CCP, he said, had long ago made up its mind to remove them.

Removing imperialism and feudalism needed the stability of the pine and the flexibility of the willow.

It is perhaps in the many stories of this period that the close affinity the people felt for Mao is best illustrated. These stories show the bold character of the fighters, viewed as heroes by the peasants, who worked for the overthrow of the 'two big mountains'. They were straightforward people, without pretensions but large in spirit, often wide in vision and deep in understanding, 'pine and willow' fighters.

Such a person was Chang Su-lien, born in Anhwei province in 1890, three years before Mao, daughter of a landless farm worker. Her father died when she was still a child. Her mother supported the family by collecting and selling firewood. At six her feet were bound, following the feudal custom. 'They said it was because small feet were more beautiful,' she said, 'but I know it was so that the girls should not run away.'

She was married when she was nine. Her husband was a

poor peasant named Chang. He rented land from a landlord and the two of them farmed it, yoking themselves to the plough since they could not afford an animal. Practically all their produce was taken as rent and tax by the landlord and government officials. They ate millet gruel once a day. When she was first told of Mao and the New Fourth Army she did not believe what she heard. 'How can it be possible, we asked, that an army should take the side of the peasants against the landlords? But the New Fourth, when it arrived, made the impossible possible . . . the rents were actually reduced . . . And the landlords held their breath and dared not say anything.'

She helped to organise women to support the New Fourth Army and care for its wounded. After the New Fourth Army incident of 1941, she threw in her lot with the communists and marched with them. The commanders ordered her to stay behind to mobilise resistance in the rear area. By then both the KMT and the Japanese had her name on their black lists. So she changed her name and assumed the role of a crazy mendicant with dishevelled hair and ash-covered face. As a beggar she wandered from village to village carrying messages by night, living in caves and feeding on berries. 'It was a hard life. As the sun set and darkness spread across the plains, I would come down from my hiding place in the hills and walk to some village. That was the loneliest moment of all, especially if the sun was gone and the moon had not come up. But then I would look up at the sky and see the stars. I would see there the face of Chairman Mao and no longer would I be alone.'

KMT agents captured this 'dangerous bandit woman' in April 1941. 'They asked me questions night and day, they asked me the names of all our guerrillas in that area, and where we had hidden the twenty-four guns that we had captured the previous year from the KMT. They asked me about the new headquarters of the New Fourth remnants who had managed to escape across the mountains. They thought I was a woman and so I would speak without difficulty and tell them all they wanted to know ... They knocked out my teeth — those that were left by the Japanese a year earlier.' The troops beat her and burnt her legs with red hot irons. 'They stuck fine-pointed bamboo splinters into my flesh and deliberately broke the points so that they remained in my flesh and caused sores dripping with pus ... All I would say was 'I don't know anything', so that they really got tired of questioning me, and after that they would beat me up every day without asking any questions. There was one thing good about my sores; they smelt so bad, so bad, that those KMT devils dared not come near me; they had to beat me with long bamboo sticks from a distance. Thus for more than a year these tortures continued.'

One day, when she fainted, her jailers thought she was dead. They threw her on a heap of bodies and crossed her name from the records, entering her death as due to 'a weak heart'. She lay on top of the corpses, warding off jackals and vultures. She thought of finishing herself off with a stone lying nearby. She lifted the stone over her forehead and was looking up at the stars when she again saw there Mao Tse-tung, the 'Saving Star' as the peasants had begun to call him. 'I decided to live.'

Hearing her body was lying outside the jail, villagers came and took it away to her sister's house intending to bury it. There they found she was alive. 'My sister had to make a thin soup of boiled flour and feed me like a baby ... The stink from the sores was now even more foul and my sister had to burn incense in my room. Without the incense even I couldn't bear my own awful smell.'

After two years' secret care, she was well enough to walk and to resume her propaganda work. Again she tramped over the hills and the KMT got to know of her 'reincarnation'. They questioned one of her daughters whom she had told to reply, 'My mother has become crazy after her long illness and has left home to wander in the hills and she will never come back.' And that was not, she said, a lie, 'for I *am* crazy — but not because of some ghost or devil — I am crazy for the revolution'.

She joined a band of guerrillas and organised villages all over the area to harrass the KMT army and authorities during the new revolutionary civil war that started in 1946. When, in 1952, after liberation, her life had become the subject of songs and stories and she was known nationally as Mother China, she found it difficult to remember which incidents in the civil war she had actually been involved in and which she only helped plan. 'There were many of us and everyone did what they must. The deed is what matters, not the name. What difference if it was me or someone else? There are thousands and thousands like me.'

The thousands are by now millions, and the process of change has still not ended. The social revolution set in motion in the Yenan years, under Mao's direction, continued throughout the new civil war and the land reform period. The Great Leap Forward and the cultural revolution are its direct descendants.

In Yenan emerged a new idea of what a man should be, in Mark Selden's words, combining 'in a single individual the values and accomplishments of the labourer, the leader, the soldier, and the student'. The intellectual, moral and physical energy generated by the Yenan experiments may yet feed further mass movements in years to come. The revolution, as Mao saw it, progresses in waves. The Yenan wave has ebbed for long periods and flowed for shorter ones. Mass movements cannot be long sustained. But the principle keeps returning, while the tactics remain flexible, the principle of the pine and the flexibility of the willow.

7   Filling the Holes and Levelling the Tops

The Third Revolutionary Civil War (the War of Liberation),
1945–1949

The reactionary, backward, decaying classes retained
[their] dual nature even in their last life-and-death
struggles against the people. On the one hand, they were
real tigers; they ate people, ate people by the millions
and tens of millions. The cause of the people's struggle
went through a period of difficulties and hardships, and
along the path there were many twists and turns. To
destroy the rule of imperialism, feudalism and bureau-
crat-capitalism in China took the Chinese people more
than a hundred years and cost them tens of millions of
lives before victory in 1949. Look! Were these not living
tigers, iron tigers, real tigers? But in the end they changed
into paper tigers, dead tigers, bean-curd tigers.

Mao Tse-tung,
from a speech made on 1 December 1958

The Russian armies cleared the Japanese from China's north-
eastern provinces in August 1945. Stalin signed a treaty of
friendship and alliance with Chiang Kai-shek while Chiang
tried to deny the CCP armies the right to accept the surrender
of the Japanese forces in the areas they controlled. Mao went
to Chungking and negotiated with Chiang for forty-three
days. He secured an agreement that preserved most of the
liberated areas as a solid nucleus of people's power.

Scarcely had the provisional agreement between the CCP
and the KMT been signed on 10 October 1945 than Chiang
resumed fierce attacks on these areas. The United States provided transport to move the KMT armies into the north-east
to take power after the Russians withdrew, forestalling take-
over by the local CCP units in many places. Mao responded

by calling for the establishment of rural base areas there, independent of the cities the KMT held.

American marines numbering 90,000 landed in China's northern ports and guarded communications for the KMT. American advisers trained KMT personnel and equipped forty-five of Chiang's divisions with modern weapons and vehicles. United States aid paid for more than half the KMT's expenditures. By mid-1946, despite further partial truces, the Third Revolutionary Civil War had begun.

Thus aided, the enemy seemed strong. But 'all reactionaries are paper tigers', said Mao in August 1946. 'From a long-term point of view, it is not the reactionaries but the people who are really powerful.' Faced by an enemy whose military supplier possessed the atom bomb, the people's army should take full account of him tactically but despise him strategically, since the outcome of a revolutionary war is finally decided not by the weapons of the ruling class but by the strength of the people. This thesis of Mao's did much to give the people confidence and turn a negative, defensive civil war into a positive, offensive war of liberation.

Re-organised and renamed the People's Liberation Army (PLA), the communist armies used the method of fighting, set forth by Mao, 'concentrating a superior force to destroy the enemy forces one by one'. Despite the KMT's seizure of big cities, the PLA had within seven months turned the war situation in a direction favourable to the people. Mao was able to announce on 1 February 1947 that the struggle against imperialism and feudalism had entered a new stage, that of 'a great new people's revolution' with the added target of the bureaucratic-capitalism of the nation's big bourgeoisie.

Closely tied to foreign imperial interests and to China's own landlord class, the bureaucratic-capitalist class owned the industrial monopolies which formed the economic basis of Chiang Kai-shek's rule. The much-hated 'four big families' headed this class, the families of Chiang Kai-shek himself, his two brothers-in-law, T.V. Soong and H.H. Kung, and Minister of Education Chen Li-fu. Mao's division of China's bourgeoisie into the unpatriotic big bourgeoisie, on the one hand, who sold out the nation's interest to foreign imperialists, and the patriotic national bourgeoisie on the other hand, was another move which increased support for the communists among the country's leading intellectuals and administrators.

Meanwhile, the communists' appeal to the ordinary people also strengthened as rampant inflation hit the KMT areas, and a speeded-up and effective land reform began to transform the liberated areas.

Land reform was initiated by the Central Committee's *Directive on the Land Question* of 4 May 1946 and was spurred on by new peasant revolts. The CCP's previous policy of reducing rent and interest, adopted throughout the war against Japan, changed to one of confiscating the land of the landlords and distributing it among the peasants, a revival of the 'land to the tillers' programme of 1926-7 and now carried out on a far wider scale. As Mao had foreseen, the KMT's decision to ally itself with the United States and pursue the war instead of seeking peace with the communists, meant that the CCP's more liberal land policy had to be reversed. Land reform became the basis for the successful waging of the liberation war since it engaged the entire peasantry in the revolutionary process.

The aim of the land reform movement, which continued after the 1949 liberation, when it eventually spread across the whole of China, was to remove all feudal forms of ownership in the countryside. The target was not to take over privately owned commerce and industry. Shops, workshops and factories belonging to landlords or rich peasants were not to be expropriated. The question to be settled first was ownership of China's vast cultivated areas. The successful transference of land ownership from the landlords to the peasants was the pivot on which the whole revolution turned.

The Directive on the Land Question started a mass campaign to 'dig out the very roots of feudalism', or, as peasants liked to put it, 'Fill the holes and level the tops'; that is, take from the rich and give to the poor. 'All our poor brothers,' they said, 'should *fanshen*', they should all 'turn over', stand up and grasp their rights.

The process was not simple. Generations of peasant fatalism towards landlord authority, nature and superstition had to be eroded. The peasants had to be convinced expropriation was the way of history. They had to be convinced there would be no restoration of landlords, for if that happened the landlords would savagely punish them.

The immediate result of the directive was a great upsurge of expropriation, in the course of which mistakes were made. In many places struggles took place against rich and middle peasants as well as landlords. This threw many rich and middle peasants on to the landlords' side, whereas the party's policy was not to overthrow, but to neutralise the rich peasants by requisitioning only their surplus land and property, and to unite with, not isolate, the middle peasants. However, the central object was achieved and feudalism in the liberated areas was rooted out by removing its economic base.

The process of reform in one small village in Kirin province in north-east China was told by Han An, the son of a landless peasant who became a national labour hero after liberation. In 1946, he said, the Eighth Route Army came to his village.

> The soldiers in this army were unlike any other soldiers that we had previously seen. Even the officers were friendly and polite, smiling all the time. They came to talk to us about land distribution and asked us if we would dare to accuse the landlord if he was brought for trial in an open people's court.
>
> To tell you the truth we were all afraid of the landlords, and even hesitated to co-operate with the Red Army officers when they asked us to speak openly

against the landlord and recount his injustices and cruelties. But then the Poor Peasants' Association was formed, and at the meetings the Red Army men came and talked to us in a friendly way, telling us that from now on the peasants would own their land and there would be no landlords to oppress us; and if the officers did anything to harrass the peasants, we would have the right to remove those officers. They talked of schools for our children that would be opened and hospitals that would be built and machines that would dig wells and provide water for the fields, and electricity that would light up our cottages.

It all seemed too good to be true and there were some old grey heads who shook their beards and said such things are only talked about but never done. After all, the landlords have always been there and will always be there, whichever dynasty ruled in Peking. But already there were some who felt that these Red Army men seemed quite serious about the things they promised us and, maybe, this time the dreams *will* become real. And then the Accusation Meeting that everyone had been talking about was actually held, and the landlords were brought face to face with the peasants whom they had oppressed all their lives, and their fathers and grandfathers before them. It looked as if the heavens were coming down to the earth and the earth was rising to the heavens; everything was so upside-down. A peasant sat in the Magistrate's chair, and the landlords and old Magistrates stood in the place of the prisoners, their heads which were so haughty once upon a time now bowed before the very people whom they had once oppressed so cruelly. Now we knew that truly enough a new life had, indeed, begun for us.

The local landlord lost not only his land which was distributed among his former tenants, but also his house which he had now to share with families of several peasants. Even the animals of the landlord were distributed among the peasants. Each poor peasant received three *mu* of land, so I got twenty-one *mu* for my family of seven.

Now at last a new life began for us. We have the land and whatever we produced belonged to us — no landlord to take it away. We paid one-sixth of the produce to the government as revenue, but the rate was fixed on the old basis, and if we increased the yield by working harder, the government share did not increase. For the first time in our life we ate our bellyful. My children, for the first time, went to school. Then I decided that, in return for all this good fortune, I too should do something. So I did two things. I joined the class for adults to learn to read and write, and then joined the Communist Party.

I was asked to tell the other villagers about the new life, so that they would learn to take advantage of the school, the hospital, the co-operative stores, and take part in the running of the village government — yes, even our little village of only ninety-four persons has its own government and we elect our officers. Mainly, though, I was to mobilise the peasants to grow more and more — and more — in our fields. You see, Chairman Mao had said that for every peasant, his land was the field of battle and that we could defeat our enemies only if we produced more food-grains, more rice, more *kaoliang*, more soya beans, more vegetables, more cotton, more eggs, more pigs, more everything. And I had to see that my village did not lag behind in this task the Chairman had entrusted to us. [1]

The poor peasants' respect for Mao began to be seized upon by his opponents in the Communist Party and used for their own purposes. Liu Shao-chi's build-up of Mao (at the Seventh Congress of the CCP in April 1945) into the world's foremost inheritor and exponent of Marxism—Leninism, was not to the taste of Mao, who had an altogether simpler, perhaps naive, way of looking at his role in history. Liu Shao-chi's views corresponded to Mao's own claim that, with the Chinese revolution, Marxism—Leninism had entered a new stage and that the Chinese way (especially the concepts of New Democracy and peasant-based revolution) had special lessons for the colonial world. However, with respect to his role in history, Mao had the ability to distance himself from his own merits. He told Snow in 1965 that he often wondered how he came to be thrown into the great events which were to dominate his life, and to be a man whose ideas grew gradually to be appropriate to China's development, when he had set out with the intention of being a schoolteacher. In any event, he could not bear the flattery of sycophants who built up his image for their own ends, though he was not always in a position to do much about it. He had to fight one issue at a time, and always the main issue first. It was ironical that in 1946 a party writer, Chang Ju-hsin, could call Mao 'the greatest genius since the beginning of the history of China ... the most outstanding descendant of the Yellow Emperor', when Mao himself had written the year before 'the people, and the people alone, are the motive force in the making of world history'.

The use of Mao's name as a red mask behind which to pursue divergent policies began on a wide scale in 1946. Then the popularity of Mao's ideas among the people meant that any communist seeking the party's and people's support could no longer do so, as Wang Ming and others had done, by openly opposing Mao. They had to invoke Mao's name as the begetter of their own opinions. This practice reached its apogee in the cultural revolution when all factions proclaimed utmost loyalty to Mao, especially those most opposed to his ideas. At times when Mao was isolated within the party leadership, as he was in 1966, he was forced to go along with such abuses. Since they came during mass campaigns in a 'leftist' guise, and the main task was then to attack the right, he could not run the risk of demoralising the genuine left by taking the weapon of 'adhering to Marxist—Leninist thought' out of their hands in an effort to forbid 'loyalty to Mao the person'. This was the position Mao was in during

1945-6, when his aim was to strengthen the forces of the left so that they could carry out the land reform effectively in the new war situation.

Meanwhile, the image of China's nationalist leader was crumbling fast. Chiang Kai-shek's response to the failing economy in the KMT areas and the land reform in the liberated areas was devious. He convened a 'National Assembly', not including the communists. He announced a truce, yet planned to attack Yenan. He promulgated a 'constitution' which in June 1947 enabled the 'Supreme Court' to order Mao's arrest. It was clear Chiang was still intent on complete destruction of the revolutionary movement.

As Chiang grew further away from the mass of Chinese peasants, he drew closer and closer to the United States for funds and for moral backing, and to China's own big bourgeoisie for domestic support. The US government continued to finance and arm him despite the fact that Chiang tolerated (in US Ambassador Leighton Stuart's words) his party's 'graft and greed, idleness and inefficiency, nepotism and factional rivalry — all the evils in short of the corrupt bureaucracy' which the KMT was supposed to have overthrown in the 1920s. Yet Chiang now relied on terror and force to crush those very people who were providing government in the border region and liberated areas that was free of those evils, and whom the people in those areas supported.

Chiang's separation from his own people was clearly shown in his use of KMT troops. His military tactics were to attack key communist points including Yenan. This ignored the fact that it was in the thousands of villages, not in one or two important towns, that the communist base rested.

Mao demonstrated the solid nature of this base when he made a tactical retreat from Yenan in March 1947. Chiang had concentrated a force of 230,000 troops against the city. It was Mao's tactics to 'keep men', that is, to preserve both his troops and the allegiance of the people, rather than to defend land at all costs. A communist soldiers' song of the period ran:

> Keep men, lose land. Land can be taken again.
> Keep land, lose men. Land and men both lost.

As Yenan was not deserted by the people, who supported the revolution, the town was not lost to the enemy, even though occupied by enemy troops. The PLA still 'held' Yenan, even though it had withdrawn, because it held the people's devotion. 'A people's war', Mao told Anna Louise Strong, 'is not decided by taking or losing a city, but by solving the agrarian problem.'

Furthermore, withdrawal before superior forces preserved the communist troops until the time came for them to use their retention of the initiative to hit back from a superior position at a time and place of their own choosing.

To back up this solid alliance of the people with the PLA, Mao re-issued the army's *Three Main Rules of Discipline* and *Eight Points for Attention* which he had first drawn up in 1928 in the Chingkang Mountains and which had done much to ensure the soldiers' close identity with the people in the intervening twenty years.

After the withdrawal from Yenan, the party's centre — the leadership organisation — was divided into two fronts, partly for greater security and partly to facilitate administration. Although it formally ended in May 1948, when the two halves rejoined, the split was still evident when the communists entered the cities and dispersed their administration, and again after liberation in the division of the centre into two lines. Mao himself was to be on the second line, while the prestige of the first line, which included Liu Shao-chi, was to be built up, 'so when I go to see God', as Mao put it in 1966, 'the country won't receive such a shock.' The conflicts over work style and policies that this administrative split gave rise to, before and after liberation, were not resolved until they were clarified in terms of class lines during the cultural revolution.

While a Working Committee under Liu Shao-chi and Chu Teh went to Hsipaipo village in Hopei province to act as coordinator between the Central Committee and the various liberated areas, Mao and the secretariat of the Central Committee directed the war from a series of new headquarters in northern Shensi. The first headquarters was at Wangchiawan, a village of less than twenty families nestling half-way up the side of a mountain not far from the Great Wall. Mao, who, like the other leaders, went under a pseudonym, his wife Chiang Ching, Chou En-lai and Jen Pi-shih lived in 'two and a half cave rooms which a poor peasant known as Old Man Wang had loaned them. Dark and dilapidated, the place was full of pickled vegetable vats. You could smell the sour odour even standing out in the courtyard. Chairman Mao stayed in the innermost room. After we put in a rickety willow-wood table, there was no space left for any other furniture,' recalled Yen Chang-lin, Mao's cook during this campaign. The leaders ate only the coarsest grain. 'The Chairman firmly demanded gruel made of flour and elm leaves.'

While technically shifting headquarters under KMT pressure and directing the PLA's battles both near and far, Mao also used the northern Shensi campaign to study local conditions. Yen Chang-lin wrote,

> No matter where we stopped, the first thing we had to do after removing the saddle-bags from the horses was to go out and spread propaganda among the people, get to know the conditions of their production and livelihood, as well as the size of the population and the number of families, how much land was cultivated and what taxes were paid — and report it all back.

The reports indicated a certain passivity on the part of the peasants, and some apprehension as to the intentions of the communist units moving among them.

For ten years or more, the people of northern Shensi province had been living a peaceful settled life. Not having known the alarms of war themselves, at first they took things rather casually . . . There had been a drought that year, with no rain to speak of since the beginning of spring. All the young men in the village had gone off to the front with their pack animals. Only the women and children were left. The sowing season would soon be over, but the only thing they could do was to look at their ploughs and worry. Seeing this situation, the Central Committee organisations immediately called an emergency meeting. Chairman Mao mobilised every man in our organisation to go out in the fields and lend a hand with the sowing; we hitched our horses to the ploughs. He also told us to assign some people to go into the mountains with the country folk and help them cut brushwood, which they needed for boiling water and for cooking. The cadres and other people of the village cheered up at once. For they began to see that, instead of giving them any trouble, we had helped them solve their greatest problem.

The PLA's behaviour contrasted as usual with that of the KMT troops. On the march one afternoon,

as we rounded a mountain top, the Chairman suddenly leaped down from his horse, then stood still. As far as the eye could see, the whole flat valley looked as if it had been swept bare by a flood . . . This area had been overrun by bandit troops. Scores of columns of men and horses had converged on this place. Where the animals' hoofs had trampled, bushes were ruined and crops were mashed to a pulp. The doors and window-frames of many cave dwellings had been wrenched off for firewood, jugs and crockery had been smashed. The Chairman stood gazing at this devastation for a long time. Only after our detachment was far ahead did he mount his horse. He spoke very little the rest of the journey. Our hearts were also blazing. We felt a terrible rage at the crimes of the enemy. [2]

Once the people's confidence had been gained, Mao's wandering group relied on the local peasants for intelligence. The activities of KMT spies were regularly reported. At the same time Mao depended on local support to keep the leaders' movements secret. The peasants had coined the expression 'six manys' to describe the main features of Mao's group, i.e. many men carrying pistols, many who ride horses, many rolls of telephone wire, many women radio operators, many flashlights and many pack animals. Mao remarked that this was indeed an accurate description. 'You can see what good analytical powers the country folk have,' he said. 'I'm afraid our own comrades may not be aware of these characteristics yet! But we must tell the people to observe secrecy. If the enemy gets hold of this kind of information, we won't be able to stay here long!'

In fact Chiang Kai-shek had sent a force of 50,000 after Mao, while the PLA had little more than 22,000 troops on all the battlefields of the north-west. It was a maxim by then that the KMT commanders 'obeyed' Mao's orders: Mao's tactics concentrated on preserving and using the initiative. Striking out west and then doubling back eastwards to the Yellow River and the Shansi border, Mao dragged Chiang's troops behind him in a brilliant series of evasive actions, feeding off the KMT by capturing their armouries and supply depots, until the PLA in the north-east turned on the tired and out-witted enemy and routed them in the battle of Shachiatien in August 1947.

Mao and his command staff settled in the village of Chiahsien and then at Yangchiakou to direct operations until March 1948, when they left Shensi for Hsipaipo in Hopei province to rejoin Liu Shao-chi, Chu Teh, and other Central Committee members. They arrived there in May 1948, investigating the results of land reform in north-east Shansi on the way.

Mao had been directing the PLA's country-wide offensive of July–September 1947 from his mountain redoubts. This offensive opened up access to the north-eastern provinces and the northern plains and forced a turning point in the war. The KMT's forces were shrinking, the PLA's growing. The strategy for the second year's fighting followed the earlier pattern of developing from small actions to larger ones, taking smaller cities and big rural areas first, to build up pressure on big cities which could be taken later. Tactically, the main aim was the annihilation of the enemy's troops, rather than the holding of any one town.

To accompany the military offensive, Mao and the Central Committee met at Chiahsien in October 1947 and decided on a land reform offensive. Mao outlined a sixteen-point basic programme for agrarian reform. This document served final notice to Chiang Kai-shek that the tide of land reform was irreversible. Land ownership rights of all landlords were abolished. The Resolution stated,

> China's agrarian system is unjust in the extreme. Speaking of general conditions, landlords and rich peasants who make up less than 10 percent of the rural population hold approximately 70 to 80 percent of the land, cruelly exploiting the peasantry. Farm labourers, poor peasants, middle peasants, and other people, who make up over 90 percent of the rural population, hold a total of approximately 20 to 30 percent of the land, toiling throughout the year, knowing neither warmth nor full stomach. These grave conditions are the root of China being the victim of aggression, oppression, poverty, backwardness, and of the basic obstacles to our country's democratisation, industrialisation, independence, unity, strength and prosperity.
>
> In order to change these conditions, it is necessary, on the basis of the demands of the peasantry, to wipe out the agrarian system of feudal and semi-feudal exploitation, and realise the system of 'land to the tillers'. [3]

The articles that followed listed the measures to be taken to transfer ownership of property via peasant associations to individual peasant families.

Two months later, after Mao had received reports of how the Draft Agrarian Law was being implemented by party cadres, a meeting was held at Yangchiakou to discuss issuing supplementary measures to clarify some of the Draft Law's articles. With the supplementary measures, the Draft Law was then announced to the liberated areas and to the whole nation.

Mao's report, *The Present Situation and our Tasks*, given at Yangchiakou on 25 December 1947, criticised both rightist timidity and leftist excesses, and explained what he thought the organisation techniques of the land reform should be. To provide for equal distribution of land per head, said Mao, 'It is necessary to organise in the villages, as lawful bodies to carry out the reform, not only peasant associations', composed of labourers and poor and lower middle peasants, '. . . but, first of all, poor peasant leagues composed of poor peasants and farm labourers and their elected committees . . . and these . . . should be the backbone of leadership in all rural struggles'.

On the other hand, the middle peasants should be won over to reform and not antagonised; the rich peasants should be treated differently from landlords. A campaign to educate and re-organise the party began removing the influence of the 'tyrant' mentality which had penetrated some organisations and which, alienating the cadres from the people, had locally held back the land reform.

In *The Present Situation and our Tasks*, Mao also presented a programme in the political, military and economic fields for the whole period of overthrow of Chiang Kai-shek and the founding of the People's Republic. The key to the political and economic movement was land reform. The key to military success was the people's war. In this war the military tactics had the advantage of a strong base in the political and economic movements. Mao's method of driving a wedge into the population and separating the good and the bad worked just as well in the military as in the other spheres. It heightened the poor's feeling of identity with the PLA, and helped create a strongly motivated, ideologically bound army. Mao's formulation was, 'Develop the progressive forces [of the workers and peasants], win over the middle forces [the middle peasants, small craftsmen, traders, students, teachers and those capitalists still free from the clutches of the big bourgeoisie and foreign companies] and isolate the die-hard forces [the landlords, big bourgeoisie and the foreign business interests].'

The confident clarity of Mao's perspectives may seem odd when we consider that he prepared the report in a mountain village when he and his Central Committee were on the run with a price on their heads. But there were good reasons for Mao's confidence.

To the KMT in Nanking, and their supporters in Washington, it seemed that Mao and his headquarters were in a last-ditch struggle, encircled and fragmented. The north Shensi episode appeared to them to be the final annihilation campaign, a little business left over from the early 1930s and now being tidied up. This view misconstrued Mao's design. While it appeared the king was surrounded, Mao was playing another game. In the Chinese game of *wei chi*, the purpose is not to concentrate on a king, as in chess, but to build the game around a number of different, widely spaced spots. Mao's design was likewise diffuse and broad. Mao, and not Chiang, had laid down the rules of the game, and the game was protracted warfare, which cannot be brought to a close in one final battle. Protracted warfare is fought in a series of running engagements at different levels of emphasis over a long period of time. Mao's Central Committee organisation was the headquarters of a dispersed and cellular movement which would continue to exist even if its head were lopped off. The future of the revolution would not be decided in the barren mountains of north Shensi, or at one or two main points in the country, but in all the base areas and in the thousands of red villages now spread over much of the north China plain, Shantung, the north-east and the north-west. To mistake the king for the people was an error the KMT and its American backers were to repeat frequently until, and also after, liberation.

The key to success of protracted warfare lay in that it was embedded in the people and was sustained by the breath of a living idea: the people's social, material and political advance. The Third Revolutionary Civil War was a war for the land in a profound sense; it was for the soil, and for ownership, certainly, but also for the deeper regeneration which people's power releases.

In this struggle the Draft Agrarian Law was vital. 'Mao's Draft Agrarian Law', wrote William Hinton, who investigated the land reform in Shansi in 1948, 'confiscated without compensation $20 billion worth of property in land; put an end to all possible compromise between the Communist Party and the Kuomintang; made country-wide overthrow of the landlords and the compradores, rather than the defence of the Liberated Areas, the main aim of the war; facilitated the capitulation and recruitment of huge blocks of Chiang's soldiers into the People's Liberation Army; inspired peasant unrest in the far corners of China; and gave impetus to demonstrations of workers, students, merchants and professional people in urban centres throughout the Kuomintang rear.' The Draft Law also acted as a yardstick for measuring the political stand of individual Communist Party members and for judging the effectiveness of the more moderate reforms previously carried out in the old liberated areas.

The Draft Law launched 'a thunder and lightning, drum and cymbal' attack on the remnants of feudal exploitation. Significantly, Hinton noted, the united front badges that had been worn on the caps of the communist soldiers since 1937 were replaced by the red star and the hammer and sickle. Red flags, unused during the anti-Japanese war, suddenly appeared in every street and courtyard and at the gateways of villages in the liberated areas. The Lunar New Year of 1948 was turned into a mass demonstration to back up the Draft Law, the CCP and Mao Tse-tung.

Work teams consisting of ten or twelve cadres went out from the party centres to survey the situation in the villages and carry through the land reform programme. The cadres of the work teams were supposed to exercise leadership, not impose control. The work team was the agent of change. The peasant was the subject of the struggle, the landlord the object.

The classification of the population into classes was undertaken by the poor peasants, led by the work teams and the peasant associations. Each family and each individual was categorised in turn, not without many mistakes, which led to reclassification, and again reclassification. Over a period of several years the peasants themselves thrashed out the question of who was on which side.)

The determining factor in deciding an individual's class status was his relationship to the means of production: was he exploiter or exploited? But in practice it was frequently by no means clear who were the small landlords and rich peasants whom the poor peasants and hired labourers could neutralise by merely requisitioning their surplus possessions, and who were irredeemably exploiters to be struggled against. The middle peasants were likewise often a nebulous category until stricter guidelines were eventually worked out; some had been on the way up to rich-peasant status, others had been on the way down to lower-middle or even poor-peasant status. It was always evident, however, who were the big landlords and who the poor peasants.

The 'leftist' tendency to draw the line too far down the scale, isolating the mass of the poor from their potential allies in the middle, was corrected during 1948 after Mao's criticisms in *The Present Situation* and his more specific directives in

Correct the 'Left' Errors in Land Reform Propaganda of 11 February that year. In these two analyses Mao again used the technique of driving a wedge into reality, dividing opposites into 'left' and right in order to unite the mass of the people along the path of revolutionary change. As one village party secretary put it to Hinton, 'This policy [of unity] is fixed by the character of our revolution at its present stage. The more the enemy is isolated the quicker can victory be won. If we say that poverty is all, and work along a narrow poor-peasant line, neglecting all our friends, we will only isolate ourselves. Whoever commits the error of isolating himself is guilty of leftism. Whoever does not isolate those who should be isolated is guilty of rightism.' New classifications were defined along Mao's lines but it was not until the post-liberation Agrarian Reform Law (1950) that the differentiation of the peasants into classes was finally settled. By that time, the movement onward to co-operative farming was already being envisaged.

The mass line process of classification was 'a distillation process.' In it the party cadres systematised the demands of the poor peasants and converted them into policies; these were tried out and studied, criticised and again systematised, and then converted into further policies. According to Hinton,

The popular demand for equalisation of land ownership that resulted in an explosion against the gentry as soon as the Japanese Army surrendered in 1945 had been studied, formulated as a policy, applied, corrected, reformulated, and applied again until it emerged as something extremely clear, sophisticated, refined, and effective ... In the end they armed the people with enough knowledge to separate with precision that which was feudal and reactionary from that which was democratic and progressive.

Thus the peasants, under the guidance of the Communist Party, had moved step by step from partial knowledge to general knowledge, from spontaneous action to directed action, from limited success to over-all success. And through this process they had transformed themselves from passive victims of natural and social forces into active builders of a new world . . .

When one applied the concept of *fanshen* ['turning over'] to a still wider canvas, it seemed evident that the word could be used to describe the rebirth of a whole country. Just as one could speak of the *fanshen* of the individual and of the community, one could also speak of the *fanshen* of the nation, that process by which a whole people 'turned over', that process by which a whole continent stood up. [4]

The basis of *fanshen* was still a united front, a unity with those who could be united with, in Mao's words. But now the united front was a revolutionary united front of different classes and groups who had in common a clear opposition to the increasingly fascist rule of Chiang Kai-shek. This policy continued to convince the vacillators. Mao's repeated call to 'unite workers, peasants, soldiers, intellectuals, businessmen [defined as the elements of the middle and petty bourgeoisie persecuted and fettered by the KMT] and other patriots' in overthrowing Chiang's dictatorship and establishing a democratic coalition government between the communists and the revolutionary wing of the KMT and other democratic parties, attracted more patriotic members of the national bourgeoisie to the CCP's side. Meanwhile the KMT's rule declined further into waste and corruption on a huge scale. By early 1948, after Chiang's outlawing of the so-called 'third force', the Democratic League, the major part of the progressive talent of all China's classes sided with the revolution.

The coalition government, said Mao in January 1948, would be a government of the People's Republic of China under the leadership of the working class through its vanguard, the CCP. To build the state power, villages and districts should go ahead and elect their local governments. People's congresses should be convened to elect governments at county, municipal, provincial and border region levels.

In several speeches and instructions during that winter Mao reminded the party that this revolution was a new-democratic, not a socialist, revolution. He was again scornful of those 'leftists' who said the poor peasants alone should conquer the country or that the democratic government should listen only to the workers, poor peasants and farm labourers, and disregard the middle peasants, craftsmen, national bourgeoisie and intellectuals. The pure fervour of the 'leftists' impetuosity might seem impressive but the immediate interests of the people were to build up production and meet the material needs of a China ravaged by war. Socialist construction, itself accompanied by class struggle, would later, according to Mao, carry the revolution to a new stage. Mao once again weighed up the short-term possibilities against long-term desirabilities.

Chen Yi's communist troops attacked Kaifeng in June 1948 and Tsinan was liberated in September. In the north-east, Lin Piao's Fourth Field Army forced the surrender of the KMT's strongest armies, half of whom had American equipment. Many of the men and all the equipment went over to the PLA who were by then superior in number and in arms. Mao drew up further instructions for the campaign against Peking and Tientsin which surrendered in January 1949. Mao and the Central Committee moved to Shihchiachuang in Hopei in February and to Peking in March. On the plains of central China, the Second and Third Field Armies encircled six army groups of the KMT: more than half a million men were killed, injured, captured or deserted. A million soldiers of the PLA advanced south to the Yangtze River which they crossed on a 300-mile front on 20 April 1949, one section capturing Nanking, the KMT capital, three days later.

Kuo Mo-jo, the poet and friend of Mao, who wrote commentaries to a number of Mao's poems, remarked, 'Before and after the campaign for the liberation of Nanking, there were well-meaning friends, within and without the country, who said we should be content with separate governments in the North and the South of China and should not provoke the intervention of, in particular, American imperialism.' It is usually assumed Stalin was one of those friends outside the country. If this is so, Mao's poem celebrating the liberation of Nanking by the PLA was a calculated expression of exultation at completing the job he had set himself to do and follow his own judgement, flying in the face of others' advice, as he had had to do at almost every stage of the revolution. The iron will of the man and a pride in the success of unifying the country after a century of breakdown and turmoil, stands uppermost in Mao at this time, and is illustrated in this poem, written in April 1949.

Over Chungshan swept a storm, headlong,
Our mighty army, a million strong, has crossed the Great
     River.
The City, a tiger crouching, a dragon curling, outshines
     its ancient glories;
In heroic triumph heaven and earth have been overturned.
With power and to spare we must pursue the tottering foe
And not ape Hsiang Yu the conqueror seeking idle fame.
Were Nature sentient, she too would pass from youth to
     age,
But in man's world seas change into mulberry fields.

Hsiang Yu was leader of a peasant force against the Chin dynasty in the third century B.C. Wishing to appear magnanimous, he refrained from killing his rival Liu Pang when he had the chance. Later he was defeated by Liu Pang and commited suicide. In the last lines, Mao says that while Nature stays the same, people can make changes. On the one hand, there is necessity; on the other, there is the objective world which is reformable.

For many party members, accustomed to work in the rural

areas, city problems were unfamiliar. The PLA began to turn itself from a fighting force into a mainly working force, its cadres learning how to administer cities, lead the workers and organise trade unions, manage industry and commerce and run schools and newspapers.

Mao was already making plans for national government and drawing up policies. In his Report to the Central Committee on 5 March 1949, Mao said that the party, relying on the working class, should 'learn how to wage political, economic and cultural struggles' in the cities, both overtly and covertly, because 'after the enemies with guns have been wiped out, there will still be enemies without guns; they are bound to struggle desperately against us'. Such struggles would revolve round the party's main task, which was to restore production and begin construction.

The task of construction was to be led by the proletariat and based on the worker—peasant alliance. At the same time, unity should be sought with those members of the urban petty bourgeoisie and national bourgeoisie who would co-operate with the 'people's democratic dictatorship'. On no account, however, said Mao, should these bourgeois representatives be accommodated uncritically or allowed a leading political role. In the event, his warning was hardly heeded and the problem of the bourgeois representatives' influence on the party was not resolved even by the cultural revolution.

As for 'diplomatic struggles against the imperialists', Mao said in the same speech, 'we are willing to establish diplomatic relations with all countries on the principle of equality, but the imperialists . . . will definitely not be in a hurry to treat us as equals. As long as the imperialist countries do not change their attitude we shall not grant them legal status in China.'

Shanghai was liberated on 27 May 1949, Kwangchow on 14 October, Chungking on 30 November and Chengtu on 27 December. By the end of the year the PLA had freed the entire mainland except Hong Kong, Macao and Tibet, and Chiang Kai-shek had fled to Taiwan.

In July 1949 the New Political Consultative Conference enunciated the party's plans for the people's government. In his address to the conference, Mao answered criticisms that after his statements on new democracy during the early 1940s he was now 'leaning to one side'. Mao agreed, 'Exactly ... All Chinese ... must lean either to the side of imperialism or to the side of socialism. Sitting on the fence will not do.' As for being 'dictatorial', he said, 'My dear sirs, you are right, that is just what we are. All the experiences the Chinese people have accumulated through several decades teaches us to enforce the people's democratic dictatorship, that is, to deprive reactionaries of the right to speak and let the people alone have that right.' As long as the party leadership did not seek to replace, but merely to give voice to, the people as 'creators of history' Mao's argument was plausible. As we shall see, even in Mao's own estimation, the party was frequently to fall far short of that promise in the decades after liberation.

He went on to answer the question of wanting to abolish state power. 'Yes, we do, but ... we cannot do it yet. Why? Because imperialism still exists ... because classes still exist in our country.' The state's role would be to defend socialism in China against imperialism without and the reactionary classes within. Again, this simple hope of Mao's was agonisingly and bitterly thwarted during the intense class struggles after liberation, in which the people challenged bureaucrats who had appropriated state power for anti-popular ends.

Lastly, Mao advised liberal intellectuals still enamoured of the 'democratic individualism' of the imperialist countries and entertaining hopes of friendly relations between China and the United States to 'cast away illusions, prepare for struggle'. It took another twenty-two years for the US government to begin to understand the resolution of the Chinese people in continuing this struggle. Meanwhile, in 1949, Secretary of State Acheson considered that the United States should 'encourage all developments in China' working towards the overthrow of the people's rule.

On 1 October 1949, standing on Tien An Men, the gateway of the old imperial palace in Peking, Mao proclaimed the founding of the People's Republic of China. China, as Mao saw it, had stood up. But revolution never wins 'final' victory. There are only stages. This was the first stage, the beginning, not the end. Seven months earlier Mao had warned,

> With victory, certain moods may grow within the party — arrogance, the airs of a self-styled hero, inertia and unwillingness to make progress, love of pleasure and distaste for continued hard living. With victory, the people will be grateful to us and the bourgeoisie will come forward to flatter us ... There may be some communists ... who cannot withstand sugar-coated bullets ... We must guard against such a situation. To win country-wide victory is only the first step in a long march of ten thousand *li* ... After several decades, the victory of the Chinese people's democratic revolution, viewed in retrospect will seem only a brief prologue to a long drama ... The Chinese revolution is great, but the road after the revolution will be longer, the work greater and more arduous. This must be made clear now in the party ... We [comrades] can learn what we did not know. We are not only good at destroying the old world, we are also good at building the new. Not only can the Chinese people live without begging alms from the imperialists, they will live a better life than that in the imperialist countries. [5]

Gradually, over the next two decades, 500 million workers and peasants began to build their better life by hard work, political struggle and profound and patient changes in thinking.

8   Building the New

The Foundations of the People's Republic, 1949–1957

> The people's democratic dictatorship needs the leader-
> ship of the working class . . . The national bourgeoisie at
> the present stage is of great importance . . . To counter
> imperialist oppression and to raise her backward
> economy to a higher level, China must utilise all the
> factors of urban and rural capitalism that are beneficial
> and not harmful to the national economy and the
> people's livelihood; and we must unite with the national
> bourgeoisie in common struggle. Our present policy is to
> regulate capitalism, not to destroy it. But the national
> bourgeoisie cannot be the leader of the revolution, nor
> should it have the chief role in state power.
>
> Mao Tse-tung from
> *On the People's Democratic Dictatorship*

On 1 October 1949 China's new red flag with its five gold
stars flew from Tien An Men. Watched by a crowd of 300,000
in the square below, Mao shouted *Wan sui* (Long live!) to
the parading, shouting, waving students and citizens, who
replied in kind. After a military march-past, when Mao
reviewed an impressive armoury of US weapons and vehicles
captured from the KMT, the crowds surged past in a great
stream for four hours, waving red banners and flowers, pushing floats, and dancing to drumbeats and the sound of gongs.

Politically, Mao now aimed at creating a unified nation
under the united front policy, led by the working class and
the Communist Party, and backed by 'international friends',
primarily, he hoped, the Soviet Union. To this end, he
encouraged the work of 'people's organisations', including
trade unions, women's groups, cultural, scientific and educational societies, as well as the people's congresses at the
various levels. Among the delegates to the People's Political

Consultative Conference held on 21 September 1949, the representatives of political parties were in a minority. An English visitor, Peter Townsend, described the motley company: 'Peasants in peasant dress, semi-literate, artless in public speaking but versed in land and its problems; a militia hero with a local reputation for manufacturing land mines; factory workers; even an old peasant woman who stolidly sewed cloth shoes in the intervals as an English housewife might knit socks; all took a simple pride in sitting and discussing with revolutionary leaders, owners of textile mills, and officials whose records traced back to the last years of the Manchus.'

Mao's opening speech to the conference made many in the audience weep with pride. 'We have a common feeling', he said, 'that our work will be recorded in the history of mankind ... Our nation will never again be an insulted nation.' The Conference went on to draw up a Common Programme outlining, according to Townsend, 'a national policy and government acceptable to all those united in hatred of the Kuomintang'. The Common Programme aimed at placing

> ... the resources of peasant, worker, petty bourgeois and national capitalist under the nation's direction in order to reach an industrialised society governed by the majority, giving to each his reward but according to peasant and industrial worker an especially privileged position, and (forcibly, if necessary) restraining any element that tries to check its advance. If its succeeds, it will lead step by step into communism, the undisguised objective of the Communist Party. [1]

The economy envisaged for the first step in the transitional period was to be divided into three sectors: state-owned, or 'socialist', the property expropriated from China's big bourgeoisie, especially from the 'four big families'; co-operative, or 'semi-socialist', using private capital for communal purposes; and private, capitalist enterprise. Whenever necessary and possible the state and private capital would co-operate to form a fourth category, state capital, or joint state-private enterprises. In every sector the state would be the ruling factor, and through it, the working class and peasantry.

The successful development of such an economy centred on two conditions, the continuation of land reform and the construction of basic industries in a series of five-year plans (to begin in 1953). The questions of where the stress should lie, in agriculture or in industry, and how and when socialisation of agriculture should take place and what agriculture's relationship to industry should be, immediately became apparent and have been the subject of continuous debate until the present time.

The state planning departments managed to convince Mao at the outset that the Russian experience of industrialisation should be taken as a model for China's. Mao was wary of adopting Russian methods wholesale but he was certainly ready to accept Russian aid for China's own plans. He pointed out that China was, and would continue to be for a long time, predominantly a country of peasants who could not be converted overnight into industrial workers. Neither could agricultural collectivisation be imposed: it could only generate itself in the course of the peasants' own mutual aid and co-operative experiments. Russia's industrial construction would serve as a constant point of reference for China's but as the foundation of industrialisation was, according to Mao, a developed agriculture, the land reform would have to be completed throughout the country.

On the one hand, therefore, China immediately set about securing Russian aid in setting up fifty major state-owned industrial enterprises which were to provide the backbone of a powerful modern industry. In December 1949 Mao went to Moscow, his first journey abroad, and after nine weeks' negotiation signed a Treaty of Friendship, Alliance and Mutual Assistance providing for credits of 60 million US dollars annually for five years.

On the other hand, land reform was pushed further forward,

systematised by the Agrarian Reform Law of 1950. Accompanying the PLA's drive across the remainder of KMT-occupied China in late 1949 and early 1950, the aroused peasants spoke out and denounced the landlords at village meetings, the very act of overthrow teaching the peasants which classes were intended to be the masters in the new state. The worst landlord tyrants, those who had committed serious and often atrocious crimes, were killed. The remainder of the dispossessed landlords were allotted the same amount of land as the poor peasants while being deprived of all voting rights. Mao's report of 6 June 1950 argued for preserving the status of the rich peasants, to restore agricultural production quickly. Rich peasants, no longer a direct political threat as they had often been in the civil war, were allowed to keep the land they cultivated themselves or by hired labour, though they were forbidden to buy more or to rent out land, or to join the peasant associations.

Writing in May 1952 in the magazine *China Reconstructs*, the social scientist, Chen Han-seng, described the stages of this 'the fiercest as well as the last battle against feudalism in China . . . a movement of the peasants to eliminate the landlords as a class and make the soil their own'. Using the experience gained in land reform in the old liberated areas, the reforms passed through three preparatory stages in the regions newly freed by the victorious PLA.

> First, remnant armed bands of reactionaries are rounded up, rural despots removed and local peace ensured by the security organs of the state. Then the peasants are organised through a preliminary movement to reduce rents and reclaim deposits, during which the Peasant Associations grow in strength as a first step in re-organising village administrations. In this stage, large groups of oppressed village people gain their first experience in successfully enforcing their will on their former oppressors.

Thirdly, many thousands of land reform workers, mobilised from the cities as well as the countryside, are trained to an understanding of their tasks and sent to the basic points to obtain practical experience. Later they are detailed to all affected localities to lead and co-operate with the Peasant Associations in the full-scale reform.

Chen went on to describe the four steps by which the land reform itself was carried out.

First, a deep study is made of conditions in one *hsiang* [an administrative unit comprising many villages] and a typical village within it. Active local peasants work together with personnel from the outside to explain the government's policy to the people. Through accusation meetings and other means, the facts of past abuses by the landlords are brought to light. The dispossessed come to understand that the wealth of the landlords is actually their own property, of which the landlord class has robbed them by force and fraud. The long-suppressed indignation of the people reaches a high tide. The people understand that they can at last act on it because the landlord class has no backing, while they are backed by the entire power of the state. Peasant Associations are cleansed of landlord agents who in many cases managed to penetrate into them immediately after liberation. By popular demand, lukewarm and wavering elements are replaced by more resolute ones in positions of leadership. People's Tribunals are set up. Despotic landlords guilty of serious crimes are tried and punished. When this has been done, the hold of the landlords over the locality is broken. No one any longer stands in awe of them. Their prestige disappears. They become isolated from the rest of the village people and can no longer dominate the course of events.

The second step is to ascertain the class status of the village people. In this way, the beneficiaries of the reform are separated from its targets. Such work is of the utmost importance and is carried out with great care.

The question is first taken up by a general meeting of the peasants, then discussed further by small groups in the Peasant Associations. Landlords and others who wish to appeal against the category in which they have been classified are permitted to present their case before a village-wide meeting. All decisions are referred to the sub-county people's government for approval and official announcement. At the end of this stage, the class status of every family in the village is established . . .

The third step is the confiscation and redistribution of landlord holdings. Practice has shown that this can be done quickly without preliminary measurement, since the local people are fully familiar with the details of land ownership. General meetings, in which the poor peasants and hired labourers play the most active role, are held in various parts of each village. Middle peasants and rich peasants are invited to participate and voluntarily declare the size of their holdings. Only in the event of unsolved disputes does measurement of land take place. Decisions on redistribution are made public on three separate occasions, during a period when applications for reconsideration may be entertained. The third notice is considered final. Generally, there is no compensation for requisitioned land and property, but compensation in varying degrees is made where the subsistence of individuals makes it necessary . . .

The fourth and final step is the surrender of old title-deeds and evidences of debt which, after inspection, are burned in a public bonfire. New title-deeds are then issued to the peasants to legalise their freshly-received holdings.

All the four steps involve sharp conflict, because the landlords submit to the law and the people only after struggle by the peasant masses.

Once this whole process has been completed in the base villages, the news is spread rapidly and widely. Representatives from all over the area are invited to witness the success. Except for those who stay for consolidation work, experienced personnel are sent elsewhere (as a rule, land reform in one place produces enough trained workers to lead it in three others).

Chen then discussed the reason why land reform started from a 'basic point' and then spread 'from point to area'.

It is because both the strength of feudal forces and the degree of political awakening of the peasants vary from place to place. Preliminary success at one point produces greater confidence on the part of those called upon to meet difficulties at others. Moreover, this is the only way of quickly training capable and experienced leaders for wider-scale work.

In the first year after the promulgation of the Land Reform Law, 300,000 additional active leaders were trained, providing an army of workers for the transformation of the countryside.

During 1951, the land reform was carried out in territory with a total of 130,000,000 rural people. Added to the old liberated areas, where it was completed earlier among a rural population of 190,000,000, this represents a total of 320,000,000 people, or 80 percent of all who live in the Chinese countryside. In 1952 the process will be completed in all China.

In the nature of things, even such a methodical reform could hardly be effected smoothly. Landlords and their agents tried to subvert the movement in many places, terrorising the superstitious and backward poor, threatening revenge, and murdering land reform workers. Elsewhere, even 'law-abiding' landlords were executed, in contravention of the party's rule that only the bullies and murderers among them should be killed. It was not until early 1953 that these excesses were curbed and the landlords finally suppressed.

A parallel and hardly less significant reform in feudal-dominated China was the Marriage Law promulgated by Mao on 30 April 1950. It abolished 'the feudal marriage system based on arbitrary and compulsory arrangements and the superiority of man over woman' and prohibited 'bigamy, concubinage, child betrothal, interference with the remarriage of widows and the exaction of money or gifts in connection with marriages'. The law thus brought the rights of men and women in sexual and family relations into line with the changes in social relations following the destruction of feudalism.

In June 1950 in the middle of these reforms and while most of the huge armies of the civil war were being redirected to productive civilian activity and sections awaited orders to liberate Taiwan, the war in Korea began. President Truman 'neutralised' the Formosa Strait. The United States thus intervened militarily to prevent the island's liberation. This open act of imperialism, as Mao characterised it, was linked with US intervention in Korea. The two developments, at a time when for the Chinese people 'the trial of war ... belongs basically to the past', brought Chinese soldiers to fight in Korea from October 1950 in the 'mass movement to resist American aggression and aid Korea' 'in the first line of defence of the socialist camp so that the Soviet Union might stay in the second line'.

Mao characterised the Korean War and the Taiwan problem in terms that would echo throughout the fifties and sixties as the United States became more and more politically and militarily entangled in east and south-east Asia. In a speech to a government council on 28 June 1950, Mao said,

The Chinese people have long since affirmed that the affairs of the various countries throughout the world should be run by the peoples of those countries, and that the affairs of Asia should be run by the peoples of Asia and not by the United States. US aggression in Asia will only arouse widespread and resolute resistance by the peoples of Asia. Truman stated on 5 January this year that the United States would not interfere in Taiwan. Now he has proved his own statement to be false, and has torn to shreds all the international agreements regarding non-interference by the United States in the internal affairs of China. The United States has thus exposed its own imperialist face and this is beneficial to the people of China and of all Asia. There is no reason at all for US intervention in the internal affairs of Korea, the Philippines, Vietnam or other countries. The sympathy of the people throughout China, as well as of the broad masses of the people everywhere in the world, is on the side of the victims of aggression, and most decidedly not on the side of US imperialism. [2]

Three further mass movements were begun in 1950-1, partly as a result of the increase in fifth column activities inside China, directed by KMT and US intelligence during the years of maximum Korean and Taiwan military action, and partly to continue putting the national house in order as the final phase of the civil war.

In the first of these, the remaining pockets of KMT troops and agents were mopped up. Investigations began into the crimes of those who had opposed the rise of people's power. Murderers and war criminals were denounced by the people and executed. A lenient policy was adopted towards those who had not committed 'blood crimes'. They were sentenced to labour reform or merely put under surveillance by the local people and re-educated. By 1956, 57.4 percent of these had been released.

Later Mao answered criticisms of the 1951-2 suppression campaign.

It was necessary . . . Who were executed? What sort of people were they? They were the people the masses hated most; they were the people who owed a lot of blood debts . . . From now on [April 1956], the suppression of counter-revolution must [follow the principles of] . . . fewer arrests and fewer executions . . . We must persist with the principle we adopted in Yenan: 'Don't kill a lone wolf; don't arrest a crowd.' . . . If [a lone wolf] can be reformed through labour, let him do that so that the useless can become useful. Besides, a head is not like a leek; it does not grow again once it is cut. [3]

The 1951-2 measures complied with the principles to be used by the people's democratic dictatorship as defined by Mao in June 1950.

In regard to the enemy, [the people's democratic dictatorship] uses the method of dictatorship, in other words, it forbids them to take part in political activity for as long a period of time as is necessary and it compels them to obey the laws of the People's Government, to work and to transform themselves into new people though labour. In regard to the people, on the contrary, it uses not the compulsory but the democratic method; in other words, it allows the people to take part in political activities and uses the democratic method of education and persuasion instead of compelling them to do this or that. This education is self-education within the ranks of the people, and the basic method of self-education is criticism and self-criticism. [4]

A two-part movement, the *san fan* (three-antis) and *wu fan* (five-antis), was directed at the party cadres and the national bourgeoisie. The *san fan*, at the end of 1951, attacked waste, corruption and bureaucracy in party and state, and struggled against the individualism and position-seeking of officials. The *wu fan*, early in 1952, attacked the 'five poisons' of fraud, bribery, tax irregularities, theft of government property and theft of state economic secrets. It helped to break down the independence of the remaining factory owners and businessmen, some of whom had used these unlawful means to challenge the new state power. The attacks in both campaigns were made at public hearings or before meetings of employees.

The third campaign had even greater importance for future struggle. It was a movement for ideological remoulding by criticism and self-criticism, and it affected mainly the intellectuals. Building on the experience of the 1942 rectification campaign, and reinforcing the change in material conditions brought about by liberation, the movement began to create the mental conditions in which the individual cadre or intellectual could become free to serve the people.

Organisationally, the cadres and the intellectuals were to carry out their work within the framework of the mass line, that is, *with* the masses and not above them. This necessitated a totally changed attitude to the nature of leadership, and indeed of special knowledge, in both leaders and led. The educated groups were expected to initiate this change, but the impulse to it came from the masses in whose interests it was. It was not until the cultural revolution, however, that organisational forms, such as cadre schools, began to be developed in an attempt to carry out the change in consciousness on a wide scale.

The 1951 campaign by no means attacked knowledge as such, examining only its use. In future there would continue to be, in Mao's formula, 'No investigation: no right to speak', but the knowledge gained from investigation, he insisted, must not be appropriated for the use of the bourgeoisie or of a ruling clique but put to the service of the masses of the people. The campaign was the beginning of a fundamental adjustment in Chinese social attitudes; this was parallel, and essential, to what the CCP regarded as the socialist transformation of the economy.

New China, starting as a poor and backward country, saw great construction projects begin in the first decade of liberation. In five years from 1950, eight major reservoirs and eleven major dams were in process of construction, and 7,700 million cubic metres of earthwork were built in the water control projects. 33 million acres were newly irrigated.

Mao issued a call for the harnessing of the great rivers that had so often brought flood and misery to millions of peasants.

The biggest water conservancy project was the scheme to control the Huai River which runs through the fertile provinces of Anhwei and Kiangsu. Over the centuries, the Yellow River to the north and the Yangtze to the south had often intermingled with the Huai to create devastating inundations of the central Chinese plains. According to historical records, the Huai River itself had flooded every two years for seventy generations, 979 floods since 246 B.C. The new scheme began the job of clearly demarcating and containing the great river systems. The control of the Huai River alone was the key to the livelihood of over 50 million peasants who tilled one seventh of all China's cultivated land.

Afforestation was begun in the denuded mountains at the headwaters of the great rivers. Tree shelter belts were planted to protect the flat lands from erosion by wind. Trees also helped to push back the encroaching sand in the desert areas of the north-west, and to reclaim land on the previously inundated plains where the wind had blown the light silt, which clogged wells and filled in irrigation ditches.

The system of dams and reservoirs was begun with Soviet aid. With their advice too, new iron and steel works and textile mills were built, oil wells drilled and collieries opened. The Han Bridge at Wuhan took the railway across the Yangtze for the first time. Power stations spread electricity into the countryside to work the irrigation pumps and to light peasant homes. New harbours and dock installations improved working conditions and the prospects of trade. In the north-east, the Number One Motor Works, which would turn out China's first lorries on a big scale, started construction in 1953. Cities like Chengchow in Honan province, which had been badly damaged in the wars, were redesigned and rebuilt to incorporate modern industry.

The changes in Chengchow were typical and striking. Whereas in the great Honan famine in 1942, in the words of a Chinese journalist, 'hundreds of thousands of peasants, in a vain attempt to seek haven, flocked to Chengchow only to die of starvation in front of the lofty mansions of KMT officials and speculators,' ten years later the same officials' houses were in the hands of organisations like the Electrical Engineering School, and the city seethed, according to visitors, with construction workers building factories, offices, hospitals, schools, cultural palaces and housing estates.

Articles of the time mentioned the 'selfless assistance' given by Russian experts. 'Soviet experts held back nothing; they showed us all they could' to help in planning and designing, and in training Chinese workers and technicians. If many of these fond expressions disappeared after the Russians' withdrawal in 1960, it is true to say that some memories of their former brothers are still treasured by the Chinese workers, especially of those advisers who 'came down' to work closely alongside their Chinese counterparts. On a visit to a remote irrigation project in 1951, an Indian visitor, R.B. Karanjia, noticed that while sanitary equipment, including commodes and bathtubs, was brought down from Peking for the use of his goodwill mission, 'a renowned Soviet engineer who was helping the Chinese on the work did not avail himself of any such conveniences. We saw him bathing behind an open shed and going with Chinese workers to the fields, spade in hand, to dig a hole and, after performing the functions of nature, closing it up with earth.' He added, in his book *China Stands Up*, that the Russian experts 'did not come to dictate as superiors or representatives of a more advanced race', and that the Chinese greeted their helpers as 'elder brothers'.

In the countryside, landlordism had been eradicated by 1952, 70 percent of the rural population having benefited by the redistribution of land. Parallel with the destruction of feudalism, Mao began to assert that 'socialist industrialisation is not something that can be carried out in isolation, separate from argicultural co-operation'. In fact, village co-operatives were already prospering on the model of Yenan's successful South District Co-operative of the 1940s, starting as supply and marketing co-ops. The co-ops provided a national market network for peasant produce by linking villages to the state trading departments and to industry. Tools, fertilisers, insecticides, cloth and other manufactured goods were sold to the villagers by the state largely through co-ops. By 1952 these co-ops had 141 million shareholders. They functioned as an economic bridge between state and people.

Initiated by the peasant associations and the co-ops, mutual-aid teams began to share animals and tools, and work fields jointly, but as a rule did not own much in common. Soon the teams fixed work points for the day's work of each team member. Labour was divided at team meetings. After summer and autumn harvests a mass meeting decided the accounts and paid grain to each team worker according to the number of work points earned. The movement mushroomed and by 1952, 40 percent of the country's peasants had organised themselves into mutual-aid teams, the first stage towards co-operative farming.

Pooling resources of animals, tools and labour stimulated production but did not solve the problem of wasteful small-field cultivation. Nor were the teams bringing in enough capital to allow them to buy machinery. A larger unit of organisation was needed. Starting in previously backward Shansi, agricultural producers' co-operatives were tried out on the basis of the mutual-aid teams. While the land remained privately owned, the peasant invested his land as shares and was paid wages for his work and interest on his investment. Fields were enlarged and the whole co-operative land was managed as a unit. A more economical use of manpower was possible in these larger units. At the end of 1953 there were 14,000 such second-stage, semi-socialist, producers' co-operatives.

By 1954 the transformation of feudal forms of land ownership and land use to co-operatives forms, and of capitalist to socialised industry, was well under way. Within five years of liberation, China's economy had been fundamentally reshaped. The years 1953 and 1954 saw the consolidation of this process and its expression in the constitutional framework.

The first five-year plan, begun in 1953, was approved in its complete form by the National People's Congress in 1955. The constitution adopted in September 1954 reasserted 'planned economic construction and gradual transformation to socialism' as the new state's goal. Mao was formally confirmed as Chairman of the People's Republic, and thus head of state.

The first five-year plan had the development of heavy industry as its focus. The nucleus of the plan was the 141 large-scale projects the Soviet Union was providing China. With this Russian aid came strong pressure from Soviet-line leaders in Peking to adopt 'one-man management' in China's new industry, such as existed in the Soviet Union. However, the man who was the outstanding proponent of 'one-man management', Kao Kang, who headed the State Planning Commission when it was founded in November 1952 and who would thus exercise supervision over the five-year plan, soon came in for criticism.

Kao Kang had been a founder, with Liu Chih-tan and others, of the Soviet movement in north-west China in the areas where Mao's Long Marchers arrived in late 1935. He accompanied Lin Piao's army into China's industrialised north-east in the war of liberation and became the chief leader of that area after 1949 in both the party and the state apparatus.

Kao is today accused of maintaining that only those with army experience, like himself, could occupy high positions. According to his critics, this was tantamount to saying 'the party grows out of the barrel of a gun', a theory which subtly altered Mao's celebrated dictum, 'political power grows out of the barrel of a gun'. He is also said to have 'carried out agitation in the PLA against the Central Committee'.

Kao had apparently claimed that his north Shensi base had 'saved' Mao and the Central Committee by providing sanctuary after the Long March. After 1949 he sponsored a novel about Liu Chih-tan to substantiate this claim. The Central Committee refused publication of the novel and replied that the north Shensi base, far from having 'saved' the party, had in fact been riven by factional strife. Adherents of Wang Ming were then persecuting Liu Chih-tan and it was only after the Red Army under Mao arrived there that the base became firmly established. Mao sarcastically referred to the novel as 'a new creation' opposing the party in the form of fiction.

The remaining accusation, perhaps the most serious, and certainly the most obscure, centres on a conference on finance and the economy held in August 1953 at which Kao and a supporter, Jao Shu-shih, director of the Central Committee's Organisation Department, are supposed to have 'conspired'. They are accused of having used their power base in the north-east after liberation to attempt to usurp the central power in three respects — power over the party apparatus, over the selection of cadres and over state finance. Perhaps Kao had used 'one-man management' to place his men in key positions in industry. In any event, he appeared to be succeeding in splitting the party leadership since, in December, when, according to party historians, Mao discovered the 'plot', Mao spoke in favour of party unity. The same theme was repeated in February 1954 when the Central Committee counter-attacked and issued Kao 'a serious warning'. Liu Shao-chi supported Mao and called for collective leadership. In a speech Liu attacked certain cadres who considered their own departments or regions 'as their personal property or independent kingdoms'. Kao's group was effectively isolated and Kao later committed suicide. Kao and Jao were finally repudiated and expelled from the party in March 1955. Mao's first struggle against the bureaucrats after liberation thus ended in the disgrace of his opponents. But this was done by intra-party struggle. The struggle never became a mass movement, never involved the people.

By the time of the Eighth Party Congress in September 1956, 'one-man management' had been, in theory, replaced by collective leadership by the party committees in the factories. Cadres thus replaced managers. But in effect many of the old managers became cadres in the collective leadership and often took a dominant position as chairmen.

Kao Kang was an advocate of concentrating resources on the development of heavy industry and might well have wanted to build up his own industrial north-eastern 'little kingdom' at the expense of other more backward parts of the country. But he was not the only state leader to stress the role of heavy industry in China's development. In 1950 Liu Shao-chi had declared that collectivisation of agriculture could take place only after the creation of an industrial base allowed the introduction of mechanised farming. In 1955, with a certain level of industrial advance assured and the evidence of the rapid growth of agricultural co-operatives in front of him, Mao began to express doubts about the wisdom of delaying socialisation of agriculture. He argued that it need not wait on mechanisation and the completion of the heavy industrial base. It could develop relatively early.

The deciding factors, he felt, were the needs and the stage of consciousness of the peasants. As to their needs, the average tillable land in China was then half an acre per person. In some places it was less than one sixth of an acre. Consequently, as individual farmers, poor peasants had little chance of achieving prosperity. If they were ready to move forward to higher stage co-ops and larger unit farming, Mao said that no one should stop them. He wanted mass mobilisation to forge good social relations and hence encourage more productive farming. He thought man's 'own two hands' were as capable of transforming nature as machines, and he held that the consciousness of the peasant, was what would lead to socialised relations in the countryside.

In June 1955 there were 650,000 second-stage agricultural producers' co-ops of a semi-socialist nature, compared with 100,000 in October 1954, mainly in the northern provinces which had been liberated earlier. In his speech to provincial party secretaries of 31 July 1955, *On the Question of Agricultural Co-operation*, Mao suggested that this number ought to be doubled in fourteen months so that there would be 'from one to several' co-operatives 'to serve as models in each of the country's 200,000-odd townships'.

He argued that socialist industrialisation itself relied for the supply of marketable grain and industrial raw materials upon a more productive use of land than could be achieved under small-scale farming. Mao now advocated pressing forward faster with second-stage, semi-socialist co-ops and entering the third stage, larger 'advanced co-operatives, completely socialist in nature' though at a low level of socialist development. In advanced co-ops, the land was owned jointly and payment was made to the individual peasant on the socialist principle 'to each according to his work'.

In his speech Mao said he thought it would take ten years for the third stage to be completed. In fact, it was basically accomplished in little more than a year. As the rural mode of life changed step by step, the Chinese peasants' consciousness rose also step by step. The advantage of the next stage, in terms of increased production and a higher standard of living, became apparent as the success of the current stage became clear.

Mao commended this upsurge when it was in its early stages and said it merited support. In the same speech, he pointed out, 'Some of our comrades are tottering along like a woman with bound feet and constantly complaining, "You're going too fast." ' He condemned party cadres who 'erected countless taboos'. He said, 'We should give this movement active, enthusiastic and systematic leadership, and not drag it back . . . Both cadres and peasants will remould themselves in the course of the struggles they themselves experience. Let them go into action and learn while doing, and they will become capable.'

He advised party secretaries not to be scared of the small co-operatives, as some seemed to be. He recommended first getting the politically conscious poor and lower-middle peasants together into the co-ops. Only later, when the co-ops were firmly established, could the upper-middle peasants be drawn in. The co-ops, he said, favoured the poor and lower-middle peasants most, and it was they the cadres should rely on. The key posts in the co-op management committees should be held by poor peasants which 'includes . . . those former poor peasants who have become lower-middle peasants since land reform'. Mao attributed the reluctance of some party members, and even leaders, to go very far along the road of co-operation to the fact that their 'eyes were on' the minority of already well-to-do middle peasants who did not stand to gain so much from the co-ops as did the poor.

Mao's argument that the co-ops would increase agricultural output, which would in turn provide funds for industrialisation, was thus only one of the reasons for his enthusiastic support for the co-op movement. The other, more basic reason was his loyalty to the poor and lower-middle peasants. However necessary it may have been to preserve the rich-peasant economy in the years immediately after liberation in order to effect a swift recovery from war and devastation, this was no way to develop agriculture in the long term. Mao explained the dangers of allowing 'the spontaneous forces of capitalism' to grow any further.

What exists in the countryside today is capitalist ownership by the rich peasants and a vast sea of private ownership by the individual peasants. As is clear to everyone, the spontaneous forces of capitalism have been steadily growing in the countryside in recent years, with new rich peasants springing up everywhere and many well-to-do middle peasants striving to become rich peasants. On the other hand, many poor peasants are still living in poverty for lack of sufficient means of production, with some in debt and others selling or renting out their land. If this tendency goes unchecked, the polarisation in the countryside will inevitably be aggravated day by day.

Those peasants who lose their land and those who remain in poverty will complain that we are doing nothing to save them from ruin or to help them overcome their difficulties. Nor will the well-to-do middle peasants, who are heading in the capitalist direction, be pleased with us, for we shall never be able to satisfy their demands unless we intend to take the capitalist road. Can the worker—peasant alliance continue to stand firm in these circumstances? Obviously not. There is no solution to this problem except on a new basis. And that means to bring about, step by step, the socialist transformation of the whole of agriculture simultaneously with the gradual realisation of socialist industrialisation and the socialist transformation of handicrafts and capitalist industry and commerce. In other words, it means to carry out co-operation, and eliminate the rich-peasant economy and the individual economy in the countryside so that all the rural people will become increasingly well off together. [5]

Mao's plan thus sought to obtain the support of the poorer of the rural population, who in any case had been the very people to have started the movement racing forward from the mutual-aid teams to the co-ops, and from the second-stage co-ops to the advanced co-ops.

As agricultural co-operation progressed, transformation in the industrial sector also gained momentum. While big industries had become state-owned at the time of liberation, the remaining medium-scale industrial enterprises were now turned over to the state, though in outward form some, especially in the older industries, stayed under joint state-private management until early in the cultural revolution.

Rather more small businesses, such as shops, rested in private or joint hands until the same period. A 'leap forward' in industry in 1955-6 prefigured the Great Leap Forward of 1958. The year 1956 was to see the basic completion of the party's programme for the socialist transformation of private ownership in agriculture, handicrafts, industry and commerce.

Local reports on progress in the co-operative movement were collected early in 1956 in *Socialist Upsurge in China's Countryside*, with Mao's introduction and commentary. Mao advanced the thesis, startling to many cadres who were to find themselves on the wrong side of the fence, that co-operatives were achieved not by administrative order but by class struggle. Where work teams, 'apparently from higher up' the party structure, were sent into the villages to monopolise leadership of the movement, Mao warned that it was the local organisers who should 'make use of their own hands and brains'; the work teams should help them and not replace them. 'Some individuals,' he wrote, 'although they call themselves communists, . . . fail to support the enthusiastic people, but on the contrary they throw cold water on the people's heads.' The slogan for the movement was to be 'Rely on the poor peasants and establish their control!' for only they could turn class struggle in the countryside into a motor of social change.

As to the methods of seeking support, Mao said the 'voluntary principle' must stand. 'We must carry out a policy of mutual benefit to both poor and middle peasants; no-one should be allowed to suffer a loss.' By making comparisons between old and new, between landlordism and mutual-aid teams, between the teams and the co-ops, between exploitation and common prosperity, communists must 'explain things . . . in vivid terms' and become 'excellent teachers'. Incompetent teachers were those who 'over-simplify the problem with such so-called slogans as "Either you follow the road of the Communist Party, or you follow the road of Chiang Kai-shek."

This is just labelling people to cower them into compliance.'
Mao said the really effective method was 'taking the peasants'
own experiences and analysing them in detail'.

An article of 9 July 1955, *Strengthening the Co-op; a Good
Example*, by the co-op department of a regional committee of
the CCP, published in *Socialist Upsurge in China's Countryside*, showed how one co-op in Fukien province, hit by
drought and with its leaders 'out of their depth' in 'work on
such a scale', managed to overcome the hesitancy of eight of
its seventy-five households towards the co-ops. These eight,
when things went badly, were preparing to pull out of the
co-op. Apart from giving training to the weaker leaders, the
co-op made 'four comparisons and five calculations,' asking
the poor and lower-middle peasants:

a Which is the best way of farming: co-op, mutual-aid
  team or individual?
b Which is better, socialism or capitalism?
c Which system is better, one that involves exploitation
  or one that doesn't?
d Which is better, individual prosperity or common
  prosperity?

a How much has been accomplished in beating natural
  calamities?
b How much income has been derived from subsidiary
  occupations?
c How many additional work points were earned as a
  result of keenness in work?
d What were the benefits and how much did output
  increase, as a result of co-operation between the poor
  and middle peasants?
e What were the difficulties in production and living,
  and how to solve them?

Then at a general meeting of all members, the benefits of
co-operation were enumerated.

In combating drought, single, centralised management combined with collective effort enabled the co-op to transplant 220 *mu* [of rice]. If the members had been working individually, no more than 170 *mu* could have been transplanted. So, with co-operation, it had been possible to transplant 50 *mu* more. Considering that 350 *catties* of rice could be harvested from a *mu* of land, the co-op made it possible to get 17,500 *catties* more than individual peasants could have done in the same year . . .

Fighting drought under centralised management, and raising water to irrigate large tracts of land instead of small plots one at a time, saved much manpower. When farming individually each household had to spend an average of 30 workdays to irrigate the fields after winter cultivation. For the 75 households in the co-op this would have meant a total of 2,250 workdays. But for its early crop in 1955, the co-op needed only 400 workdays to carry water, push waterwheels and tend the irrigation channels. The saving was no less than 1,850 workdays. Reckoning a workday at ten *catties* of rice, the total savings here were 18,500 *catties*.

With a large pool of manpower under its management, the co-op was able to get work done more efficiently. During the spring drought, when everything had to be done very quickly, over twenty members were sent to villages as far as 20 *li* away to look for seedlings. About a dozen worked on the waterwheels day and night. All draught animals and seedling planters were organised for emergency works. As a result, 40.27 *mu* of rice fields were planted. It was reckoned 250 *catties* would be grown on each *mu*, raising total output by 10,067 *catties*. Scattered farming could not have solved such difficulties in seedlings, draught animals, manpower and irrigation, and only five *mu* could have been planted under such conditions . . .

Poor peasants in the co-op had 100 *mu* of land pooled in the co-op. Yield on their plots could increase by over 20 percent on the average, and much more in some cases. The 1.67 *mu* of paddy field owned by Lin Chun-mu, a former farm labourer, could yield 2,000 *catties* in the early crop season as against 800 *catties*. If an additional 140 *catties* could be harvested on each *mu* of land owned by the poor peasants, the total increase would be 14,000 *catties*.

The middle peasants also benefited from the co-op. They began to understand that if they stood together with the poor peasants both would share the benefits, while if they farmed separately both would lose. Some middle peasants had had the mistaken view that 'joining the co-op means to slave for the poor peasants', but the facts caused them to give it up. In changing small plots into large tracts for cultivation, 27 boundary ridges between the fields were removed. The new land thus acquired could yield 540 *catties*, in addition to the savings in manpower.

Division of labour and specialisation by trades brought higher income from subsidiary occupations. During the long period of the fight against the drought, the mutual-aid teams could not prevent all their land from being affected. The co-op not only saved its crops, but managed to earn 1,545 *yuan* from side occupations. 'In such a serious drought,' said Lin Yu-tou, a middle peasant, 'you'd have had to work in the fields all day. If there was no co-op, how could we get anything from side-line production?

These practical examples and calculations were a good lesson to the members ... Take the case of Lin Tien-teh, a middle peasant, who had been wavering all the time in the co-op, taking two steps back every time he took one forward. After the calculations he no longer repeated his old refrain: 'My buffalo is strong and I can work hard. On my own I could carry my rice seedlings and plough too the fields and transplant 2 *mu* a day. Better pull out of the co-op and farm by myself.' Instead, he was determined to stay in ...

Of the eight member households that had decided to pull out, six changed their minds after the calculations, and the remaining two decided to think it over. [6]

Mao commended this co-op for its method of analysing in detail the experience of its members.

Many of Mao's remarks in his commentary on the *Socialist Upsurge in China's Countryside* prefigure themes which he advanced more fully in the Great Proletarian Cultural Revolution. Recognising the co-operative movement was essentially an ideological and political struggle, Mao drew attention to the presence of 'old ideas reflecting the old system [which] invariably remain in people's minds for a long time. They do not easily give way'. Already struggle against the old ideas of bourgeois leaders in the academic world had come out into the open.

Typically, Mao lined himself up with the 'nobodies' against 'the big shots' in this struggle. On 16 October 1954 he wrote a letter to the Political Bureau of the CCP defending two Youth League members for writing an article refuting the scholar Yu Ping-po. Yu had written a work on the classical novel, *The Dream of the Red Chamber*, and his protectors had tried to prevent the youths' criticism of it being published in the party press. Their main excuse, commented Mao ironically, was 'that it was "an article written by nobodies" and that "the party paper is not a platform for free debate".' Mao went on,

It seems likely that the struggle is about to start against the ... school of bourgeois idealism which has been poisoning young people in the field of classical literature for more than thirty years. The whole thing has been set going by two 'nobodies', while the 'big shots' usually ignore or even obstruct it, and they form a united front with bourgeois writers on the basis of idealism and become willing captives of the bourgeoisie ... Towards such bourgeois intellectuals as Yu Ping-po, our attitude should naturally be one of uniting with them, but we should criticise and repudiate their erroneous ideas which poison the minds of young people and should not surrender to them. [7]

Three significant facts can be traced in this letter. Mao claims that elements in the party leadership itself were not only obstructing criticism, they were actually protecting the perpetrators of what he called the 'poison' of bourgeois idealism. Secondly, Mao saw criticisms by the youth as a possible means of bringing pressure to bear on such leaders. Thirdly, Mao regarded himself as isolated at that time, like the two Youth League members, at least from influence over a part of the party's press and perhaps over certain 'big shots' in the party to whom he was a 'nobody'. Mao pressed co-operation forward in 1955, when a campaign was indeed waged against bourgeois idealism and its influence on China's scholarship. But by 1956, the right was retrenching.

Delaying tactics were being used inside the party leadership to thwart the changes in ideology and in agriculture; so much so, in fact, that Mao's further plans for accelerating the socialist development of agriculture were put aside early in 1956, not to re-emerge for eighteen months; the movement towards advanced co-operatives slowed down during the course of that year. A great wage reform in early 1956 stressed material incentives rather than mass mobilisation as a means of encouraging production. It gave greater rewards than before to skill and productivity in industry. It is not likely this reform had Mao's backing.

In the spring of 1956 Mao was struggling to shape new and creative solutions to the problems of China's transition to socialism. On the one hand, there existed China's 'poverty and blankness', her economic and cultural backwardness, inherited from the old society. On the other, there were her awakened millions. How should the latter be organised to transform the former? What type of leadership should the party provide during and after the transitional period?

Mao concluded that the party should not be afraid to admit that contradictions continued to exist in socialist society. Rather such contradictions had to be analysed and used as a motor of social change and material transformation. The party regarded the transition to socialist forms of ownership as completed with the take-over of industry and the consolidation of 'fully socialist' advanced agricultural co-ops. But what concerned Mao was that after the transition the party leadership should face the fact that there were still two roads, two possibilities of development. The first was to adopt capitalist methods of economic development, relying on managerial strata in industry and on a rich-peasant economy in the countryside. The second was to go forward on a socialist road towards higher forms of collective organisation, relying on the skill and resources of the workers and the poor and lower-middle peasants. For the next decade Mao would wrestle with this problem, at first struggling mainly within the party and by 1966 opening the struggle up so that it involved the whole people in a fight to control their destiny.

In a speech of April 1956, *On the Ten Major Relationships*, Mao argued again in favour of treating agriculture as the key to economic advance. To concentrate on heavy industry alone was to disorganise the economy and limit the number of consumer goods available to the people, a mistake which Mao admitted the Soviet Union had made under Stalin. He agreed China must certainly develop heavy industry, and indeed give it priority, but greater attention must be paid to light industry and agriculture than had been done in the Soviet Union.

Mao was formulating the policy of 'taking agriculture as the foundation and industry as the leading factor, with grain as the key'. It was a question of getting the relationship right. A concern for the people's immediate living standards need not clash with the need to accumulate funds to develop industry and to mechanise agriculture. The standard of living of the people should correspond with the stage of development of productive forces and no section of the population, and certainly not the leading groups, should seek a standard higher than the remainder. As production increased, so too would the people's livelihood improve, neither more nor less than the increased production permitted. This equal and gradual rise in living standards laid a good basis for a harmonious relationship between workers and peasants, and provided a widespread, though not complete condition of equality among the people that enabled later attacks on privilege and luxury-seeking among some cadres and intellectuals to be deemed reasonable and just.

Mao chose this course for hard economic reasons, too. In a country the size of China, with its backwardness and its huge population in the countryside, the question of food was the essential one to solve. A minimum living standard at such a stage of development was guaranteed by agriculture, not by industry. A successful agriculture would raise living standards which would in turn generate the development of light industry. 'The more the output of daily necessities,' he said, 'the more the accumulation [of capital. Thus] after a few years, there will be more capital available for heavy industry.

A more productive agriculture, basically grain, would create a surplus. The surplus, invested in light industry as capital, would create light industry's own surplus for re-investment in heavy industry. The spiral would thus also create its own market as it went along.

The 'ten major relationships' Mao enumerated were ten contradictions in China's socialist society. To resolve these contradictions meant to mobilise 'all the active factors and all the available strength'. From the defensiveness of this remark and of his whole speech, it is evident he regarded the passive, backward factors as entrenched elements, a conservatism that exerted a ruling and debilitating effect over many aspects of society, including the party and the party's policies. Significantly, the speech was not published until twenty years later.

Through the ten contradictions ran a common thread, that the main divisions in China were between economic backwardness and economic progress, between political backwardness and political progress. The theme of Mao's speech was that a backward economy could not be converted into an advanced one if political backwardness thwarted political progress. He was beginning to thrust to the fore a principle that in the cultural revolution he would insist was paramount, the principle of 'putting politics in command' in China's development of a modern economy.

A month after his speech, in May 1956, Mao swam the Yantze River at Wuhan from Wuchang to Hankow. At a period which can only be considered as uneasy for him, and one in which he was dwelling upon and planning the next movement forward, Mao seemed to gain power from combating the elemental force of the great river. The poem, *Swimming*, which he wrote to celebrate his feat, suggests that only in struggle did Mao feel free. Mao also uses the images of building to show that China's current stage of socialist construction was only one stage of a much longer struggle that had to be undertaken before reaching freedom, which to Mao meant a true dictatorship of the proletariat. He was to swim the Yangtze twice more that summer.

> I have just drunk the waters of Changsha,
> And eaten the fish of Wuchang;
> Now I am crossing the thousand-mile long river,
> Looking afar to the open sky of Chu.
> I care not that the wind blows and the waves beat;
> It is better than idly strolling in a courtyard.
> Today I am free!
> It was on a river that the Master said:
> 'Thus is the whole of Nature flowing!'
>
> Masts move in the swell;
> Tortoise and Snake are still.
> Great plans are being made;

A bridge will fly to join the north and south,
A deep chasm become a thoroughfare;
Walls of stone will stand upstream to the west
To hold back Wushan's clouds and rain,
And the narrow gorges will rise to a level lake.
The mountain goddess, if she still is there,
Will be startled to find her world so changed.

A further sign of consolidation by the rightists came in September 1956 when Marxism—Leninism and Mao Tse-tung's thought, officially the guiding principle of the party since 1945, was set aside at the Eighth Congress of the CCP in favour of plain 'Marxism—Leninism'. At the congress Mao warned repeatedly against conceit and arrogance, 'which makes one lag behind': most arduous tasks lay ahead of China, he said, in the great work of socialist construction. In particular he pointed to the need to strengthen ties between party and people. But despite his warnings, the year 1957 was to see a further shift away from mass movements by elements in the party leadership, as the agricultural producers' co-operatives began to come under the influence and even control of the well-to-do middle peasants.

Furthermore, a change was beginning to take place in the leadership principles of the Soviet Communist Party, following Khrushchev's criticism of Stalin at the Twentieth Congress of the Communist Party of the Soviet Union (CPSU) in February 1956. If, as was then clear to Mao, the mere taking of power by the forces of the people did not put a stop to class struggle, but that such struggle continued to exist in socialist society, was that struggle to be dampened and even extinguished by administrative measures, as was the case in the Soviet Union? If, on the contrary, it was to be encouraged, how could it best be handled so that contradictions were resolved in ways which consolidated the people's power?

Stalin had made gross errors but, Mao considered,

Khrushchev's method of criticising them itself lacked self-criticism. The evaluation Khrushchev was making of Stalin was one which affected the whole of the Soviet Union, and indeed the whole of the world revolutionary movement, yet it was made in secret session with no opportunity for the people to express their opinions through class struggle. The intense 'centralism' of Stalin's and Khrushchev's Russia was forcing Mao to re-examine the other aspect of 'democratic-centralism' — democracy. If China was a dictatorship of the proletariat, what were the forms through which the people could speak and dictate to the bourgeoisie?

Another warning signal came with the counter-revolution in Hungary, in October 1956. Again Mao felt that it was wrong for the Hungarian leadership to have allowed the people's criticisms to grow without freedom of class struggle, to the point where counter-revolutionaries could take advantage of the discontent to stage an uprising. The Hungarian party had mishandled the problem of debate and criticism by the working class.

The evident lack of dictatorship by the proletariat in Hungary and the Soviet Union caused Mao concern that the lesson should be learnt in China. He had already called for an airing of views in public in the hope of challenging the entrenched rightists in the party. In a speech on 2 May 1956 he had launched a campaign, which continued throughout the following winter, to 'let a hundred flowers bloom, let a hundred schools of thought contend' in the arts and sciences.

The Hundred Flowers Campaign was both summed up and deepened by Mao's speech of 27 February 1957, *On the Correct Handling of Contradictions among the People* which he had prepared for nearly a year and which he revised again before its publication on 18 June 1957. In it he pointed out the moral of the events in Hungary and the Soviet Union. In a socialist society,

we are confronted by two types of social contradictions
— those between ourselves and the enemy and those

among the people themselves ... The contradictions between ourselves and the enemy are antagonistic contradictions. Within the ranks of the people, the contradictions among the working people are non-antagonistic ... There are still certain contradictions between the government and the people. These include contradictions among the interests of the state, the interests of the collective and the interests of the individual ... The only way to settle questions of an ideological nature or controversial issues among the people is by the democratic method, the method of discussion, of criticism, of persuasion and education, and not by the method of coercion or repression ... [The democratic method was] epitomised in 1942 in the formula 'unity, criticism, unity' ... It means starting from the desire for unity, resolving contradictions through criticism or struggle and arriving at a new unity on a new basis. [8]

With these principles Mao intended to give a firm structure to class struggle under conditions of socialism. Continued struggle was the way by which the people raised their consciousness and Mao saw consciousness as the essential element generating the people's creation of their own wealth in a socialist society.

In the same speech Mao reminded the people that he included himself among those who had to remould their ideas. There was no-one so advanced that he needed no change at all. He himself had to continue to learn, he said, if he was to make further progress and not lag behind. Mao exempted no leader from the necessity to keep pace with the people's advance. This was as much a challenge to the conservative elements as a confession of his own shortcomings.

On 12 March 1957 Mao announced to a conference of cadres the Central Committee's decision to embark on a new rectification within the CCP to criticise its 'subjectivism, bureaucracy and sectarianism'. The rectification was designed to take note of the criticisms of the party in the Hundred Flowers Campaign and to study documents about the changes in the Soviet Union, all with a view to examining 'one's own thinking and work . . . learning from past mistakes to avoid future ones'. Would such rectification 'undermine our party's prestige'? asked Mao. No. It would enhance it. It would analyse conditions in China dialectically: and 'by analysis, we mean analysing the contradictions in things'. Though confined within the party at first, the rectification movement must 'open wide' and not 'restrict' debate. That, said Mao, is the method the party must adopt 'in leading our country . . . Let all people express their opinions freely, so that they dare to speak, dare to criticise and dare to debate . . . Marxism develops in the struggle against bourgeois and petty-bourgeois ideology, and it is only through struggle that it can develop.'

Mao went on to expand this theme into a greater warning.

In our country . . . in the ideological field, the question of who will win in the struggle between the proletariat and the bourgeoisie has not really been settled yet. We still have to wage a protracted struggle . . . One of our current important tasks . . . is to unfold criticism of revisionism . . . There is still class struggle . . . – and it is very acute, too. Even great storms are not to be feared. [9]

Mao's analysis of the contending forces was driving him closer to the conclusion that 'a great storm' must soon come. While declaring that 'the large-scale, turbulent class struggles of the masses characteristic of the previous revolutionary periods have in the main come to an end', he found that in whatever area he pursued the policy of continuing the class struggle under conditions of socialism there were obstacles put in his way. Local party committees, he said, should 'tackle the question of ideology' but in many places they had not – they were 'too busy'. Apparently, ideology was not even on their agenda.

The right wing in the universities who, in the early summer of 1957, came out with individualist and elite criticisms, such as that politics should be 'divorced' from study and that socialism, while perhaps suitable for the economy, had nothing to do with education or culture, exposed their assumptions before the people and were themselves criticised. A few frowned on the very existence of the Communist Party in the universities: these critics were struggled against at public meetings. Criticism of bureaucracy from the proletarian left, on the other hand, Mao took as an indication of the feeling among the people about aspects of party work. Mao, unlike the party bureaucrats, held that such criticism tended to consolidate the dictatorship of the proletariat over the reactionary classes. Meanwhile, 'some people' on non-party newspapers, wrote Mao in June 1957, were waging 'a struggle from the standpoint of the bourgeoisie against the proletariat' by printing 'many seditious reports' reflecting 'confusion' and 'anarchy' under guise of letting 'a hundred schools contend'.

The youth, the problem of 'successors to the revolution', was much on Mao's mind. Would they be a possible agent of fundamental criticism to 'tackle the question of ideology' if the party proved incapable of rectifying itself? When Mao travelled to Moscow to the conference of world communist parties in November 1957 he took time off to address a meeting of Chinese students and trainees.

> The world is yours, as well as ours, but in the last analysis, it is yours. You young people, full of vigour and vitality, are in the bloom of life, like the sun at eight or nine in the morning. Our hope is placed on you ... The world belongs to you. China's future belongs to you. [10]

This was only Mao's second visit abroad. It was hardly a happy one. Khrushchev had espoused the doctrine of 'transition to socialism' by 'peaceful means', through parliamentary majorities rather than through revolution. The Chinese delegation regarded the doctrine as quite unrealistic and saw it as an expression of Soviet weakness in the face of imperialism.

Khrushchev's other doctrine, peaceful co-existence with imperialist countries, was not bad in itself, but the Chinese claimed it could not be regarded as dealing with the primary contradictions between imperialism and socialism which would remain antagonistic and which could only be resolved by the revolutionary overthrow of the capitalist ruling class.

If Khrushchev's doctrines were born of fear of war with imperialism, Mao reminded the conference that war bred revolution as well as wreaked destruction and although it was better avoided, to fear it was to fear imperialism which was its perpetrator. Moreover, fear of war was something the imperialists relied upon to weaken the revolutionary will of the people and in general to preserve their rule. The effect of Khrushchev's doctrines would be to lower the consciousness of the people and so to vitiate the growth of socialism not only in the West but also in the socialist countries.

As we have seen, Mao recognised the tendency towards power being usurped in China by those favouring the well-to-do peasants in the countryside and a managerial elite in industry. Following the rightist trend of 1956-7 in China and the growing estrangement of the Chinese and Russian parties, Mao became even more convinced that only a further growth in the political consciousness of the poorest peasants and the workers could prevent a revision of socialist priorities from taking place in China. Such a revision, in a country at a low level of industrial advance, could only mean a return to poverty for the majority of its inhabitants, while a few regulated production to their own material advantage.

9   The Clash of Models

*The Great Leap Forward, the Communes and
the Emergence of 'Two Roads', 1958–1964*

> Throughout the country, the communist spirit is surging
> forward. The political consciousness of the masses is
> rising rapidly . . . China is forging ahead in her economic
> revolution . . . In view of this, our country may not
> need as much time as previously thought to catch up
> with the big capitalist countries in industrial and agri-
> cultural production. The decisive factor, apart from
> leadership by the party, is our 600 million people.
> The more people the more views and suggestions, the
> more intense the enthusiasm, and the greater the energy
> . . . Do the working people of China still look like
> slaves as they did in the past? No, they have become the
> masters.
>
> > Mao Tse-tung, from an article of 15 April 1958

The shift in the thinking of the Chinese people, which
marked both the formation of the co-operatives and the great
debate around the rectification campaign in 1957 criticising
the opinions the rightists had voiced in the Hundred Flowers
Campaign, generated two far wider and deeper movements.
These were the Great Leap Forward, beginning in the spring
of 1958, and the movement to set up communes which
started in the same summer. Both movements were expressions of the theory of 'continuous revolution' developed by
Mao and proclaimed by the Chinese leadership at the onset of
the Great Leap Forward. Both were in line with Mao's conviction that freedom of class struggle was the precondition
for economic growth under socialism. Both were concrete
examples of how to synthesise the enthusiasm of the people

so that its power became not only a spiritual but a productive force.

The Great Leap Forward policy was conceived by the Central Committee in the autumn of 1957 as 'a new high tide' of production using the slogan 'Overtake Britain in Fifteen Years'. It was endorsed by the National People's Congress after much discussion at all levels of the party. Two conferences of the party centre in January 1958 mulled over questions of the work methods the party should adopt in the Great Leap. After the second conference, Mao wrote down *Sixty Points on Working Methods*, a draft resolution to be sent back to regional bureaux to be 'refuted or developed' before a final version was drawn up and used as a guide to action.

According to Mao's theory of continuous revolution, which he advanced in the *Sixty Points*, 'ideological and political struggles between men ... will never cease'. The development of socialist society, and even of communist society, from one phase to another 'must necessarily be a relationship between quantitive and qualitative changes. All mutations, all leaps forward, are revolutions which must pass through struggles. The theory of the cessation of struggles is sheer metaphysics'.

The solving of contradictions among the people, including the contradictions between the people and 'the bourgeois rightists', must be through 'the bloom-contend type of mass debate', not by suppression. In pursuing mass debate, ideology and politics 'are the commanders, the "soul" '. To ignore ideology and politics, to be concerned only with 'business matters', to be 'expert' while neglecting 'redness', would 'lead our economic and technological work astray'. On the other hand, those who 'have no practical knowledge are pseudo-Red, empty-headed politicos'.

In an article published in a party journal on 15 April 1958, Mao introduced a report on a co-operative, and incidentally summed up the spirit following the rectification of

1957, heralded the Great Leap and even looked forward to the cultural revolution, with the words,

> Never before have the masses of the people been so inspired, so militant and so daring as at present. The former exploiting classes have been completely swamped in the boundless ocean of the working people and must change, even if unwillingly. Undoubtedly there are people who will never change, who would prefer to keep their thinking ossified down to the Day of Judgement, but that does not matter very much. All decadent ideology and other incongruous parts of the super-structure are crumbling as the days go by. To clear away the rubbish completely will still take some time, but there is no doubt of their inevitable and total collapse ... The working people on the 9,600,000 square kilo-metres of the People's Republic of China have really begun to be the rulers of our land. [1]

A few weeks later, on 5 May 1958, Liu Shao-chi announced the Great Leap Forward policy to the Second Session of the Eighth National Congress.

During the Great Leap Forward, 500 new factories were com-missioned. With most industry transferred to state ownership, the working class had its first major experience of socialist con-struction without the national bourgeoisie, albeit under managerial direction. In town and country, small-scale or backyard industry, such as iron and steel making, though the products were often poor, familiarised hundreds of thousands of ordinary people with industrial processes for the first time. Compensating for the lack of expertise common to all countries that begin their development 'poor and blank', the backyard workers (office and service staff, teachers, students, peasants) learnt new skills through practice. Some small-scale enterprises were superseded once their educative function had been fulfilled, but many remained or were developed into medium-scale operations, while many workers used their newly gained experience at a higher level of production in local factories.

All over the country the construction by the peasants of reservoirs and pumping stations for irrigation showed the advantages of large-scale rural organisation. As word of the great changes spread, peasants began to unite the co-operatives into communes big enough to use machinery effectively, plan construction on a proper scale, set up plants for repairing farm tools and make better use of labour and land. The central government's practice of setting up state farms to reclaim waste areas was extended.

Those rural communes which had started off an unwieldy size were soon divided up. The urban communes were abandoned as premature. Where rural and urban production units had combined to form a commune, the rural part retained its commune structure while the urban part was dismantled, though many rural communes continued to run individual small factories and workshops. These moves in 1959 indicated a retraction of the 'crest' of the original 'high tide' of 1958. However, the basic gain, the three-level system instituted within the rural commune (the commune, the production brigade and the production team) is the system existing today.

The initial 27,000 communes of 1958 were reorganised into 74,000-odd units by 1961. (In 1973 there were said to be over 50,000 communes which means that some have again been enlarged). In these rural units, the peasant, or commune member as he is called, is paid according to his work, while each household's sideline occupations, such as the rearing of a pig or chickens or growing vegetables on his private plot, provide supplements to the family income. The state grain tax is paid by the commune at an effective rate of 5—6 percent; the tax is reduced if the harvest is poor and waived in disaster years and in communes which are in the poorest and most backward areas. Backward communes may indeed depend on state grain supplies, transferred from other communes or even other provinces. A small percentage of grain is stored against bad years and for seed the following season.

The commune's income is gained mainly from selling a quota of its produce to the state. The quota is set according to the wealth of the brigades: rich communes sell most, poor ones sell least. The quota is calculated after the brigades' food needs have been met. The share-out of the resulting income is in the hands of each brigade or production team and, after costs have been met, it is split up between investment and welfare funds and the brigade members' own private consumption. This latter amounts to 55—75 percent of income, distributed to commune members according to work points, which are themselves set by the mass decision of the brigade members. The personal income of the household thus increases with the increase of the production of the whole brigade. Funds accumulated by the brigades can be used by the commune to buy tractors or other machines, or to develop large scale services and enterprises such as hospitals, small factories, irrigation works and small power stations.

For the next decade, the commune system, which is not a state system but a type of 'collective ownership by the labouring people', succeeded in achieving a balance, or relationship, in Mao's term, between state, collective and individual interests in China's countryside. After three unsettled years, the communes settled down to a decade of good harvests unknown in China for centuries. This transition to a higher stage of collective ownership was done without a mass slaughter of rich peasants as had occurred in the Soviet Union under Stalin and with a maximum of poor peasant involvement and local leadership, again an advance on the methods used by Stalin's activists. It was, in other words, a rural economic revolution brought about by class struggle, by education and persuasion, by political consciousness.

The commune system transformed rural ownership so that

the units of production were large enough for economical collective effort and for gradual mechanisation. China's small-field agriculture at last raised itself to a level of co-operation that enabled it to modernise its methods, introduce machines and begin the long transformation of the peasant landowners into wage labourers and finally into machine-operators and industrial workers. Mao showed by this method of communisation that a certain degree of collectivisation of the peasantry not only could be achieved before mechanisation but, in the context of China's small-unit farming, was a necessary precondition of agricultural mechanisation.

The communes were also a new type of management unit, reponsible for local education, culture, health, trade, industry and militia. They were a combined political and economic organisation at the local level. As such, they tended to reduce the imbalance between village and town and to hold out the prospect of a new type of industrialisation.

The scale of the changes in the hinterland was described by Rewi Alley, who reported the movement from several score communes during the Great Leap Forward. In January 1959 he drove through the hills of north-east Hunan.

> The countryside was a blaze of lettering, slogans painted on the front face of each terraced rice field, big wooden characters three feet high making up slogans along the roads, bill boards with slogans, pictures and poems painted on them with a thatched roof covering to protect them from the rains, 'Communism is Good,' 'All for Each, Each for All' . . . 'The Communes are Good' and 'Leap Forward, Still Leap Forward.'

Alley visited the Chinching Commune, near Changsha, in an area that had been important in the time of the first soviets in the early thirties. The commune was by no means a model or an exceptional one.

Its chairman was a local man in his late forties . . . We came in to see him through a meeting hall where commune workers were in [training] class, and he told how his commune was formed last summer out of the people in four townships of the county. They demanded to be organised in this way, following news of the setting up of the first commune in Honan. The overall figures . . . show that it has 12,530 families, made up of 45,735 people, of whom 18,979 are wage earners. In round figures, 3,000 are workers in small industries, 6,000 in local construction projects, and 9,000 farm the 51,000 *mu* of irrigated land and the 6,600 *mu* of dry land . . .

'It was too bitter in the old days,' the chairman said quietly . . . In 73 families, for instance, husbands had had to sell their wives, and 1,200 families sold one or more of their children; 4,000 families depended on being hired, and over 3,000 families had sold all their possessions at one time or another to procure food to get through a winter. In 500 families young men had sold themselves to be sons of others. Six thousand families had to seek outside work as well as work their rented land. Young widows often had to give away their children and sell themselves in order to live. [In one village] out of 103 families, 49 were without bedding quilts, 42 had no winter clothing, 41 were in debt, 34 had some members of their family out begging. All ate rice bran and wild vegetables for a good portion of the year. In other words, it was a bankrupt village . . .

In 1949, the area did not have more than 2,000 farm tools. Now it has over 40,000. The 50 pairs of rubber shoes that the landlord and rich peasants owned in 1949 had by last year given place to over 8,000 pairs owned by commune members. It would be hard to find any young man without his fountain pen. The 13 small primary schools in 1949 have given place to 71 large ones, concentrated last year from a good many more. The commune also has 5 middle schools, and its adult training schools . . . Crops are mainly rice and sweet potatoes. In the 35,000 *mu* of paddy fields, grain which averaged 200 *catties* a *mu* in 1949, averaged 767 *catties* in 1958. Average income per head was 18 *yuan* in 1949 and 112 in 1958. [2]

Mao spent the summer of 1958 touring the country, inspecting progress. He celebrated the Great Leap Forward and the commune movement as a nation-wide upsurge of creative energy. 'During this trip,' he told a news agency reporter, 'I have witnessed the tremendous energy of the masses. On this foundation it is possible to accomplish any task whatsoever.' The more the people carried out a conscious revolution in their social relationships, in response to the qualitative changes in reality brought about by the present and previous stages of struggle, the more they could command the development of productive forces. The Yenan spirit and the politics of the mass line spread throughout the country in the first production movement after liberation to mobilise the power of the people fully.

Its mass nature, however, was anathema to some CCP members who, according to Mao, called the movement in industry 'irregular' and disparaged it as 'a rural style of work' and 'a guerrilla habit'. Its community base was likewise scorned by those who emphasised centralism at the expense of democracy: it was not easy to encompass its enthusiasm in the confines of a neat state plan. Bureaucracy in China and in the Soviet Union therefore derided it. As a result, the Great Leap and the commune movement brought into active contradiction the different approaches of the Russian managerial and the Chinese mass-line methods of leadership.

It was Mao's thesis from then on that a managerial system dominated by experts and technicians was inherently revisionist (*ie* it tended to re-assert the values of the defeated classes) whereas proper adherence to the mass line would eventually produce a new system asserting the communal values of the revolutionary classes. Such a new system indeed showed signs of arising in 1967-8 during the cultural revolution in the form of revolutionary committees, composed of representatives of the workers and peasants who, along with revolutionary cadres, were supposed to establish political domination for the first time over experts and technicians in factories and communes, in administration and in education. After 1958, however, 'three bad years' of natural calamities and poor harvests obscured the conflict between the two methods of leadership for the time being and gave bureaucratic methods the chance to spread again.

As he had planned to do since the previous January, Mao retired from the chairmanship of the People's Republic in December 1958, though he remained party chairman. Liu Shao-chi was elected head of state in his place the following April.

Mao visited his native village of Shaoshan in June 1959 and in a poem to commemorate the visit he happily contemplated the fertile commune fields and the hero-labourers whose 'bitter sacrifice' in 'the long-fled past' had given rise to the growing prosperity of the present.

> Like a dim dream recalled, I curse the long-fled past —
> My native soil two and thirty years gone by.
> The red flag roused the serf, halberd in hand,
> While the despot's black talons held the whip aloft.
> Bitter sacrifice strengthens bold resolve
> Which dares to make sun and moon shine in new skies.
> Happy, I see wave upon wave of paddy and corn,
> And all around heroes home-bound in the evening mist.

A week later he wrote another poem, *Ascent of Lushan*, in which he dwelt on themes of retirement.

> Perching as after flight, the mountain towers over the
>   Yangtze;
> I have overleapt four hundred twists to its green crest.

Cool-eyed I survey the world beyond the seas;
A hot wind spatters raindrops on the sky-brooded
waters.
Clouds cluster over the nine streams, the yellow crane
floating,
And billows roll on to the eastern coast, white foam
flying.
Who knows whither Prefect Tao Yuan-ming is gone?
Perchance to till the ground in his Land of Peach
Blossoms.

Tao Yuan-ming was a fourth-century prefect in Kiangsi who left office, according to tradition, rather than bow to others. He became a hermit at the foot of Lushan. In an essay, *Peach Blossom Spring*, Tao wrote of an ideal land where people lived in peace and happiness free from tyranny and exploitation.

Mao's own retirement released him from the duties of head of state and gave him more time to devote to party work. Certainly he soon returned to the thick of intra-party struggle. At the Lushan meeting of the Central Committee in July—August 1959, Defence Minister Peng Teh-huai attacked some aspects of the mass-line method, as used in the Great Leap and in setting up the communes. Mao answered with a spirited defence of the movement's enthusiasm and aims, some self-criticism regarding the production targets which he admitted had sometimes been over-ambitious, and a demand for Peng's dismissal for seeking to turn legitimate criticism into hostile attack.

As Mao saw it, 'we have sympathy for the person, but not for his mistake'. Peng was busy attacking the 'leftism' of the commune movement, including the communal canteens (which were abandoned), the 'equalitarianism', the distribution of free food when stocks would not last until the next harvest, and other over-extended tendencies which had emerged and which were too utopian for the stage of consciousness and the level of production to sustain.

Mao admitted these were problems, but he claimed that by August 1959, after several months of opposing the left tendency, they had been overcome. 'There is no more pompous exaggeration,' he said, meaning that production figures had been scaled down and were no longer being ludicrously inflated by over-enthusiastic cadres at the lower levels, and that communes were no longer being declared a short cut to instant communism. He now charged that the real danger by the autumn of 1959 came from the right. It was natural a rightist tendency would come up, while a leftist mistake was being corrected. Mao said that the rightists, including Peng, 'are still making demands for correction . . . They attack the general line [of socialist construction] and try to lead [it] astray.' The rightists were attempting another consolidation after the galloping mass movement of 1958.

By 1960 — the middle year of 'the three bad years' of natural disasters — and, until 1963, the counter movement against the general line of the Great Leap was laid down by directives issued by the Central Committee against the spirit and advice of Mao. They were not made public but were transmitted to the particular spheres where they applied. They only came to light in the cultural revolution when Red Guards used them to expose the 'bourgeois line' of the 'capitalist roaders', in particular Liu Shao-chi.

The Central Committee's directive for industry had seventy clauses. It emphasized the authority of management and of professional engineers and technical staff. It tightened labour discipline and laid stress on rules and regulations, while increasing material incentives for individual workers.

The directive for agriculture made the production team the main accounting unit, instead of the production brigade, thus returning this important function from the level of the village to the level of families. Individual incentives, tied to work points, were emphasised. During this period, too, a further set of four policies was applied throughout the country, known as the 'three freedoms and one responsibility'. The 'three freedoms' were freedom to develop a free market, freedom to develop small enterprises with sole responsibility for profit and loss, freedom to increase the size of private plots for individual families to cultivate. The 'one responsibility' was the fixing of output quotas, hence the responsibility for cultivation of given fields belonging to the collective, on individual households.

The directives for schools and higher education stressed academic achievement, staff authority and professional qualifications. Leadership in universities passed to old scholars who planned courses, took no part in teaching and concentrated on research, at the same time being allowed certain personal privileges such as special food rations, special seats on buses and the right to jump queues. These privileges hardly reflect the great power the scholar groups in fact wielded in China's higher learning, nor does it suggest the extent to which children from worker and peasant background were excluded from university education and, even when some were admitted, as during the Great Leap Forward, to what an extent they were discriminated against at college.

In the international sphere, too, the communist movement continued to show what Mao regarded as unhealthy signs. In April 1960 an article partly attributed to Mao, *Long Live Leninism!*, defended the political analyses of Marx and Lenin, especially on questions of revolutionary overthrow of capitalism, against the reformism of the Yugoslavs and, by extension, of Russia. In June 1960 Khrushchev denounced Mao, saying that he had become 'an ultra-leftist, an ultra-dogmatist, indeed, a left-revisionist' and that the Russian leadership did not approve of the Hundred Flowers Campaign, the Great Leap Forward or the communes. In July Khrushchev withdrew Soviet experts from all industrial projects they were aiding in China, tearing up hundreds of agreements and contracts.

Mao's response was not only to continue to oppose the

Russian revisionist policies of peaceful transition to socialism and avoidance of all wars at all costs, in which Mao could rely on the support of Liu Shao-chi and of most of the 'first line' of leadership in the Chinese party. He also continued to try to seek out the seeds of that revisionism inside the CCP, by challenging its basic methods on two fronts; first, in industrial management and, two years later, in the more general relations between party cadres and people which he tried to rectify in a 'socialist education movement'.

He issued a direct rebuff to Soviet industrial management methods in 1960 by drawing up a new charter for the huge iron and steel complex which the Russians had helped to rebuild near Anshan in previously Japanese-occupied Liaoning province. The Anshan charter was to replace the Russians' charter of the Magnitogorsk Steel Plant, which had laid down a managerial policy based on giving free rein to expertise and management privileges. More important, the Anshan charter was a direct alternative to the Central Committee's own seventy-point directive on industry. It is a sign of Mao's isolation at this time that he could draw up a charter for a single factory while the Central Committee was issuing a directly contrary directive to be applied to the whole of industry.

Although supported locally in the early 1960s, the Anshan charter was not adopted as a nation-wide model until the Great Proletarian Cultural Revolution had defeated Liu Shao-chi's 'first line.' The charter declared,

> Keep politics firmly in command; strengthen party leadership; launch vigorous mass movements; institute the system of cadre participation in productive labour and worker participation in management, of reform of irrational and outdated rules and regulations, and of close co-operation among cadres, workers and technicians; and go full steam ahead with the technical revolution.

Mao, still in the 'second line', was paying less and less attention to everyday affairs. He later complained that some comrades in the 'first line' did not even bother to consult him on major policies. It appeared he was being cold-shouldered and the 'first line' was trying to ease him out of a position of having a say in whole areas of decision-making. He was later to claim that there was no proper discussion at the party centre from 1959 to 1964 and he complained of military and propaganda leaders doing their work in secret.

On the surface, Mao's life at Chungnanhai in central Peking seemed sober and contented enough when Edgar Snow visited him there at the end of 1960. Cut off from day to day detail, it seems he used his time inspecting the provinces and planning a wider strategy for the years to come.

He lived in a small part of the imperial palace of the Ming and Ching emperors, across the wide boulevard from the new and monumental Great Hall of the People. He was then sixty-seven years old, and his wife, Chiang Ching, was forty-eight. Within the compound, wrote Snow,

> ... no guards were visible along a willow-fringed drive that skirted the palace lakes, past beds of gladioli and chrysanthemums, to the graceful old one-storey yellow-roofed residence. It was one of a group of palace buildings formerly occupied by court mandarins and later by Kuomintang officials. Most members of the Politburo were similarly quartered, close to each other. The great chambers and audience halls of the main palaces were now museums or playgrounds and in one corner of Pei Hai stood a model nursery ...
>
> The large, comfortable living room of Mao's home was tastefully furnished in Chinese style; directly adjoining it were a small dining room and his study and living quarters. The meals he ate and served his guests were a few home-style dishes of Hunanese cooking. He drank with me a bit of *mao-tai*, the fiery liquor of Hunan, in raising toasts for the occasion. He also served the Chinese red table wine which was for sale (unrationed) in the liquor stores of north China at one *yuan* a bottle.

Mao was much heavier than he used to be; he ate moderately and smoked fewer cigarettes . . . Across the park were imperial Manchu buildings in which he could have outshone the White House, but these were kept for 'people's palaces' . . . Mao was still relaxed, deliberate in his movements, quick to perceive any nuance in a remark, and a man with not exactly a twinkle but a quizzical beam in his eye. He had an infectious laugh and thoroughly enjoyed a witty remark. He also had an incandescent temper. [3]

Snow reckoned that Mao spent about four months of each year in Peking and toured China the rest of the time. He kept contact with provincial party leaders and with others lower in the party ranks. He made a point of calling, sometimes unexpectedly, at new projects, communes, factories, nurseries and kindergartens. He told Snow that he inspected 'reform-through-labour' farms, and when he visited farms or local workshops 'he had long talks with the peasants and tried their food'. Snow noticed that 'he knew close to the calorie what the average child and adult were eating; in a time of successive natural calamities, he knew how far it was from adequate'. Today, many oil paintings and posters still depict him on the 'tours of inspection' he made at this time, surrounded by workers at a Shanghai steel works or walking in white shirt, baggy trousers and huge straw sunhat in the wheatfields of Hopei. Sometimes, when Mao disappeared from public view, his time was being spent in solitary study. He might read for a whole week. Snow had earlier noted how, in Yenan, when a new pile of books of philosophy arrived in the middle of a series of interviews, Mao excused himself and retired to consume them in three or four nights of intensive reading.

In these years of watching and waiting, Mao seems to have been able to depend on the company and loyalty of a few friends. More than once he exchanged poems with the poet and scholar Kuo Mo-jo, in which the two friends expressed their dismay at the 'confusion of right and wrong'. As the split with the Russian party deepened and Mao was not yet sure how far he could check revisionism in his own party, he wrote a reply to a poem of Kuo's saying that though revolution had broken over the earth like a thunderstorm, the 'evil spirit' of revisionism had brought back 'a noxious fog', 'a spectral dust that fills the world', which only a true faithfulness to basic Marxist–Leninist principles could 'disperse'.

In another poem he praised the plum tree, well-known for blossoming in adverse conditions of frost and snow. The poem betrays an intense feeling of isolation and a deep sense of the need to follow his own convictions.

> Wind and rain escorted Spring's departure,
> Flying snow welcomes Spring's return.
> On the ice-clad rock rising high and sheer,
> A flower blooms sweet and fair.
>
> Sweet and fair, she craves not Spring for herself alone,
> To be the harbinger of Spring she is content.
> When the mountain flowers are in full bloom,
> She will smile, mingling in their midst.

According to Kuo Mo-jo, Mao circulated this poem among Central Committee members to keep up their spirits during the Sino-Soviet dispute. But he was also, perhaps, trying to gain sympathy for his own views by drawing attention to the strength of his sense of what was right.

Still dwelling on the image of plum blossom he resolved on his sixty-ninth birthday, 26 December 1962, to welcome difficulties. He seems to have felt attacked from all sides.

> Winter clouds snow-laden, cotton fluffs flying,
> None or few the unfallen flowers.
> Chill waves sweep through steep skies,
> Yet earth's gentle breath grows warm.
> Only heroes can quell tigers and leopards
> And wild bears never daunt the brave.

> Plum blossoms welcome the whirling snow;
> Small wonder flies freeze and perish.

This last poem, *Winter Clouds*, came shortly after the tenth
plenary session of the Eighth Central Committee, held in
September 1962, during which Peng Teh-huai, though
officially dismissed, produced an 80,000-word document
defending himself and renewing his attack on Mao for 'putting politics in command' in the Great Leap Forward. Liu
Shao-chi and Teng Hsiao-ping, the general secretary of the
party, advocated the reversal of the verdict on Peng. Mao
fought against Liu at this meeting and warned the Central
Committee 'Never forget class struggle!' a motto that would
echo through the years of upheaval of the cultural revolution.
Mao called for a socialist education movement to try to
correct the rightist tendency in the party's work methods.
His spirit at this conference, reflected also in *Winter Clouds*,
suggests that by then he had decided to fight back strongly
and had formulated ways of doing so.

In a further poem replying to Kuo Mo-jo on 9 January
1963, he sounded in an even more ebullient mood. Writing
two days after an attack in Moscow's *Pravda* had brought
the Sino-Soviet discord into the open, Mao seems to have
made up his mind that a counter-attack against Russian
revisionism could best be made by an all-out attack on its
influence in the Chinese party.

> On this tiny globe
> A few flies dash themselves against the wall,
> Humming without cease,
> Sometimes shrilling,
> Sometimes moaning.
> Ants on the locust tree assume a great nation swagger
> And mayflies lightly plot to topple the giant tree.
> The west wind scatters leaves over Changan,
> And the arrows are flying, twanging.
>
> So many deeds cry out to be done,
> And always urgently;

The world rolls on,
Time presses.
Ten thousand years are too long,
Seize the day, seize the hour!
The Four Seas are rising, clouds and waters raging,
The Five Continents are rocking, wind and thunder roaring.
Away with all pests!
Our force is irresistible.

In the same May he wrote that if the Chinese Communist Party did not conduct class struggle at the same time as developing production and technical expertise, 'it would not take long . . . before a counter-revolutionary restoration on a national scale inevitably occurred' and the whole of China would 'change its colour'.

Measures to correct that drift during the socialist education movement beginning in 1962-3 included relating education to production, extending the practice of cadres taking part in manual labour alongside workers and peasants and stirring the masses to act against poor leadership.

Mao had put these Yenan principles forward again during the Great Leap Forward. 'In future', he told a Tientsin University meeting on 13 August 1958, 'schools should have factories and factories schools. Teachers should do manual work. It will not do to move only their lips and not their hands.' In the 1957 rectification he had praised the use of the *tatsepao*, big-character wall posters on which people could write up criticisms of the leaders in their work places. In that year, too, the system of cadres doing a certain period of labour in their factories, offices and communes had been established, only to be eroded by the Central Committee's counter directives of 1960-3.

Ko Ching-shih, Mayor of Shanghai and one of Mao's closest regional supporters in the Great Leap and in the years up to the cultural revolution, described some of the good effects of this cadres' labour system. 'Leading cadres have discarded their bureaucratic airs and haughty attitude. Their merging with the masses as common labourers has become the new prevailing practice.' He had also warned, in December 1959, 'A single rectification campaign, however, cannot put things to rights once and for all.' Some cadres grumbled that labour ' "takes them away from their proper work" . . . According to them, the natural "work" of leading personnel is to issue orders from above, and there is no need whatever for them to concern themselves with how the masses think and live and to be one with them . . . We must continue to use the method of the rectification campaign to further develop relations of comradely mutual help between leading cadres and the workers.'

Mao used his inspection tours and his studies of regional reports to look for alternative models of China's growing industry and agriculture to those in the Central Committee's directives. He wanted to present the people with a direction closer to what he thought were their interests: he was already seeking to outflank the Liu-dominated Central Committee and party apparatus.

Khrushchev's tearing up of contracts had compelled China to develop her own resources. But Mao chose to expound a policy of self-reliance as a matter of principle as much as of necessity. Certainly China had to become an industrial state with modern technology: but if that state developed other than on the basis of the people's own consciousness, decisions and hard work, if it was in any sense done *for* them, and their initiative dominated by experts or by machines, then there would be a dangerous breach of Marxist–Leninist principles. There would be the risk of the dictatorship of the proletariat through the party becoming the party's dictatorship over the proletariat. Mao felt convinced that China was constructing socialism. It followed that if the means of production were socially owned, they should be socially used, and should not be appropriated by the experts, technicians, managers and leaders of the party's 'bourgeois headquarters', the 'first line'.

Mao therefore drew attention to two major models of self-reliance. China was most in need of oil. At the end of 1959 new oil deposits were discovered on the wild prairies of the north-east. In the spring of 1960, in tough natural conditions of a marshy wasteland in summer, a frozen wilderness in winter, with a minimum of tools and equipment and a maximum of ingenuity and sheer hard work, the determined oil workers supported by housewives and new recruits, managed to open up the oilfield and start the oil flowing so quickly that by 1963 China was self-sufficient in petroleum. After a century in which she had been reliant on imported oil, this was an achievement fundamental to China's continued political as well as economic independence. Many songs, stories and films were created praising the successes of the workers of the Taching oilfield.

Mao's call — 'In industry, learn from Taching' — was matched by a similar call to adopt a style of self-reliance and hard work in the rural areas: 'In agriculture, learn from Tachai.' Tachai was a poor brigade in a north Shansi commune whose small labour force had started to transform their stony hillslopes and eroded gullies into cultivable land. Using their own hands, they built walled terraces on the hillsides and, filling them with soil, created small, flat fields. In 1963 a flood washed away much of their work and destroyed their village. In the face of 'the worst deluge of the century' the party secretary of the brigade, Chen Yung-kuei, summed up the villagers' arguments for not asking for state aid. There were, he said, ten advantages:

1 It was in the interest of the state. Money was needed to build up the country. If Tachai did without state aid, that was equivalent to aiding the state and to building up socialism.
2 It was in the interest of the collective. Overcoming difficulties by their own efforts would further reveal the strength of their collective economy and make the villagers love the collective more.

3 It was good for the cadres. Self-reliance would temper them and force them to use their brains more.

4 It was good for the commune members. It would overcome any idea of depending on others and would spur them to strive hard and work tirelessly.

5 It would greatly strengthen the determination of the poor and lower-middle peasants and deflate the arrogance of the class enemy.

6 It was good for the socialist emulation campaign for overtaking and learning from the advanced and helping the backward.

7 It was good for developing production.

8 It was good for maintaining the honour of being an advanced unit.

9 It was good for unity.

10 It was good for training successors. [4]

The state had sent messages of good wishes; it had also sent relief. 'We'll accept half the help offered us by the state,' said Chen Yung-kuei, 'and send back the other half: we'll accept the moral support, but send back the money and supplies . . . The money and grain from the state could only solve our problem for a time, whereas the spirit of self-reliance taught us by the Central Committee and Chairman Mao will always be of use. That's what we want; — it's an inexhaustible treasure!' This last comment can be taken as a broad hint by Chen to Liu Shao-chi's men in the agricultural ministry to fall in behind Mao's outright support for the 'Tachai spirit'. Chen had already suffered from the attacks of Liu's adherents who wanted to abandon support for Tachai and concentrate on holding up rich brigades as models.

As promised by Chen, Tachai's villagers set to work and rebuilt the village and fields with their own hands. That year they reaped a good harvest, and even extended the terraced area before the next spring. The Tachai example, in the words of British economist Joan Robinson, 'appeals to the poor commune to pull itself up by its own bootstraps, and offers rewards in pride and honour.'

As the nation's harvests grew better from 1962 on and the gains from the large-scale construction of reservoirs and other water conservancy measures in the Great Leap became apparent, the credibility of the right's attacks on Mao became weaker. The ground was becoming clear for another movement forward.

The years 1963-4 saw Mao beginning his counter-attack on three fronts: the repoliticising of the army, under Lin Piao, with a course in basic Marxism—Leninism and a reform of its work style; the training of 'red successors' among the youth; and an attack on the bourgeois cultural superstructure, especially on the traditional opera companies. Mao finally chose education and the arts as the two arenas for the initial battle. In the event, surprised by the ardour of the awakened youth and the resistance of the rightists entrenched in their cultural enclaves, Mao used the Red Guards as a battering ram against reaction, and cultivated the army as a secure bastion of proletarian defence when the cornered rightists, mainly in the provinces, tried to precipitate armed conflict.

In May 1964 the publication of *Quotations from Chairman Mao Tse-tung* started the political education movement in the army, led by Minister of Defence Lin Piao. The movement was designed to counter the example of the Soviet Red Army, which laid heavy emphasis on rank, promotion and weaponry. It aimed to revive the principles of comradeship between officers and men, as in the Yenan days, and of man's primacy over weapons. Insignia and uniforms defining rank were abolished in June 1965. During the following six years the *Quotations* were to prove themselves indispensable in raising political consciousness in China on a mass scale and in introducing young foreign readers to the new Chinese thinking and often indeed to Marxism.

The *Quotations*, with an introduction by Lin Piao, selected passages from Mao's works which stressed class struggle, self-reliance, putting politics first, combating elitism, serving the people, hard work and frugality, investigation, criticism and self-criticism, political study and the importance of revolutionising the state's superstructure. In the hands of the Red Guards the *Quotations* would serve as an object lesson in Mao's applied dialectics. Mao had developed the theory that once the revolution had changed the economic base, it could not be assumed that the superstructure (of education, the arts and culture in general, as well as the ministries and other administrative organisations) would automatically transform itself to suit the base. The state itself, devising new organs of social control and reviving old ones, tended to allow a group of administrators to preserve a dominance impermeable to proletarian criticism and potentially contrary to proletarian dictatorship. 'Even today,' Mao told André Malraux in 1965, 'broad layers of our society are conditioned in such a way that their activity is necessarily oriented towards revisionism. They can only obtain what they want by taking it from the masses.' The preponderance of such people in the leadership would not necessarily lead to a full restoration of capitalism (capitalism had, in any case, never properly established itself in China) but it would restore modes of conduct appropriate to capitalist development, and even prolong feudal habits and customs. In particular, it would re-establish inequality. Defending equality, though not 'absolute equalitarianism', Mao claimed, 'The revisionists mix up cause and effect. Equality is not important in itself; it is important because it is natural to those who have not lost contact with the masses.' The dialectical answer to this creeping revisionism, in Mao's mind, was for representatives of the proletarian base to hit back, using its ideas in an attempt to revolutionise the superstructure. Despite their proneness to over-simplification, the Red Guards were on the whole to use the *Quotations* in exactly this way.

In 1963 Mao had named another model for emulation, the

young soldier Lei Feng, who had died in an accident a few years before. Lei Feng's life was used as a model both in schools and in the army's campaign to train its recruits to be political activists with a penchant for thrift, hard work and service to the people. Lei Feng, according to Premier Chou En-lai, 'worked for the public welfare and forgot himself. His words and deeds were consistent. He made a clear distinction between love and hatred.' Lei Feng overcame self-seeking: 'We should be as relentless as the autumn wind on individualism,' wrote the good soldier in his celebrated diary. The moral for the army, as for the schoolchildren who studied the soldier's short life, was to hate the bourgeoisie and love the workers and poor peasants. Lei Feng was a hero of the mundane. He elevated small details of everyday thoughfulness, kindness and thrift to the level of magnificent revolutionary gestures, thereby demonstrating that the least person, the 'nobodies' and not the 'big shots', were the heroes who made history. His view of the life of the ordinary man as one of heroic drama explains why Lei Feng was loved by millions of young people and why they could identify with him so easily and, through him, identify with 'revolutionary purity' and with Mao. When they began to see through the facade of the bureaucrats in their school and university party branches, they increasingly believed revolutionary purity emanated from Mao.

Since the Great Leap Forward, Mao had shown great concern that the generation born since liberation should become successors to the Yenan tradition and join in struggle to educate themselves in the realities of people's power. Part-work, party-study schools, combining physical and mental labour, were extended in 1964 and students took part in the socialist education movement in the countryside.

In a series of talks and directives over a period of two years, Mao probed away at the basis of the bourgeois authorities' preconceptions. In May 1963 he re-expressed the dialectical process, the interchange of idea and action in revolutionary work, in a ten-point *Draft Decision of the Central Committee on Certain Problems in our Present Rural Work*. 'It is man's social being that determines his thinking. Once the correct ideas characteristic of the advanced class are grasped by the masses, these ideas turn into a material force which changes society and changes the world . . . Among our comrades there are many who do not yet understand this theory of knowledge. When asked the source of their ideas, opinions, policies, methods, plans and conclusions, eloquent speeches and long articles, they consider the question strange and cannot answer it.' If at that time some of 'our comrades' could not answer it, within two years China's youth were busy answering it for them.

But Liu Shao-chi issued his own counter-order to the ten-point draft decision in September 1963. Its title, echoing Mao's, was *Decision Concerning certain Concrete Policies in the Socialist Education Movement in the Countryside*. It purported to come from the Central Committee, too, and no-one at lower levels knew then that the new directive was not Mao's. It was supplemented by a further directive from Liu in September 1964.

Liu Shao-chi's wife, Wang Kuang-mei, had been developing a novel method of rural political work while directing the socialist education movement in Taoyuan Brigade, Hopei province. She had been ordering work teams to go to the villages and find out one reliable family from whom to solicit information on the work of party officials in the area. Villagers who spoke out openly against local cadres, on the other hand, her men denounced and even imprisoned. A similar fate awaited those lower cadres who criticised the 'reliable family'. This came to be called 'taking root in one family' and it was quite opposite to Mao's concept of the socialist education movement which was to provide conditions for the whole village community to speak out in criticism of their local party leaders. Since the 'reliable family' was most often a better-off peasant and a senior local party cadre himself, the effect of Wang Kuang-mei's methods was to suppress the poor and lower-middle peasants, as had happened previously under the 'commandist' efforts of some of the land reform work teams. While appearing leftist, the work teams were, Mao soon claimed, 'right in essence' and were adopting methods designed to protect the party apparatus. Their methods had been popularised by the party and carried out in the socialist education movement all over China in direct contravention of Mao's original draft decision which the unknowing cadres at lower levels, acting many of them in good faith, must have assumed had been superseded by Liu's new one. In fact Liu's directive of 1963 gave the official seal to methods that had been in use for some time, pushed by energetic propagators of Liu's line in the party apparatus.

But an even more fundamental divergence of methods between Liu and Mao in the socialist education movement was over the question of models for agricultural development. Wang Kuang-mei had built up the rich brigade at Taoyuan, on the fertile plain of north-east Hopei, as a model of an economically advanced unit situated in an area favoured by nature. To hold up a well-to-do unit was, to Mao, to invite the wrong sort of emulation: it appealed to the self, the spirit of 'What's in it for me?' and tended to release rich peasant class forces.

Mao had advocated the Tachai Brigade as a model because it was poor and faced tough natural conditions, but more importantly because of its political consciousness, because of the method it had chosen to become better off. Tachai showed how a poor brigade could develop its wealth collectively. To Mao, Tachai was an advanced unit because of its collective work methods which were appropriate to thousands of similar brigades, for he knew that the harshness and backwardness of Tachai's conditions were more familiar to China's poor peasants than the wealth of Taoyuan.

It was in answer to this move of Wang's and Liu's, and as a result of the deformations that the apparatus had succeeded in making in the socialist education movement, that Mao drew up his Twenty-three-Point Directive at the end of 1964, which he presented to the Central Committee in January 1965. And it was this directive for a 'four clean-ups' campaign that was to provoke a breach with Liu's line which would never be mended.

The Twenty-three-Point Directive explicitly demanded the rooting out of 'persons within the party who are in authority and are taking the capitalist road'. From a study of Wang Kuang-mei's methods, it had become clear to Mao that the most urgent problem was 'revisionism in the centre'. He realised that most members of the work teams sent into the countryside to investigate party activities were themselves either 'capitalist-roaders' or directed by 'capitalist-roaders', and their main intention on arrival was to see that the people's criticism of party methods was deflected and turned back on to the critics. According to Mao's new directive the 'wrong tendency' of these bourgeois authorities, who disliked disturbance and upset and who propagated the line of "peaceful evolution" in order to re-establish capitalism', must be rectified by mass criticism; they must 'clean up' their methods in four spheres — political and economic matters, organisation and ideology.

These contradictory orders of 1963-5, all in the name of the Central Committee but only the last specifically in Mao's name, must have alerted party workers at lower levels at least to the existence of a fundamental struggle within the party. But other, and earlier, warnings from Mao had indicated the issues, and yet mass criticism was still being muzzled. Mao had issued a general instruction on 'Learning from each other, and overcoming complacency and conceit' in December 1963. In it he said that 'the faults common to all our comrades' were:

> To refuse to apply Marxist dialectical, analytical method, that is, the method of splitting one into two (both

achievements and shortcomings); to work in one's own field, studying only the achievement but not the short-comings and mistakes; to like flattery but dislike critical words; to have no interest in organising competent high and middle cadres to learn and investigate the work of other provinces, cities, regions, or departments so as to link the result with one's own circumstances and improve [one's] work ... to be blindly conceited, that is, to limit oneself to one's own district, the small world of one's department, the inability to widen one's scope, and the ignorance of other spheres of work; to show and talk to foreigners, visitors from other places, and people sent by the Centre only about the achievements, not the weaknesses, in one's own area of work; and to talk only superficially and perfunctorily.

The Centre has more than once raised this problem to our comrades ... All matters (economic, political, ideological, cultural, military, party, etc.) are always in a process of development; this is common sense to a Marxist. However, many of our comrades in the Centre and regions do not use this method of thinking and working. There is a formal logic deeply planted in their minds which they cannot uproot. [5]

In another warning, of February 1964, Mao attacked distortions of education:

The present examination system is more suited for enemies, than for the people; it is like an ambush, because the questions are remote, strange, and still in the tradition of the [stereotyped, feudal] eight-legged essays. I am against it. My suggestion is to publish the questions first, let the students study them and answer them with the help of their books ... Students should be permitted to doze off when a lecturer is teaching. Instead of listening to nonsense they do much better taking a nap to freshen themselves up. Why listen to gibberish anyway? ... The present system strangles talents, destroys young people. [6]

He recommended developing the students' initiative and curbing the arbitrary power of their teachers. In revolutionary education the teachers were the problem. Teachers, as much as anyone else, should have the spirit of serving the people.

Further, the campaign for the army to reform its work style and study politics turned outwards in 1963 and spilled over into the whole of society. Using this campaign as a device to try to undermine the complacency of the bureaucracy, Mao had hoped to arouse the revolutionary spirit of the cadres by exhorting them to take the PLA as a model of a correct attitude to their work.

> Now the whole country is learning from the PLA and Taching, and schools too should learn from the PLA. What the PLA excels in is the field of political ideology. It is also necessary to learn from the advanced units in the cities, agriculture, industries, commerce, and education, throughout the country.
>
> There are people who suggest that the industrial departments at all levels (from the departments [ministries] to the factories and communes) throughout the country should learn from the PLA by setting up political departments and political bureaux and appointing political commissars, and by adopting the 'four firsts' and the 'three-eight style'. It seems that this is the only way to arouse the revolutionary spirit of millions of cadres and workers in the industrial (as well as agricultural and commercial) departments. [7]

The 'four firsts' were as follows: in man's relationship with his weapons, man comes first; in all activities, political activities come first; in political work, ideological work comes first; in ideological work, creative study comes first. The 'three-eight style' of the PLA consisted of three phrases, *ie* correct political orientation, plain, hard-working style, and flexible strategy and tactics, and, in Chinese, eight characters, meaning unity, alertness, earnestness and liveliness.

But none of these opening shots proved to be so shattering as the attacks he and Chiang Ching began making on the cultural departments of the superstructure. Mao had given two instructions on literature and art in 1963 and 1964. In the first, of 12 December 1963, he had written:

> Problems abound in all forms of art . . . in many departments very little has been achieved so far in socialist transformation. The 'dead' still dominate in many departments . . . The social and economic base has changed, but the arts (as part of the superstructure, which serve this base) still remain a serious problem. Hence we should proceed with investigation and study and attend to this matter in earnest.
>
> Isn't it absurd that many communists are enthusiastic about promoting feudal and capitalist art, but not socialist art? [8]

In the second instruction, of 27 June 1964, Mao extended the attack to embrace almost the entire cultural superstructure.

> In the last few years these [mass cultural] associations, most of their publications (it is said that a few are good) and *by and large* the people in them have not carried out the policies of the party. They have acted as high and mighty bureaucrats, have not gone to the workers, peasants and soldiers and have not reflected the socialist revolution and socialist construction. *In recent years*, they have slid right to the brink of revisionism. Unless they remould themselves in real earnest, at some future date they are bound to become groups like the Hungarian Petofi Club. [9]

Mao identified the members of the Petofi Club with the instigators of the 1956 uprising in Hungary.

In 1965 Mao urged that the historical play *Hai Jui Dismissed from Office*, written by Wu Han in 1961, which covertly defended Peng Teh-huai, should be repudiated with other works by bourgeois authorities. In 1963-4 Chiang Ching had started to transform the content of Peking opera so that it should express the past and present history of the proletariat instead of the lives of feudal princes and officials. The army entered this struggle when Chiang Ching organised a forum in Shanghai sponsored by the PLA in February 1966. There she raised criticism of the 'black line' which, she said, had dictated the culture of China since liberation, forcing art and literature away from agitation by and for the people and towards a culture by and for an elite. The published summary concluded,

> As a result of the influence or domination of this bourgeois and modern revisionist counter-current in literature and art, there have been few good, or basically good, works in the last decade or so ... which truly praise worker, peasant and soldier heroes and which serve the workers, peasants and soldiers ... A lesson to be drawn from the last decade or so is that we began to tackle the problem a little late. We have taken up only a few specific questions and have not dealt with the whole problem systematically and comprehensively. So long as we do not seize hold of the field of culture, we will inevitably forfeit many positions in this field to the black line, and this is a serious lesson ...
>
> The last few years have seen a new situation in the great socialist cultural revolution. The most outstanding example is the rise of Peking operas on contemporary revolutionary themes ... Under the irresistible impact of this offensive, Peking opera, formerly the most stubborn of strongholds, has been radically revolutionised, both in ideology and in form. This has started a revolutionary change in literary and art circles. [These] are pioneer efforts which will exert a profound and far-reaching influence on the socialist cultural revolution. [10]

These conflicts over methods and content of the new proletarian forms of art, deriving from the contradictory class viewpoints of the protagonists, marked the first stirrings of the Great Proletarian Cultural Revolution.

10   The Beauty of Our Age

The Great Proletarian Cultural Revolution and After,
1965—1976

> Although the bourgeoisie has been overthrown, it is still
> trying to use the old ideas, culture, customs and habits
> of the exploiting classes to corrupt the masses, capture
> their minds and endeavour to stage a come-back. The
> proletariat must do the exact opposite: it must meet
> head-on every challenge of the bourgeoisie in the ideo-
> logical field and use the new ideas, culture, customs and
> habits of the proletariat to change the mental outlook
> of the whole of society.
>
> *Sixteen-Point Decision of the Central Committee,*
> August 1966

'When did you finally decide Liu Shao-chi had to go?' Edgar
Snow's question in an interview after the cultural revolution
assumes that Mao had the power to decide the issue. The
reality was the reverse. Mao had rather to fight to preserve his
own line against the inroads of Liu's, meanwhile struggling to
launch a counter-attack.

In answer to Snow's question, Mao said that Liu had
strenuously opposed the very first point in the programme
for the 'four clean-ups' in January 1965. It was Liu's opposition to this point that decided Mao that, if it came to a
head, the struggle against the rightist headquarters must not
baulk at removing its highest representative. Yet as late as
October 1966 Mao was saying, 'We must not get rid of Liu
Shao-chi by a stroke of the pen.' He had committed mistakes,
said Mao: let him correct himself. It was Mao's aim to create
conditions for the masses of the people to voice what those
mistakes were. This voicing, or 'extensive democracy', was

what came to be known as the Great Proletarian Cultural Revolution. Yet the cultural revolution was much more than the greatest mass criticism China had yet known. It was an attempt to revolutionise the whole of the state superstructure. Literally translated, the Chinese term for this mass movement is 'a full-scale revolution to establish a proletarian culture'. And it is by this yardstick that one must judge the achievements and the failures of the ensuing four years of turmoil.

The point Liu opposed so strongly was, not surprisingly, the one that demanded the removal of 'those in the party in authority who are taking the capitalist road'. Evidently Mao intended the 'four clean-ups' as a programme for overturning the party's superstructure. Naturally he found the plan blocked. Just as the socialist education movement had been accepted in theory but distorted in practice by Liu's cadres, the 'four clean-ups' could hardly be expected to get off the ground if it was to be conducted by the very officials whom the programme called upon the people to eliminate. Liu's 'first line' had taken Mao's socialist education movement as a warning. They had marshalled their forces against any mass campaign of the sort Mao envisaged where the people would speak out against the apparatus. So carefully had they managed their opposition that by January 1965, Mao was to claim, the essential power of the party (the power over propaganda work, the power of the provincial and local party committees, power even over the Peking party committee) was against him over this issue and was effectively out of his hands.

It is debatable if it was ever in them. Ever since the 1947 division of the administration into first and second lines, Liu had built up a following among leading intellectuals from the old gentry and the city bourgeoisie. After liberation, this power base widened when his apparatus formed ties with Soviet-oriented technicians and engineers, and with part of the working class who were before 1949 organised by Liu in more or less classical European and Soviet ways through unions and party cells. Mao, on the other hand, concluded Snow, 'personified the total indigenous revolutionary experience that was deeply rooted in the vast countryside, with egalitarian traditions realised in the armed forces and their close ties with the peasantry.' Mao concentrated on principles and strategy, the broader outlines of progress to socialism, while he relied on Liu's first line to see to everyday business. This was a damaging mistake.

When it came to power, in order to achieve its aim of unifying a disrupted and fragmented country, the Communist Party had to have a trained administrative apparatus. Mao had said that the first line had to be built up in order to make the succession of power after his death an easier task. 'So,' he remarked in 1966, 'I thought I'd establish their prestige before I died. I didn't expect the contrary to happen.' Instead of the two lines working collectively, Mao and his second line had been gradually displaced and the apparatus had taken over. The first line agreed to carry out collective decisions modelled on Mao's precepts but in practice worked primarily to build up their own 'little kingdoms', the bureaucratic power bodies at every level which Mao so detested. 'I had too much trust in them,' he admitted. The apparatus, while acknowledging the supremacy of 'Mao Tse-tung's Thought' in word, followed a policy of *yu-ming wu-shih*, *ie*, the name without the reality.

In the first years after liberation this uneasy alliance worked well enough so long as one side or the other compromised and while unity was in both their interests. The division into two lines was even legitimised under the terms of the new party constitution at the Eighth Congress in September 1956, making it easier for Mao to 'retire' two years later. But by 1965 neither Mao nor Liu could pursue his own goals by any further shaky liaisons. So far as Liu was concerned, Mao was an irritant, a thorn in his flesh, as he tried to pursue 'rational' economic ends by bureaucratic means. So far as Mao was concerned the power was with the apparatus and he found that by compromise he could only make dents in the regime of the officials, or slightly deflect its revisionist course. 'I became aware of this at the time of the Twenty-three-Points [January 1965] . . . It was in September or October [1965] when this question was raised: If there was revisionism in the centre, what would the regions do about it? I felt that my views couldn't be accepted in Peking.' What Mao had intended as a mechanism for the rational transference of power after his death (by establishing collective leadership on two levels while he lived) was converted by rightists into its opposite: a lever to create a split between the revisionist and revolutionary wings of the party. The answer, for Mao, lay in struggle and overthrow along class lines.

As a result Mao had to look for others outside the ministries in Peking who would accept his views. He felt himself to be 'alone, alone with the people'. Who would respond to his vision? His instinct was to go to the common soldiers, the tested and true guerrilla army, whose earlier struggles in the mountain strongholds had established a tradition of plain living and high consciousness. Though their spirit of self-sacrifice and hard struggle had been eroded by the trend towards professionalism, medals and sophisticated weaponry introduced by Peng Teh-huai, it was largely restored under Lin Piao's leadership. By 1965 the PLA was once again a stronghold of militant egalitarianism, deriving its spirit of 'serve the people' from the revolutionary traditions of three civil wars among the poorest of Chinese peasants. Mao sought and gained Lin Piao's support and through him the loyalty of the army and an important (though minority) section of the Central Committee.

Mao sought a second base of support among the young people. Since his own experience in the May 4th Movement he had always regarded the youth as the spearhead of ideas unwelcome to the ruling power. The campaign to learn from Lei Feng and the PLA (carried on in the schools since 1963) had stirred many students' belief in selflessness and the glory of heroic struggle. When criticism of bourgeois authorities erupted on China's campuses in the summer of 1966, Mao issued his own *tatsepao*, *Bombard the Headquarters*. His poster would have the effect of directing future criticism even to the highest levels of the party apparatus. It threw Liu into consternation: the students were up in arms against his bureaucrats.

Mao's third base from which to mobilise the attack was Shanghai, in particular some younger members of the party's propaganda department in that city, including its director Chang Chun-chiao. With the Peking press closed to him, Mao eventually went to Shanghai in November 1965 to encourage the press there to publish an article by the young writer, Yao Wen-yuan, criticising Wu Han's play about Peng Teh-huai and other works favoured by the apparatus's first line.

It was in Shanghai that Mao had had the consistent support of the city's mayor, Ko Ching-shih, who had backed Mao's ideas on industrial management until his death in May 1965. And it was in collaboration with Shanghai producers and actors that Chiang Ching had been working on the reform of Peking opera against the wishes of Peking's Ministry of Culture, where the literary theorist Chou Yang had been most successful, with Peng Chen (Mayor of Peking), in blocking Mao's second line in cultural matters. The young and articulate propagandists of Shanghai were ideal allies in the fight against the entrenched authorities of Peking.

Having given notice of the coming counter-attack in his Twenty-three-Points, Mao spent the spring and summer of 1965 waiting for the reaction. When opposed and in the minority it was his instinct to wait and make no false move, watching his opponents' manoeuvres. In conversation and in his writing at that time, he talked much about bureaucrats. Commenting on the report of a friend who had described the administration of a factory where he had done his stint of manual labour, Mao assailed the factory managers. 'Such people are already becoming capitalist vampires to the workers ... The bureaucrats and the workers ... are acutely antagonistic classes ... [The managers] are the object of struggle and revolution ... In the end they will be knocked down like capitalists by the workers ... We can only rely on those cadres who are not hostile to the workers.'

Talking to André Malraux in the same summer, Mao attributed the 'legacy' of the bourgeoisie, which was 'also our fate', to the particular course the revolution in China had taken. 'We made the revolution with peasant rebels; then we led them against the cities ruled by the Kuomintang. But the successor of the Kuomintang was not the CCP, however important that may be: it was the new democracy. The history of the revolution, like the weakness of the proletariat in the big cities, forced the communists into collaboration with the petty bourgeoisie.' Mao's counter-attack on Liu's first line resulted from a recognition that it was they, and not the workers, who at liberation had assumed the power in the government, the provinces, the cities and even the factories.

Mao's eagerness to work with Lin Piao in a co-ordinated attack on every manifestation of privilege and rank was not, therefore, for the sake of equality alone. Mao did not want 'absolute equalitarianism'. He sought instead an equality of shared experiences between leaders and led, sufficient to undermine the re-establishment of the old classes and to stop the formation of new elites. 'The forces tending toward the creation of new classes are very powerful' he told Malraux. 'It isn't simply a question of replacing one bourgeoisie with another, even if the other is called communist ... The thought, culture and customs which brought China to where we found her must disappear; the thought, customs and culture of proletarian China, which does not yet exist, must appear.'

In his notes of 3 July 1965 on a report concerning the Peking Teachers' Training College, Mao made his attitude to leaders clear.

Democracy means allowing the masses to manage their own affairs. Here are two ways: one is to depend on a few individuals and the other is to mobilise the masses to manage affairs. Our politics is mass politics. Democratic rule is the rule of all, not the rule of a few. Everyone must be urged to open his mouth. He has a mouth, therefore he has two responsibilities — to eat and to speak. He must speak up wherever he sees bad things or bad styles of work. He must follow his duty to fight.

Nothing can be done well, if it depends entirely on the leader, not on the leadership of the party. [We] ... must rely on the party and [our] comrades to deal with matters, not on a solitary leader. An active leader followed by inactive masses will not do; it must be established as practice that the masses use both their hands and their mouths. [1]

That summer Mao made a sentimental journey to the cradle of the revolution, the Chingkang Mountains, where in 1927 he had led his 800 defeated soldiers to form the first red base and initiate a new style of rural-based revolution. He seems to have gone with a longing to re-identify himself with the mainspring of the revolution at its original site, a desire to fortify his strength by absorbing inspiration at the sources from which all the events of the intervening years had flowed. It was a dangerous time for him, and in a poem, *Chingkangshan Revisited*, he warned, 'Do not look down the precipices.' He seems to have felt his life was at an all-or-nothing stage: 'Reach the ninth heaven ... or the five oceans deep ... either is possible.' But gaining strength from his visit, he ended with a vow he would persevere.

A long cherished wish to approach the clouds
Once more, by climbing Chingkang Mountains.
After a journey of a thousand leagues
The old view seen in a new visage.
Everywhere orioles sing, swallows dart,

Brooks murmur,
And the tall tree brushes clouds.
Once past Huangyangchieh
Do not look down the precipices.

Wind and thunder rumbled;
Banners unfurled;
The realm was made stable.
Thirty-eight years have elapsed
Like a snap of the fingers.
Reach the ninth heaven high to embrace the moon
Or the five oceans deep to capture a turtle: either is possible.
Return to merriment and triumphant songs.
Under this heaven nothing is difficult,
If only there is the will to ascend.

At the end of September 1965, at a conference of the Central
Committee, Mao announced that revisionism at the centre
must surely be challenged and he asked the meeting what it
would do to act against it. He seems to have attempted to
divide the Central Committee: who would be on which side
in the coming struggles?

Liu Shao-chi was forced to take further counter-measures,
not only by Mao's attack on him at this conference, but also
by the publication of an article by Lin Piao that month, *Long
Live the Victory of the People's War*. In this polemic against
the military technocrats, Lin had extended Mao's 'countryside surrounding the cities' concept to the world at large.
He described the third world countries, where national
liberation movements, such as Vietnam's, would be sure to
break out, as a world-wide backward or peasant force that,
united in people's wars, could surround and strangle the
advanced, industrialised countries of the capitalist West, and,
by extension too, of the revisionist East. Lin's programme
was a counter-blow to Liu Shao-chi's pragmatic foreign
policy (which critics later said he had been pursuing since
1962), known as the policy of 'three peaces' (peace with

imperialism, revisionism and reactionary forces in the world) and 'one less' (give less aid to the revolutionary forces). Despite this programme of Lin's, Liu Shao-chi continued his own line and in March and April 1966, even as the cultural revolution began, went on a state visit to Pakistan, Afghanistan and Burma as President of the People's Republic of China.

Awaiting the repercussions of his first move against the centre, Mao opened up his Shanghai front with Yao Wen-yuan's article denouncing Wu Han, the vice-mayor of Peking, published in the Shanghai press on 10 November 1965. From that month until the following summer, Mao did not return to Peking and he did not recover his leadership role in the capital until August 1966.

At first the bourgeois authorities themselves tried to grasp the leadership of the cultural revolution. In an *Outline Report* on problems of culture (drawn up in the name of the Central Committee without the approval of Mao and issued on 6 February 1966) Peng Chen, protector of Wu Han, tried to turn the rising criticism of *Hai Jui Dismissed from Office* into a purely academic question about how history should be treated.

Mao was meanwhile retaliating on two more fronts, culture and education, linking both fronts to his secure base in the army. The forum which met in Shanghai from 2 to 20 February 1966, under PLA auspices and guided by Chiang Ching, reviewed the transformation of Peking opera so far and discussed the further revolutionisation of art and literature. The forum's summary served to broaden the attack in the cultural sphere.

On 7 May, writing to Lin Piao, Mao made some notes on a report concerned with improving the PLA's agricultural work, a seemingly innocuous and narrow subject which, however, he used as a starting-point to describe his vision of how to eradicate the differences between town and country-side, and between mental and physical work. This document later became a blueprint for transforming the state and party organs and also the work of everyone in society, after the 'criticism and repudiation' of the cultural revolution had demolished the old structures. It became celebrated as the *May 7th Directive*.

The directive was intended to force the party to open the issues to the people and at the same time to provide the opportunity for the people to widen the horizons of their lives. The army, it said, should not only be a military and productive force: it should also take part in 'the struggle against capitalist culture'. Likewise, workers and commune members should not confine themselves to their own special work in factory and commune but should attempt to combine agriculture and industry; workers should engage in agricultural production 'under adequate conditions . . . following the example of the Taching oilfield', and peasants should collectively set up small-scale factories 'when circumstances allow'. Workers and peasants should also 'criticise the capitalist class' and 'learn military affairs, politics and culture'.

Students were in a similar position. 'Their studies are their chief work; they must also learn . . . industrial, agricultural and military work . . . School courses should be shortened, education should be revolutionised, and the domination of our schools by bourgeois intellectuals should by no means be allowed to continue.'

Mao outflanked the Central Committee with this directive. He next retaliated against Peng Chen's *Outline Report* by ordering the Central Committee to revoke it. He dissolved Peng Chen's Group of Five in Charge of the Cultural Revolution and set up a new Cultural Revolution Group directly under the Standing Committee of the Political Bureau, with Chen Po-ta and Chiang Ching as two of its members closest to him. Peng Chen himself was ousted from power in Peking.

'We were very happy about this,' an economics student from Sian told the Swedish writer Jan Myrdal, 'and immediately organised a demonstration. We demonstrated outside party headquarters in Sian and shouted: "Down with the

handful of party persons in power taking the capitalist road.'
We could see them behind the windows.'

Mao and the Central Committee issued another circular,
the May 16th Notice, 'opening wide' the cultural revolution
to let the proletariat 'express their opinions freely, so that
they dare to speak, dare to criticise, and dare to debate'. Mao
warned that some of the 'capitalist-roaders ... we have
already seen through, others we have not ... Some are still
trusted by us and are being trained as our successors, persons
like Khrushchev, for example, [*ie*, Liu Shao-chi] who are
nestling beside us.'

On 1 June Mao commended the authors of an attack on Lu
Ping, principal of Peking University, and said that their poster,
or *tatsepao*, calling for his downfall and put up outside the
dining room of the universtiy, was 'a Marxist—Leninist one'
because it raised the question of taking power from the university's bourgeois academic authorities. The poster, a traditional form of protest written in big Chinese chararacters,
was signed by a young woman instructor, Nieh Yuan-tzu, and
eleven teachers and students. Mao managed to get it published
in the press and broadcast it over the radio. Throughout June,
rebel groups made thousands of similar posters and stuck them
up in universities and streets all over the country. It seemed
the mass movement started by the students was in full swing.
On 2 June, Mao was quoted as saying 'Wind will not cease even
if trees want a rest.' Six days later the *People's Daily* again
revealed Mao's exultation at the upsurge; 'Without destruction
there can be no construction; without blockage there can be
no flow; without stoppage there can be no movement.'

But by mid-June Liu Shao-chi had succeeded in setting the
party apparatus in a contrary motion, intervening to halt the
tide. He adopted the earlier tactic of sending work teams into
institutions (mainly the universities, where his followers were
under pressure) to channel criticisms away from the party
leaders and on to the rebels themselves, a policy of attacking
the many to protect the few.

By early July Mao seemed more isolated within the party than ever. He later recalled how his arguments for the May 16th Notice had been received by the Central Committee. 'I had to take charge of the drafting of the May 16th Notice, in which the question of lines and the question of the two roads was clearly brought up. Most people thought at the time that my understanding was out of date, and at times I was the only person to agree with my own suggestions.'

It was at this crucial stage that he decided to depend yet more heavily on Lin Piao's support. Lin had been urging his supporters to build up Mao's image and appeal to the people over the heads of the party apparatus in the name of Mao. Mao had told Edgar Snow in January 1965 that he saw the need for this, in order to convert loyalty to the party into loyalty to his own line. But by April 1966 he was more wary of Lin Piao's motives. At a meeting in Hangchow he criticised 'those formulations of my friends' which recommended using the Little Red Book of quotations for what he called a 'miraculous' effect.

On 8 July Mao wrote to Chiang Ching in a divided mood, a mixture of resignation and confidence. On the one hand, Lin Piao was pursuing the course of elevating Mao to the position of 'greatest genius', the Great Helmsman and Great Supreme Commander, and using Mao's portrait 'to frighten away spirits', just as pictures of the ancient hero Chung Kuei had been used in the past. On the other hand, Liu Shao-chi had to be 'knocked down' and Lin's forces were the only ones capable of carrying the criticism movement through.

In the letter he told Chiang Ching that he had had to give in to Lin Piao on this issue, and remarked that it was the first time in his life he had had to compromise on a major point of principle. When could this fact be made known, he asked? Perhaps not until after his death, when rightists could well use even the letter he was writing in order to attack the left, using his name. But at that perilous juncture in the spring and summer of 1966, Mao could do nothing but lend weight to the general forces of the left and form an alliance with Lin Piao, since it was not the moment to demoralise the revolutionary forces by criticising the 'ultras' among the leftists: the main task was to hit the rightists.

Mao said he hoped he would be able to struggle against, and overcome, Lin's distortions at a later stage, after the right had been dealt with. In a paragraph of profound self-analysis, he admitted his own limitations were the limitations of any one man. 'When there is no tiger in the mountains the monkey becomes king.' For lack of heroes, he said, a little man became famous. 'There is in me something of the tiger, which is the main thing, and something of the monkey, which is secondary.' He was, he said, a mixture of the tiger's self-confidence and the monkey's diffidence. He was never the complete tiger, any more than he wished to be the complete king.

The letter also shows a broad vision of history, of his own part in it and of the Chinese revolution's significance. He foresaw a time when reaction would very likely restore an anti-revolutionary power in China, even using Mao's name to justify it. The pain with which he expresses this fear suggests his conviction that, indeed, this restoration was inevitable, given the wave-like movement of human history. As he had remarked to Snow, perhaps in a thousand years' time all the revolutionary efforts of man this century, including the ideas of Marxism–Leninism, would appear faintly ridiculous. And yet, Mao wrote to his wife, man advances. He concluded that the progress to socialism and communism would prove to be the factor determining world history in the end, and not the temporary fury of reaction in the trough of a wave.

Mao said in the letter that he gained courage from the hard and bitter soul of Lu Hsun with whose spirit 'he had gone to commune' in a 'cave' that summer. In Mao's eyes Lu Hsun had the ability to strip pretension of its mask and preserve his critical spirit from erosion and compromise. Mao seems to have felt a deep and temporarily enervating disappointment with himself for having lost his April fight with 'my friends' over the use of his image in a desperate attempt to preserve a unity against his, and the revolutionaries', enemies. After the experience of these months he returned to the battle a still ebullient, if sadder, man.

Once again Mao sought to gain courage in a personal victory over natural elements, a victory he could hold up to the nation, especially to the youth, as a symbol of regenerative power. On 16 July he performed the remarkable exploit of swimming fifteen kilometres in the Yangtze River near Wuhan in an hour and five minutes, presumably aided by the strong current. Two days later he returned to Peking, triumphantly announcing his good health and strong determination to a surprised propaganda department who did not issue a communiqué hailing the olympic event until 25 July. On the 26th, to rub the point into a startled party, *People's Daily* quoted Mao as saying, 'No need to be afraid of tidal waves; human society has been evolved out of "tidal waves".'

The next three weeks were a critical stage in the counter-attack by Mao and the Cultural Revolution Group to recover the initiative. Rebel groups, many calling themselves Red Guards, had retaliated against the work teams in the universities in June and July. Cultural Revolution Group leaders Kang Sheng, Chen Po-ta and Chiang Ching had visited the campuses of Peking and Tsinghua universities in the capital to read the big-character posters and to argue in support of the student movement.

On 21 July Mao gave a talk to leaders of the party centre.

Nieh Yuan-tzu's big-character poster of 25 May [put up at Peking University] is the declaration of the Chinese Paris Commune of the sixties of the twentieth century; its significance far surpasses that of the Paris Commune. It is beyond our ability to write this kind of big-character poster.

Much to the rightists' consternation, Mao now charged those who had rounded on the students, including some in his audience, with trying to sabotage the cultural revolution.

> On my return to Peking, I feel sorry that things are so quiet. Some schools are shut; some even suppress student movements. Who [in the past] suppressed student movements? Only the northern warlords. It is anti-Marxist for the Communist Party to be afraid of student movements. Some people talk about the mass line, talk about serving the people every day, but they actually follow a capitalist line and serve the bourgeoisie ...
>
> It will not do to impose restrictions on the masses. Seeing the students rise up, Peking University imposes a restriction on them, euphemistically calling it 'to direct them to the right way'. In fact, it was directing them the wrong way. [2]

On 22 July Mao gave a talk at a meeting of regional party secretaries and members of the Cultural Revolution Group, recalling the work teams from the campuses. He said that the cultural revolution should be led at the local level, not by work teams from outside, but by those who knew something about local conditions, the people themselves, in their own workplaces. He bitterly attacked leaders who ignored or feared criticism.

> So the newspaper offices in Sian and Nanking were besieged for three days and [everybody] was scared stiff. Frightened like that? Oh, you, you do not want a revolution; but now the revolution has come to you. At some places it is forbidden to surround newspaper offices, to go to the provincial [party] committee, or to send people to the State Council. Why are you so scared? When [the revolutionaries] got to the State Council, they were received by some small fry who could not explain a thing. Why was it done that way? If you do not want to step out [and see them], I will. However you argue, it is just a matter of fear ... Go

down to the levels below, stop your routine work, and get some real feeling for things . . .

Comrades at this conference should go to Peking University and the School of Broadcasting to read their big-character posters and to take a look at the places stricken with problems. But perhaps not today, because we are dealing with documents. When you go there to read the posters, say that you are there to learn, to help the revolution, and to ignite [the revolution] in support of revolutionary teachers and students. You are not there to listen to rightist gibberish. For two months now, there has not been an ounce of real understanding, only bureaucratism. Students will surround you. Let them. You will be surrounded as soon as you begin to talk to them. More than a hundred people have been beaten up at the School of Broadcasting. This is the beauty of our age — the left beaten up by the right and thus disciplined. Nothing will be achieved in six months or in a year if we only send work teams. You have to depend on the people on the spot. First, struggle, and then reform. To struggle is to reform and to reform is to construct. [3]

Through Chiang Ching, who went to investigate and to speak at Peking University on 25 July, Mao next told the students themselves that their fight was just. Those who had called their attacks on the party 'counter-revolutionary' and 'against communism' were holding up a shield to protect themselves from criticism. Under the influence of PLA units, Red Guards at the middle school attached to Tsinghua University in Peking had put up a *tatsepao* in July which said, 'We will rebel as long as there are classes and class struggle! We will rebel as long as there are contradictions!' Mao wrote to congratulate them for their spirit on 1 August: 'I am fully behind you.'

An even more explicit public demonstration of Mao's support for the student movement came five days later. From 1 to 12

August the Eleventh Plenary Session of the Eighth Central Committee met to discuss the cultural revolution. In the middle of the meeting, on 5 August, Mao startled all China by issuing his own *tatsepao*, *Bombard the Headquarters*, at what was a decisive point of the deliberations. In his poster he declared his unreserved approval of Nieh Yuan-tzu's poster and the Red Guards, against their party detractors.

> China's first Marxist—Leninist big-character poster and commentator's article on it in the *People's Daily* are indeed superbly written! Comrades, please read them again. But in the last fifty days or so some leading comrades from the central down to the local levels have acted in a diametrically opposite way. Adopting the reactionary stand of the bourgeoisie, they have enforced a bourgeois dictatorship and struck down the surging movement of the great cultural revolution of the proletariat. They have stood facts on their heads and juggled black and white, encircled and suppressed revolutionaries, stifled opinions differing from their own, imposed a white terror, and felt very pleased with themselves. They have puffed up the arrogance of the bourgeoisie and deflated the morale of the proletariat. How poisonous! Viewed in connection with the right deviation in 1962 and the wrong tendency of 1964 which was 'left' in form but right in essence, shouldn't this make one wide awake? [4]

With Mao's authority behind the students' attacks, it was no longer possible for Liu's 'White terror' (as repression by the work teams had come to be called) to be carried out openly and the rightists were forced to change their tactics. Liu was knocked off balance and never recovered. His apparatus thereafter began to shift allegiance, some members coming over to the side of the revolutionary storm, either because of last-minute conversion or of opportunism, others forming new cliques and continuing their struggle under other guises. With Peng Chen and Liu in disgrace for attempting to seize control of the cultural revolution in order to defuse it, the stage became clear for the mass student movement to spread across the nation and convert itself by stages into a workers' and peasants' revolution against party bureaucracy.

Mao's poster helped him to manoeuvre into a dominating position at the eleventh plenary session. Mao had gone to the conference, he later recalled, with the spirit of finally fighting off his isolation. His arguments at the session, which were to be set out in the Central Committee's Sixteen-Point Decision, were supported, he said, by 'a fairly narrow majority'. Liu was very ambiguous, but actually, Mao told Edgar Snow, he was dead against the Sixteen-Point Decision. Yet the decision went through, backed no doubt by representatives of the revolutionary teachers and students for whom Mao had arranged to attend the meeting. Mao had turned the tables. At last he had succeeded in outflanking and isolating Liu.

This achieved and the Central Committee's loyalties narrowly won for the time being, Mao proceeded to publish the outline principles the session had laid down to guide the cultural revolution as it entered its first period of maximum velocity. On 8 August the Central Committee issued its Sixteen-Point Decision, based on Mao's draft.

The opening paragraphs made a distinction between what was desirable in the long term and what was necessary and possible immediately. Sketching the long-term movement, they said:

> Although the bourgeoisie has been overthrown, it is still trying to use the old ideas, culture, customs and habits of the exploiting classes to corrupt the masses, capture their minds and endeavour to stage a come-back. The proletariat must do just the opposite: it must meet head-on every challenge of the bourgeoisie in the ideological field and use the new ideas, culture, customs and habits of the proletariat to change the mental outlook of the whole of society.

As for what could be done now:

At present, our objective is to struggle against and over-throw those persons in power taking the capitalist road, to criticise and repudiate the bourgeois reactionary academic 'authorities' and the ideology of the bour-geoisie and all other exploiting classes, and to transform education, literature and art and all other parts of the superstructure not in correspondence with the socialist economic base, to facilitate the consolidation and development of the socialist system.

Noting that the cultural revolutionary groups, committees and other organisational groups which had already begun to emerge in the course of struggle were 'something new and of great historic importance', the Sixteen-Point Decision went on to spell out how these new forms should best develop.

It is necessary to institute a system of general elections, like that of the Paris Commune, for electing members to the cultural revolutionary groups and committees and delegates to the cultural revolutionary congresses. The list of candidates should be put forward by the revol-utionary masses after full discussion, and the elections should be held after the masses have discussed the lists over and over again.

The masses are entitled at any time to criticise members of the cultural revolutionary groups and com-mittees, and delegates elected to the cultural revol-utionary congresses. If these members or delegates prove incompetent, they can be replaced through election or recalled by the masses after discussion.

This extremely significant decision would have transferred power at all levels from the party alone to elected assemblies made up mainly of workers, peasants and students, and only partly of functionaries. Thus the dictatorship of the prolet-ariat over the bourgeoisie would be strengthened. The decision had a galvanising effect on the workers in the cities and their radical spokesmen; and it gave a firm backing to the Shanghai Commune, which was established for three weeks in February 1967 before it was superseded in a resurgence of power by representatives of the old administrative apparatus and the PLA. The question of whether local organs of power should consist of elected representatives of the masses at their workplace, in counties and in cities, was one that was never successfully settled. But the fact that the question was asked made it certain that the ideal of the Paris Commune would be kept alive for a later generation to fulfil.

A similar spirit is manifest in the instructions on methods of struggle.

> In the Great Proletarian Cultural Revolution the only method is for the masses to liberate themselves, and any method of doing things on their behalf must not be used. Trust the masses, rely on them and respect their initiative. Cast out fear. Don't be afraid of disorder . . . The method to be used in debate [among the masses] is to present the facts, reason things out, and persuade through reasoning. [5]

The decision also recalled that a key problem was the training of 'Red successors' to carry the revolution into the next generation. School courses, it pointed out once again, should be combined with productive labour so that students would 'become labourers with socialist consciousness and culture'.

On 18 August 1966, at the first of a series of Red Guard rallies in Peking, Mao, wearing army uniform, allowed a girl student of Tsinghua University to pin on him the red armband of the Red Guards. He stood on the rostrum on Tien An Men in central Peking from where he had read his speech founding the People's Republic on 1 October 1949. Now he presided over the demolition of the upper echelons of the party that had made the People's Republic possible, for the sake, he would say, of the party's — and the Republic's — rejuvenation. With Lin Piao standing beside him and Liu Shao-chi significantly apart, he reviewed columns of marching young people totalling one million. There would be six further rallies, each of as many students and young people, during the next three months. From the second rally onwards Liu was never again photographed on the rostrum. During the winter, street posters denounced Liu, and in the spring a nation-wide movement was begun to study and criticise his writings.

Red Guards travelled throughout China 'exchanging revolutionary experiences' and attacking the Four Olds — old ideas, culture, customs and habits — according to the thesis, deriving from Mao, that the ancient must be made to serve the modern, and the old be displaced to establish the new. Violence and chaos were attendant on the students' activities.

On 23 August at a work conference of the centre, Mao advised, 'Let the chaos go on for a few months . . . It does not matter if there are no provincial party committees. [Most of these had had their offices surrounded and their work incapacitated by the Red Guards.] The *People's Daily* has published an editorial, calling on the workers, peasants and soldiers to stop interfering with students' activities, and advocating non-violent, not violent, struggles.'

In fact, young workers were already forming their own rebel groups in the big cities and turning criticism onto their factory managements. Factory party committees were already being overthrown. On 24 October Mao called on the country as a whole to 'Grasp Revolution, Promote Production', a slogan that showed Mao's conviction that a truly revolutionised working class, with no bureaucracy putting brakes on them, would turn their spiritual force into a material force, and output would increase.

The following day at another work conference of the centre, Mao said, 'The great cultural revolution raised havoc . . . my comment on Nieh Yuan-tzu's big-character poster, my letter to the Tsinghua Middle School and my own big-character poster . . . It was done . . . in a short space of time but it had tremendous momentum — both exceeding my expectations. The tidal waves strike you with all their might. Since I am responsible for this havoc, I can hardly blame you if you grumble.' He went on first to praise the effectiveness of *tatsepaos*, next to examine what the attacks were aiming at and then to apportion the blame for the deterioration of relations inside the party which had made the cultural revolution necessary.

> [From January to May], . . . there were many articles and directives from the centre [about the cultural revolution] which failed to attract much attention. But big-character posters and the Red Guards attacked, and they succeeded in attracting attention. It is impossible to ignore them. The revolution has come to your door-step . . . Who wants to knock you down? I do not. I do not believe that the Red Guards want to do that either . . . [We] cannot shift all the blame to Comrade [Liu] Shao-chi and [Teng] Hsiao-ping. They are to be blamed: so is the centre [as a whole]. The centre has not done its job . . . in seventeen years, the first and second lines have led to disunity. The responsibility belongs to others and myself. [6]

As the struggle 'opened wide' and began to be taken up in the factories and communes, the Central Committee drafted two documents under Mao's direction to guide the cultural revolution in industry and agriculture. The first stressed that the struggle in industry

> . . . is developed for the purpose of promoting revolutionisation of one's mind and moving production forward . . . The leading bodies of factories and mines are not permitted to attack and retaliate upon the masses who have conducted criticisms and brought facts to light, nor are they allowed to deduct wages and dismiss the workers because the latter have conducted criticisms and brought facts to light . . .

The worker masses have the right to set up revolutionary organisations during the cultural revolution . . . Don't let the undesirable characters make a cat's-paw of you, and don't bring about a state of antagonism [between workers]. Persist in struggle by reasoning and refrain from struggle by violence. Don't strike others with your hand . . .

The working personnel of workers' organisations must not, as a rule, detach themselves from production . . .

Students may go to factories and mines according to plan to build revolutionary ties and exchange revolutionary experiences with the workers in the latter's leisure hours. They may also go to work, labour and study with the workers according to plan and discuss problems of cultural revolution together. Workers may also send their representatives to local schools to build revolutionary ties. All those who go to build revolutionary ties with others must not monopolise things and interfere with the cultural revolution of other units.

The second repeated the theme of 'stimulating production' and went on to state that the main aim in the countryside was to allow the masses 'to be their own masters' by removing rightist cadres, attacking the Four Olds and fostering 'the new ideas, new culture, new customs and new habits.' It went on,

The organ of power leading the great cultural revolution in the countryside shall be the cultural revolution committees formed of poor and lower-middle peasants. These committees shall be elected democratically by congresses of poor and lower-middle peasants, and may be re-elected or dismissed at any time if they are incompetent. The leading groups in charge of production, after being consolidated or re-elected through discussion among the masses, shall be responsible for the work of production, distribution, purchase and supply . . .

The great cultural revolution in the countryside should be conducted by means of free contending, free airing of views, big-character posters and great debates, *ie* the practice of extensive democracy . . . It is . . . permissible to organise groups of revolutionary students to go to the countryside for the purpose of establishing revolutionary ties. They should eat, live and labour together with the poor and lower-middle peasants and take part in the great cultural revolution in the countryside, but they may not take everything into their own hands. [7]

Three peasants of Liuling, near Yenan, later told Jan Myrdal how Red Guards had come to their village in September 1966.

First, seven of them. The second time, ten . . . Each group stayed for a week or ten days. That was how the cultural revolution began among us.

The Red Guards came with the book of quotations. They read out to us quotations we'd never heard before. They made speeches and arranged discussions. We welcomed them by beating on drums. They came to us in our caves. We warmed the *kang* for them, so they shouldn't catch cold. They paid their way. All of them . . .

I had eight of them living in my home [said the second peasant]. They all came from Sian. They were about eighteen years old. They spread Mao Tse-tung Thought. They asked whether we had any problems in the brigade, whether the cadres had been making any mistakes. They mobilised the masses and held big discussions. They urged us to speak out openly and write big-character posters. 'You must pluck up courage and criticise things that are wrong,' they told me. 'We are Chairman Mao's Red Guards. Chairman Mao supports the poor peasants. We aren't afraid of criticising.'

The Red Guards wanted to hear everything about how we used to live in the old society . . . how we'd had to sell my two youngest brothers during the 1928 famine.

After they left Liuling, Red Guards managed to trace one of

this man's missing brothers. 'And so,' he said, 'after all these years, we found each other again.'

The third poor peasant, who was prone 'to get angry with folk and bawl them out', was secretary of the local Youth League; he had never been criticised by the masses before, but the arrival of the Red Guards changed this.

> For the Red Guards from Peking . . . talked with our youngsters in the village and formed a Red Guard section and began to criticise our cadres. That's something they'd never have dared to do before they met the Red Guards from the big cities. [8]

Mao was already beginning to pick up the pieces. With the left mobilised and the revolution passing through the country, he began to examine what possible forms of power could grow out of the creative chaos. He was moving the revolution into a long period of 'criticism and repudiation of bourgeois ideology' and an even longer period of 'transformation' to a new administration that would hopefully be more answerable to the people. Disturbed at the increasingly pointless disorder, Mao decreed on 29 January 1967 against 'arbitrary treatment' of reactionaries. Much of this disorder was provoked by the old party authorities themselves to set worker against worker in an effort to protect themselves.

Provincial and urban party leaders, most notably in Shanghai, split up Mao's directive, 'Grasp Revolution; Promote Production', into two parts, at first stressing the latter at the expense of the former. They manoeuvred workers' groups to oppose the revolutionary students, while encouraging them to confine their own activities to production. They next adopted the opposite tactic, emphasising only the first part of the directive, and paid workers bonus wages and travel allowances to leave production and 'Grasp Revolution' in the hope of bringing economic chaos. They fomented strikes and instigated workers to flock to the banks and withdraw their deposits by force. Becoming wise to this manipulation, Shanghai workers formed dozens of rebel groups and rose in the 'January Storm', 1967, and seized power from the municipal authorities.

On 5 February the Shanghai People's Commune was set up, modelled on the Paris Commune and composed of a number of rebel workers' and students' groups. It omitted a number of others who, in the next few weeks, bitterly contested their exclusion or equally bitterly condemned the commune as yet another creation of the functionaries. A similar commune was set up by workers in the industrial city of Taiyuan.

For twenty days Mao and the Cultural Revolution Group in Peking deliberated whether to support the Shanghai Commune. They were anxiously awaiting the formation of new power bodies which could provide models for the rest of the country where the situation was becoming rather too turbulent even for Mao. Chen Po-ta and Chiang Ching said that Peking, too, should have its commune.

Although it had arisen 'from the bottom up', part of the power of the Shanghai Commune had already been appropriated by local functionaries and by members of the Cultural Revolution Group, led by Chang Chun-chiao. Nevertheless it did by and large represent a genuine unit of proletarian power. But while Chang Chun-chiao was in Peking trying to sort out whether the Cultural Revolution Group should come out in support of the Shanghai Commune, another power seizure in the north-eastern province of Heilungkiang provided more conservative elements with an alternative model to the risky Shanghai venture. Heilungkiang's new organ of power was a 'three-way alliance' between rebel leaders, high party officials who were considered loyal to Mao's line, and high army officers.

Worried that recent attacks on the Cultural Revolution Group itself would lead to attempts to overthrow all party cadres, and not merely the rightists, Mao apparently concluded that the Shanghai Commune was unrepresentative of a power structure suited to China at that stage of economic and political development. If before the cultural revolution Mao had been particularly worried about the 'democratic' side of democratic-centralism, as the revolution got under way he began to see the need again for centralism. In the event Mao went along with those, especially Chou En-lai and some PLA leaders, who wanted the re-imposition of centralism to be clearly expressed in whatever new organs were to be built up.

Chang Chun-chiao therefore returned to Shanghai with the message that the Shanghai Commune should change its name to the Shanghai Municipal Revolutionary Committee and follow the model of Heilungkiang, which by then the party press was extolling as the way forward for the whole country. On 24 February the Shanghai Commune was dissolved and the Shanghai Municipal Revolutionary Committee set up in its place. This was a body much more inclined to reinstate those '95 percent of cadres' who, once criticised, had 'reformed' and who, though they had committed mistakes, were in essence 'good.' The revolutionary committee and not the commune was to be the model for the rebuilding of the power structure throughout China. Thereafter, under PLA auspices, revolutionary committees were to be created as provisional organs of power at all levels. These 'three-way alliances' were made up of soldiers, revolutionary cadres and workers or peasants, including Red Guards. In factories and other units they were at first elected by the mass of workers at the workplace, but by 1971, with no new elections held, the revolutionary committees had largely been superseded by the restored, and unelected, party committees.

The communes, which were intended to have made the administration, including the party, permanently responsive to the base through elected representative assemblies of workers, were not mentioned again by the leaders of the Cultural Revolution Group, although the formation of organisations along the lines of the Paris Commune had been one of the aims of the cultural revolution spelled out six months previously in the Central Committee's Sixteen-Point Decision. Supporters of the idea, however, continued to praise the initiative of Shanghai and Taiyuan in the months to come and some of its Red Guard adherents turned on Mao and Chou as having sold out the cultural revolution to the old bureaucracy.

The resort to the more conservative organ of the revoltionary committee did not, however, have the immediate effect the Cultural Revolution Group hoped for. Although power seizures followed quickly in the rest of the country, they faced heavy opposition, not only by the entrenched rightists in the old administrations but by new leftist rebels who claimed legitimacy by their part in the earlier struggle and who now accused the centre of betraying the principles of the proletarian left. In many provinces old party leaders formed armed bands of workers and peasants in bloody attempts to suppress these rebel groups. Mao instructed the PLA to intervene to separate the contestants in the interest of a greater unity, but few listened. The rebel groups themselves also degenerated, engaging in pointless factional combat, which, aided by overreaction on the part of some army commanders, soon involved virtual armies of warriors, all claiming they spoke in Mao's name, joining battle with stones, swords, sticks, rifles, machine-guns and even artillery, in prolonged attempts to establish their own righteousness. These mock-heroic — and in some cases genuinely heroic — battles were quickly exploited by old and new power seekers in the party, especially in the more remote southern and western provinces.

In an effort to lay a better basis for the period of 'transformation', Mao mapped out a nation-wide criticism of Liu Shao-chi, still referred to in public not by his name but as 'China's Khrushchev' or 'the top party person taking the capitalist road'. Mao said that Liu should be criticised 'until he stinks', but he did not want to vilify Liu as a person. It was Liu's ideas that should be repudiated. Mao described this campaign of criticism as 'a phenomenon affecting the destiny of China and the world'. Beginning in Shanghai in February 1967, extending throughout the country by April and continuing until September, workers, peasants, soldiers and students undertook a systematic analysis of Liu's writings, speeches and actions, especially of his stress on self-cultivation, slavishness and blind obedience in party members.

A number of further counter-currents, however, developed in the first half of 1967. The 'February Adverse Current', in which Tan Chen-lin, a member of the Central Committee, tried to 'reverse the verdicts' on Liu Shao-chi and Teng Hsiao-ping, was resisted by the Cultural Revolution Group and the Red Guards of the departments in his Ministry of Agriculture and the agricultural colleges. A second counter-current, the 'March Evil Wind', was an attempt to reverse the verdict passed on the February Adverse Current.

A third setback, the 'Wuhan Incident', occurred in July. Chen Tsai-tao, commander of the Wuhan Military Region, staged a 'counter-revolutionary coup' by abducting two emissaries from Peking, vice-premier Hsieh Fu-chih and Wang Li (the latter a member of the Cultural Revolution Group) who had arrived in Wuhan to sort out the factions and had sided with rebel groups against Chen. They were held for two days and then released when local revolutionary organisations overcame the rightists with the aid of PLA units sent by Lin Piao.

A more complex and longer lasting attempt to resist the Cultural Revolution Group's new line was made by what came to be called the 'ultra-left' May 16 Corps, led by some members of the Cultural Revolution Group itself. Reacting against the army's intervention and the re-instatement of many cadres, the May 16 Corps tried to commandeer the leadership of the cultural revolution and raise further anti-rightist storms that would topple the majority of cadres and would also extend the cultural revolution into the army. For a time in May and August 1967 they succeeded in winning control of the Foreign Ministry. Their leaders, Wang Li, Kuan Feng and Chi Pen-yu, were Chiang Ching's assistants in the Cultural Revolution Group. Their opponents claimed that they and other 'small reptiles' tried to isolate Chou En-lai from the Cultural Revolution Group, and 'sow dissension in Chairman Mao's headquarters.' The Corps was exposed and 'pulled out' by September 1967 but it was later asserted that they had had connections with a higher protector, Lin Piao. These conspiracies, factional struggles and 'incidents' pulled the level of struggle down to that of personal rivalries in many places.

Other 'ultra-leftist' groups lower down in the party and many Red Guard groups outside it continued to advocate getting rid of 95 percent of the cadres and all the leaders, saying they were tainted with the ideology of capitalism. This persistent upsurge of 'ultra-leftism' forced a partial retraction by those in the Cultural Revolution Group, led by Chou En-lai and now backed by Mao, who were concerned to get the destructive stage converted into the constructive stage as soon as possible, to avoid any further dislocation of China's economy.

During the Wuhan Incident at the end of July Mao had sanctioned the use of force to defend the revolutionary left. But seeing his instruction distorted ('Arm the left!' echoed Chiang Ching in a number of speeches to students and rebel groups), by September he had changed tactics. After touring north, central-south and east China to see developments for himself, summarise them and make recommendations, he appealed to the conflicting and often fighting groups to reason things out from the point of view of class struggle in their efforts to create revolutionary committees and said they should judge the cadres they were criticising from the same angle.

Even in June, in the wake of the Shanghai storm, he had declared,

> The method of simply rejecting everything and negating everything, of directing the struggle against the cadres who shoulder most of the responsibility and do most of the work, or against the 'heads' of departments, must be abandoned.

On 8 August, *People's Daily* quoted him as saying,

> Cadres who have made mistakes can re-establish themselves, provided that they do not persist with their mistakes, but reform them, and are forgiven by the revolutionary masses. [9]

But now he began to stress unity. The workers' rebel organisations should unite. An editorial in the same paper on 14 September said that Mao thought

> ... within the working class, there is no basic clash of interests. Under proletarian dictatorship, the working class has absolutely no reason to split into two hostile factional organisations. [10]

The old slogan, 'Unity- criticism and self-criticism -unity' was rebroadcast. Mao called for unity too amongst students whose 'grand alliances' he said should accord with the principle of alliance with the masses, not with other factions against yet more factions.

These 'grand alliances' of the 'proletarian revolutionaries' were to preserve the newly created 'extensive democracy' (that is, widespread debate) and were not to stifle it. The three-way alliances created out of the grand alliances, despite their increasing reliance on old cadres and military representatives, were still intended to carry over the gains of the cultural revolution into the renovated and rebuilt administrative structure. As the three-way alliances were also the basis of the new revolutionary committees, it is clear Mao hoped to salvage something of the mass participation which had been the hallmark of the cultural revolution, 'the mobil-isation of the masses from below', 'the emancipation of the masses by the masses'. In the stage of transformation that had now begun, Mao intended the struggle to preserve more than a token of mass involvement.

In every factory, commune, office, school and university where issues had been opened wide, the twin methods of alliance and debate gradually began to cohere the disputing elements into something like a constructive peace. But it would take another year of even more widespread factionalism for the process to work itself out. The stages of struggle-criticism-transformation, beginning in 1967, continued until 1969 and in some units until later still.

The revolutionary committees were built on the principle Mao put forward, 'Combat self and criticise revisionism', which he claimed in November 1967 was 'the basic ideological programme' of the cultural revolution. On the road to trans-formation, 'struggle' was defined as the process by which the people 'exposed, repudiated, overthrew and discredited' the leaders who followed the bourgeois line. 'Criticism' meant to dispute and repudiate the ideas emanating from those leaders. 'Transformation' itself consisted in simplifying the adminis-trative structures, changing irrational rules and regulations and organising cadres to go to the grassroots to take part in production. By September 1968 revolutionary committees had been established in all provinces, except Taiwan, and work went ahead on rebuilding party committees.

Mao underlined the need for the working class to lead this transformation of the superstructure, especially in education. In August 1968, workers' propaganda teams entered schools and universities to revolutionise education under their leader-ship in co-operation with soldiers, students and teachers. The teams, Mao said, should remain in schools and universities permanently and 'take part in fulfilling all the tasks of "struggle-criticism-transformation" and they will always lead the schools'. In the countryside, schools were to be run by the poor and lower-middle peasants. In some case, soldiers joined the workers in trying to forge a unity between student factions, employing not the gun but political argument. Some workers and soldiers were killed or injured when they refused to fight back in confrontations with university students which were often prolonged, sometimes lasting months.

School and university courses in all subjects began to be tied in more closely with work in factories and communes. Workers became teachers, and teachers became workers. This accorded with Mao's cycle, 'Practice, knowledge, again practice, and again knowledge', by which he described the process through which people learn. Workers and peasants lectured in university and school classrooms. Qualifications for enrolment at universities were revised in favour of labouring people: 'Students,' said Mao, 'should be selected from workers and peasants with practical experience, and they should return to production after a few years' study.'

Mao had become so unimpressed by Red Guard factionalism that, addressing some of their warring leaders on 27 July 1968, he told them bluntly, 'You have let me down and, moreover, you have disappointed the workers, peasants and soldiers of China.' He turned to another method to try to train these 'red successors.' From the end of 1968, millions of university students and middle school leavers were settled in the countryside in the hope they would gain knowledge through work, the lesson of the soil. These young settlers were detailed to relate their consciousness, raised, or at least enflamed, by political work in the Red Guard groups, to the practical problems of rural development. Apart from learning how peasants transformed nature, they also served the useful purpose of teaching old peasants how to read and write and introducing younger peasants to the history of their urban struggles.

Realising that one explanation for the various factions' espousal of mindless action was that they were short on theoretical knowledge, Mao set in motion a vast campaign of study, which he hoped would 'liberate materialist philosophy from the confines of the lecture-rooms and textbooks' and place it where he believed it belonged — in the minds of the workers and commune members as they worked in the factory and field. From the relatively simple 'three constantly-read articles' [11] which, with the *Quotations*, were the staple reading matter of the cultural revolution, factory and commune study groups went on to read and discuss major works of Marx, Engels, Lenin, Stalin and Mao. It had long been Mao's intention to convert the Marxist canon from a prerogative of scholars into 'sharp weapons' for class struggle, thus attempting to transform Marxism from a philosophy of practice into the practice of philosophy.

For the remoulding of higher intellectuals, officials and party workers, Mao backed the setting up in October 1968 of May 7th Cadre Schools. Established mainly in wastelands, which the cadres were expected to open up into fertile lands, these schools were attached to all government departments and other big units, including universities. In the course of this labour the cadres' thinking would hopefully be changed; they would identify with the labouring people and recognise, by creating it themselves, that it was labour that created wealth and that therefore it was the masses of labouring people, and not one or two heroes, or leaders, still less intellectuals, who created history. All cadres were to attend these schools in rotation for one or two years.

Thus the struggle returned to where it had begun, in education. The cultural revolution, coming full circle, at last provided, in a planned national movement, for three of the main points in Mao's programme since the Great Leap Forward — the reformation of the university and school system; the remoulding through labour of young people and cadres, especially intellectuals; and the popularisation of Marxist theoretical study.

The Ninth Party Congress of April 1969 drew together the strands of the cultural revolution in what Mao called at its start 'A congress of unity and a congress of victory.' But it was a flexible unity and a short-term victory. In the report he read to the Congress, Lin Piao quoted Mao as insisting,

> We cannot speak of final victory. Not even for decades ... The final victory of a socialist country ... involves the victory of the world revolution and the abolition of the system of exploitation of man by man over the whole globe. [12]

The new party constitution, which the congress adopted, restated — and wrote into the party rules — the principles that there are classes, class contradictions and class struggle in the period of transition from socialism to communism, thus officially rejecting the line of Liu Shao-chi who, in 1956, had said that the question of whether socialism or capitalism wins in China was already solved. Far from ending class struggle, the cultural revolution was seen by the two leading speakers at the Ninth Congress as opening the way for more in the future. As Mao had said many times before and repeated not long after the cultural revolution began, a victory is not a conclusion but a stage.

> The victory or defeat of the revolution can be determined only over a long period of time. If it is badly handled, there is always the danger of a capitalist restoration. All members of the party and all the people of our country must not think that after one, two, three, or four great cultural revolutions there will be peace and quiet. They must always be on the alert and must never relax their vigilance. [13]

It seems, however, that Mao and Lin, the latter backed by Chen Po-ta, differed at this Congress over the extent to which party cadres, once criticised and 'remoulded', could be brought back to their posts. The draft political report, drawn up by Chen, was rejected as erroneous by the Central

Committee, and the report that Lin Piao read at the Congress was a further one, drafted under the supervision of Mao.

Meanwhile, rebuilding the party continued throughout 1969, using the revolutionary cadres and reformed cadres as a nucleus and bringing in new talent, especially from among the young. The new party constitution added 'Mao Tse-tung Thought' once again to the Marxism—Leninism which was held to be the theoretical basis guiding it, thus restoring the legitimacy of Mao's Thought which had been lost when it had been omitted from the 1956 constitution.

Mao's stress on unity at the Ninth Congress reflected the need for preparing against war as well as grasping revolution and promoting production. Skirmishes and minor battles along the Russian border early in 1969 reminded the country that the Soviet Union's political opposition to China's revolutionary advance was expressed militarily in a formidable army equipped with rockets and nuclear weapons, much of which were poised for use against China. China's development of atomic weapons and space satellites showed she had advanced technically. Her strategy for preparing against war was defensive and involved millions of civilians digging air-raid shelters and underground escape routes for the populations of the big cities. Grain reserves were built up. More power was devolved to the provinces and the structures of military and civil administration were simplified to provide more flexibility and self-sufficiency at local levels in the event of an attack.

With the decrease in US power, shown by its defeat in Vietnam and its inability to intervene openly in China since liberation, China's relations with the other 'paper tiger', the Soviet Union, took on new importance. Mao's analysis that the Russian people would resume struggle in the long run did not dispose of the fact that China had to continue to have state relations with the revisionist leaders. Negotiations began on the border dispute and the party's policy remained 'to develop relations of friendship, mutual assistance and co-operation with socialist countries on the principle of proletarian internationalism.'

On 20 May 1970, following the US intervention in Cambodia and the successive waves of international protest against American aggression in Vietnam, Mao wrote a message of support for all those fighting US imperialism. He said that the new upsurge in the world-wide struggle against the United States indicated that, though there was still the danger of world war, 'Revolution is the main trend in the world today.' The United States seemed big and powerful, but a small weak nation could defeat it, if the people 'rise in struggle, take up arms and grasp in their hands the destiny of their country.' The example of the Indo-Chinese peoples in particular showed that it was not the people who feared US imperialism, but the US imperialists who feared the people.

It was not until August and September 1970 that Mao was able to begin to deal with the major power that had occupied the ultra-leftist wing of the party during the cultural revolution. For more than two years the affairs of the May 16 Corps had been investigated. As the layers of protectors began to be uncovered, Lin Piao was forced into a corner. At the August–September second plenary session of the Ninth Congress, convened at Lushan, Lin, whose succession to Mao as party chairman was now written into the party constitution, began to push a desperate, if at first veiled, attack. He tried to get Mao to fill the post of chairman of the Republic, sometimes referred to as president, which had been vacant since the deposing of Liu Shao-chi and his expulsion from the party in October 1968. Lin Piao's aim was to succeed Mao in this post too. Mao replied by making it clear he no longer approved of this office, and had always regretted its existence even when, until December 1958, he had occupied it himself. Mao thought it put too much power in the hands of one man, above the party and the administration.

Ascribing Mao's 'development of Marxism—Leninism' to 'his genius', Lin Piao used Mao's praise of his originality during the cultural revolution to prove that he was not only a successor to Mao's office but to his 'genius' too. This spirit even transmitted itself, in a redoubled state, to the next generation: Lin called his own son 'a supergenius' and gave him an important post in the air force. After his downfall, Lin was accused, among other things, of having wanted to set up a Lin family dynastic rule after Mao's death. But in 1970 Lin felt his power, as he conceived it, shaking, as the role of the PLA diminished following the rebuilding of the party.

The army's very success in the cultural revolution had prevented it playing the classical role in militarised states, that of a power force independent of the civil force. Its democratic spirit of joining in production in order to 'serve the people' and not 'ride on the people's backs' had merited Mao's call to the people to learn from its example. It had preserved itself as a genuine 'people's army', close to the workers and peasants, relatively free of political careerism among its lower-ranking officers and encouraging an advanced socialist consciousness among all its ranks through cultivating its close ties with the poorest people. Now that the party and civil administrations were being restored, the PLA's representatives on revolutionary committees in factories, communes and other establishments were gradually withdrawn or reduced in number.

Mao told the French foreign minister, Maurice Schumann, in July 1972 that Lin Piao had resisted this reminder of the army's secondary status, wanting military power to be elevated to the position of main political force. At the Lushan conference in the late summer of 1970 Chen Po-ta spoke for Lin in pushing forward the idea that Mao's 'genius' should be rewarded with the chairmanship of the Republic. Led by Mao and Chou En-lai the Central Committee rejected Lin's line on 'genius', the chairmanship and the role of the military. Chen Po-ta was defeated and his motives called into question; after investigation, it transpired that Chen was a leader of the May 16 Corps, so Lin resorted to conspiracy.

Though repudiated politically, Lin was not dismissed. Indeed, he retained his official position as Mao's successor up until his conspiracy was exposed. After his line had been defeated, Lin offered no political threat, since he had no power base outside a few armed service leaders and his own personal relationship with Mao. Evidently, Mao thought Lin's previous history estimable enough, and his present known opposition was not sufficiently severe for him not to continue to occupy the post of vice-chairman of the party. Meanwhile, Mao hoped to win him over.

At the same time, a swing to the right was evidently gathering momentum. The new foreign policy line from the end of 1970 was distinctly conciliatory to those who a year before had been China's bitterest enemies, among them the government of the United States. At home, many old cadres were easing themselves back into important positions, after rehabilitation, fully in conformity with Mao's view that cadres could be re-instated, once reformed.

The ultra-left was being attacked for using certain works, or even just single sentences, of Mao's writing out of context; the new line was to study Marxism—Leninism comprehensively. It was being restressed that in the combination of theory and practice, the element of theory must not be neglected. The militant utilitarianism which had led some party activists to uphold 'the two hands' over the 'mind' was being corrected.

Furthermore, Mao's superhuman image, so assiduously built up by Lin and the propaganda apparatus and which Mao had been so unhappy about in the spring of 1966, was being dismantled on Mao's orders. The language used in reference to Mao was rationalised. Little Red Books of the quotations grew scarcer and the omnipresent portraits, statues, busts and bill boards were steadily removed.

Lastly, and most significantly, the power of the revolutionary committees, elected in 1967-8 as representatives of the people in their workplaces, was passing back into the hands of the party committees. The party was in command, supposedly refreshed by 'new blood' but in practice dominated in many of its organs by a majority of old rightists. The 'capitalist-roaders' had suffered a defeat but they were not defeated. They were weaker than before the cultural revolution but they were still there.

By 1969 many leaders in the Central Committee believed that US imperialism was beginning a tactical shift brought about by defeats suffered in Indo-China. Chou En-lai sought and won Mao's backing for an attempt to take advantage of the contradictions in Washington's new position. Mao's 'revolutionary diplomacy' (talking with his enemies as a method of fighting them, such as he had employed in previous negotiations with the United States in Yenan, and with Chiang Kai-shek in Chungking in 1945) was revived as a tactic. China began to plot a course of developing direct contacts with the American government, of which Nixon's visit to Peking in February 1972 would prove to be one stage. The Chinese government launched a new international propaganda campaign to dispute the right of either the United States or the Soviet Union to exercise overlordship of the earth. The communists' taking of China's seat in the United Nations provided them with a forum for pursuing this policy.

Defeated in his attempt to oppose Mao and Chou En-lai, Lin Piao began his plot in December 1970. From 22 to 24 March 1971 his agents, including his son Lin Li-kuo, drew up an Outline for Project 571, the Chinese for the figures 571 being homophonic for 'armed uprising'. In their project, the conspirators made various plans for removing Mao, either by arrest at home or on tour, or by surrounding a meeting of the Central Committee and arresting its members including Mao; or, in the last resort, by a palace revolt and assassination.

After the power was taken, a White terror would reign, eliminating all cadres at every level who opposed Lin's supremacy.

While this plot was being hatched in the spring and summer of 1971, Mao continued to make efforts to 'recover' his old comrade after the failure of Lin's bid to 'take over power, and usurp the leadership of the party, the government and the army' at the plenary session the previous autumn. In this Mao was markedly unsuccessful.

It seems the conspirators, who counted among their number Lin's wife, Yeh Chun, and some service chiefs, finally decided to assassinate Mao when he was touring south China in September 1971. Mao had spent the previous three weeks touring the Kwangchow and Nanking military regions, talking to local commanders about the need for the PLA completely to submit itself to party orders. 'I don't think the armed forces will rebel,' he challenged the commanders in one talk.

According to the Central Committee's Document Number 24 of July 1972, Mao left Shanghai on 11 September by train and arrived in Peking on the afternoon of the 12th. Lin's conspirators had thought he would travel by plane and their first plan was to make an attempt on Mao's life at Shanghai airport. Mao's change to a train brought a second plan into operation – to dynamite Mao's train and to attack it by plane with rockets. This plan misfired because the junior officer entrusted with the task refused to carry it out. Depending on the success of these moves, an attack was to have been made on the leaders' headquarters in Peking to capture the entire Central Committee.

Lin's contingency plan had provided that if all these attempts failed, he was to flee to Kwangchow (Canton) and set up an alternative Central Committee there. He had planes standing by for this eventuality. But at some stage Lin Piao's daughter, Lin Li-heng, tipped off the air force unit in which she worked and told them about her suspicions of her father's activities. Premier Chou En-lai found out about a plane waiting at Shanhaikuan airport north-east of

Peking. This was one that Lin had standing by to take him to Kwangchow on the morning of the 13th. Chou ordered all flights grounded and the PLA alerted.

On the evening of the 12th Lin got wind that the plot was discovered, perhaps through a service chief in Peking, or perhaps, according to one version, because Mao phoned him at the seaside resort of Peitaiho, near Shanhaikuan, where Lin was staying, and from some remark of Mao's assumed he was discovered. At 2:30 on the morning of the 13th Lin rushed to the plane at Shanhaikuan with his wife and son, his car being damaged in the dash. He climbed aboard up the pilot's ladder — 'his wife's feet knocking his bald pate below, he was in such a hurry', the airport staff said later — and the plane took off without proper take-off instructions or routine, without a navigator and without a second pilot. Instead of going to Kwangchow in the south, the plane headed north-west towards Russia. In one story, Chou is supposed to have asked Mao, watching the plane on the radar at the air operations room, whether he should order it to be shot down. Mao objected, saying 'How would we explain it to the people? Let him flee. That will expose him.' Two hours later the plane crashed in Mongolia. No reason for the crash was given in the Central Committee's document. Lin, his wife and son and other chiefs of the army, navy and air force were killed. In the plane were found a collection of secret party documents and currency of various countries.

Documents related to the conspiracy, including a photostat of the Outline for Project 571, were circulated in the party and later among the people for discussion in early 1972. Mao ordered a rectification campaign in the PLA: whereas the people had learnt from the army in the cultural revolution, the army had now to learn from the people.

At the forty-fifth anniversary of the founding of the PLA, on 1 August 1972, an article in *People's Daily* turned the page on the Lin Piao episode.

Since the second plenary session of the Ninth Central Committee of the party [the August—September 1970 meeting at Lushan] the People's Liberation Army, with the warm attention of Chairman Mao, has carried out education in ideology and political line and achieved remarkable results. Armed with the three basic principles put forward by Chairman Mao [after Lin's attempted coup], namely 'practise Marxism and not revisionism; unite and don't split; be open and above-board and don't intrigue and conspire', the commanders and fighters have made a deep-going criticism of Liu Shao-chi and other swindlers [*ie* Lin Piao]. This has raised the political consciousness of the People's Liberation Army. It has become a common practice among the cadres and fighters to make a serious study of works by Marx, Engels, Lenin and Stalin and Chairman Mao's works ... Any careerist or conspirator who wants to undermine this army is only daydreaming ... Chairman Mao has pointed out: 'The correctness or incorrectness of the ideological and political line decides everything.' When the party's line is correct, we have everything; if we have no men, we will have them; if we have no rifles, we can get them; if we do not have state power, we will be able to seize it; if the line is incorrect, we will lose what we already have ... The PLA is a genuine people's army under the absolute leadership of the party and an instrument for carrying out the party's programme and line. [14]

For the time being, the party had succeeded in re-asserting its full authority over the military.

Unlike most previous struggles against 'left' and right in the party since the Yenan days, that against Lin did not extend into all parts of the party and wide sections of the people until his posthumous repudiation. This fact reflects Lin's isolation from the people and the lack of potency of his ideas. It also demonstrated the need for the people to possess new mechanisms of control as a check on their leaders.

It is clear that Mao saw this need, and he accelerated the national programme to study Marxism to train the people and party to recognise a sham Marxist when they saw one. It seems Lin's incumbency as vice-chairman was almost entirely determined by his relationship with Mao. Apart from that relationship, his ideas had little social basis. While his earlier ideas, especially just before and during the cultural revolution, were sometimes original and certainly useful in the struggle against the right, his latter-day conversion to militaristic opportunism would have held little attraction in the eyes of the people.

The virulent anti-Mao sentiment in the Lin clique's manifesto, Outline for Project 571, which, in illiterate calligraphy and on ordinary ringbook notepaper, called Mao 'a feudal-patriarchal autocrat' and his rule 'social-feudalism', and even referred to him by the code name 'B 52', after the notorious US saturation bomber, may just have had some influence, especially on the youth, if Lin had taken power and conducted propaganda along the same lines. But the clique's espousal of terror and its lack of a social programme would have given it a shaky start in leading the country away from what the clique regarded as Mao's suffocating dominance.

The campaign to repudiate Lin Piao after his death first took the form of an attack on his militaristic leftism and he was branded as an ultra-leftist. But by the time of the Tenth Party Congress, held in Peking in August 1973, at which Lin was posthumously declared a renegade and expelled from the party, the repudiation of Lin was already being used by the entrenched elements in the party to pursue a rightist line. As Chou En-lai said in his report to the Congress, one tendency may easily mask another; and 'when a wrong tendency surges towards us like a rising tide, we must not fear isolation and must dare to go against the tide and brave it through. Chairman Mao states, "Going against the tide is a Marxist–Leninist principle." '

Wang Hung-wen, a young leader from Shanghai, gave a report to the Congress on the new party constitution in which he made it clear there were still cadres, especially some leading cadres, 'who will not tolerate differing views of the masses inside or outside the party ... It is quite serious in some individual cases.' Suppression of criticism and even arrest had been used, he said, in handling problems among the people. In 1973 Mao had had to issue an order to the security bureau to 'stop beating people' while they were in prison. Revisions to the constitution, apart from writing out Lin as Mao's successor, included a new sentence, 'It is absolutely impermissible to suppress criticism and to retaliate.'

On the other hand, the Congress strongly reaffirmed party control. The 1968 slogan, 'The working class must exercise leadership in everything', became in 1973, 'The party must exercise leadership in everything'. A few weeks after the Congress, it was announced that Teng Hsiao-ping, general secretary of the party until he was denounced as a rightist in the cultural revolution, had rejoined the political bureau. Attempts were being made within the party at the same time to 'reverse the verdict' on Liu Shao-chi, and an opera in Liu's defence was briefly staged in Peking in January 1974.

The left tried to defend its gains. In the autumn of 1973 university students in Peking and other critics once more campaigned against revisionism in education. Primary-school children attacked 'the absolute authority of the teacher' as being a relic of the past. A movement to discredit Confucianism began in the provinces. By late January 1974 all these new manifestations of protest were embraced by the party leadership in a national campaign to 'repudiate Lin Piao and Confucius'. The campaign was 'personally initiated' by Mao.

In this campaign of *tatsepaos*, criticism meetings and, to a lesser extent, struggle meetings against his remaining followers, Lin Piao was clearly labelled, not merely 'an ultra-leftist, in essence a rightist', but actually an ultra-rightist. The previous tendency to criticise the cultural revolution in criticising Lin, was declared incorrect. The cultural revolution, which, during 1972 and 1973 was referred to as having already ended, was now affirmed as still continuing and in need of 'consolidation'. Praise of the 'new things' emerging from it became widespread.

These 'new things' were five in number, all associated with Mao's line: the development of a barefoot (or amateur) doctor service in the countryside, the practice of sending 'educated youth' to the countryside to settle, the entrance of workers and peasants into universities in a big way and the 'revolution in education' in general, the setting up of cadre schools, and the writing of the eight 'revolutionary model theatrical works' under Chiang Ching's aegis. Each of these gains had come under covert attack in the previous two years.

The position of the 'educated youth' in the countryside was especially doubtful. City parents had used various strat-agems, such as putting their child's name down for university, to get them home. Girls had been mistreated and overworked. The youth had sometimes not been paid for their work: in April 1973 Mao even sent 300 *yuan* to a desperate parent in Fukien province for his son who was in financial difficulties. In July 1973 the Central Committee ordered the local leaders responsible to provide proper facilities for these new rural youth.

The 'three-in-one teams' in the factories, composed of cadres, technicians and workers, were sometimes also counted as a 'new thing' of the cultural revolution, and they seem to have been retained as an encouragement to the technical innovation for which they were responsible. But the most outstanding embodiment of the three-in-one principle, the revolutionary committees, which represented the central gain of the cultural revolution so far as the masses of workers and peasants were concerned, being composed after 1967 of PLA, revolutionary cadres, workers or peasants and Red Guards but by 1972 mainly of reinstated cadres with one or two worker representatives, were not at first included as a 'new thing' to be defended, presumably because they were by 1974 so far in decline they could not be acclaimed as successes: the party committees had appropriated their power. Mao may have clutched at the five peripheral gains to try to open a campaign to restore the more important one that had been forfeited. In June 1974 posters went up in Peking and other cities charging local party leaders with, among other things, forcing workers off the party committees and reducing workers' supervision over the party to a formality. The revolutionary committees institutionalised by the revised state constitution of January 1975 were very different bodies from the ones envisaged in 1967.

Mao persisted in his efforts to cut the ground from under the feet of the new bourgeois class. In a major speech towards the end of 1974 he analysed the nature of 'bourgeois right' in a socialist society, saying that China still practised a commodity system and perpetuated various inequalities in the scales of wages and the distribution of products. He said that 'bourgeois right' could either be restricted or it would be allowed to spread unchecked, providing fertile ground for the development of the new bourgeois class which the Lin Piao episode had shown to be waiting to consolidate its power. And he began a national campaign in early 1975 designed to examine the real meaning of the dictatorship of the proletariat: to what extent could that class be said to be 'dictating' in China today?

A few months later, in August 1975, Mao raised a negative criticism of the classic tale of peasant uprising, *Water Margin*, which in his youth he had read with an admiration that was tempered by a feeling that the story's heroes, for all their romantic daredevilry, were little more than rebel gentry, and not of the people. His criticisms drew attention to tendencies in the party towards 'capitulating', as he charged the novel's main hero, Sung Chiang, with doing — capitulating to revisionism at home and to one or other of the superpowers abroad.

It seems the newly re-instated Teng Hsiao-ping again resisted Mao's continued assaults on emerging bourgeois forces. Early in 1976 Teng was accused of stirring up a 'right deviationist wind' in education and the economy the previous summer. Renewed criticism charged him with distorting the 'three directives' Mao had given for the development of the economy. The directives referred to studying the theory of the dictatorship of the proletariat so as to prevent revisionism; stability and unity; and pushing the national economy forward.

Teng advanced a programme of 'taking the three directives as the key link'. By treating all three directives on an equal footing, he effectively reduced their political meaning, while inflating their economic meaning. It was always class struggle, and not economic factors, that Mao described as 'the key link' in development. 'What "taking the three directives as the key link"!' Mao is said to have retorted. 'Stability and unity do not mean writing off class struggle. Class struggle is the key link and everything else hinges on it.' And on 10 March 1976 Mao opened a campaign to try to prevent the reversal of any more of the 'correct verdicts' passed during the cultural revolution, with an unsettling announcement to the people: 'You are making the socialist revolution, and yet you don't know where the bourgeoisie is. It is right here, in the Communist Party.' Six months later, on 9 September 1976, Mao was dead.

Mao's warning of 10 March 1976 has a resonance that will surely be heard repeatedly in the years to come. It encapsulates Mao's testimony, his restless message for the future. It is a cry, clear and painful, that contains the sound of much future conflict. It will be quoted by faithful followers, and by inveterate enemies of his thinking. Each will use it to give validity to his own line. It is fitting for such a restless seeker that one of Mao's last known pronouncements appears to envisage not an ending but a new beginning.

A week after his death, at the funeral ceremony for their

'great teacher', as the millions wept in Tien An Men Square and down all the wide streets of central Peking, in all the towns and villages across the country, the young revolutionaries in the mourning crowds no doubt found the challenge of life without Mao as difficult and as immense in significance as the challenge Mao set them while he was alive. They, and the Chinese people, are born of him, as he was born of them.

Meanwhile the Central Committee developed its analysis of the contending forces in the world, dividing the world into the developing countries, which included China, on the one hand, and the two superpowers, Russia and the United States, on the other, with the other advanced industrial countries in the middle, exploiting the developing countries but trying to preserve some independence of the superpowers. When Teng Hsiao-ping spoke at the United Nations' special session on the problems of raw materials and development in April 1974, he pursued the line that the Soviet Union was now unquestionably not merely a revisionist country but a 'social-imperialist' power: having restored capitalism at home, it was now seeking world hegemony. *Détente* between the two superpowers was a smokescreen. They were 'contending and colluding', but, Teng reminded the assembly, between imperialist powers, it was always the contention that was the ruling factor. And he ended his speech with an appeal, strange from a state leader, and one which, having the ring of Mao about it, is very likely a quotation from him, 'If one day China should change her colour and turn into a superpower, if she too should play the tyrant in the world, and everywhere subject others to her bullying, aggression and exploitation, the people of the world should identify her as social-imperialism, expose it, oppose it and work together with the Chinese people to overthrow it.'

Judging from some of his statements of the past decade, it is not too much to suppose that Mao saw that day as not far off. 'The rise to power of revisionism,' he said, 'is the rise to power of the bourgeoisie.' After more than twenty-five years of the People's Republic, the question of state power is by no means settled.

The comments of some Chinese labourers which I recorded in 1972-3 reflect something of the attitudes to life of the working people in the aftermath of the Great Proletarian Cultural Revolution. The comments were made in a period when peasants and workers had been called upon to relate to the young the lessons they had learnt from 'the bitter past', and at the same time to raise their own political level by a study of Marxist philosophy and history. In the past, Mao felt, the Chinese revisionists had followed their Soviet counterparts in holding back theoretical knowledge from the masses in order to parade themselves as authorities. They had appropriated Marxism to bolster their own power. Now Mao wanted the people to grasp Marxism for themselves.

In recounting their lives and in commenting on their study, these peasants and workers revealed something of their view of Mao and of his place in history. In their ritualism the stories contained a pull to the feudal past. In their continuing acceptance of authority at face-value, the story tellers showed how much has still to be achieved. But in their intense concern with doing what will bring benefit to the community and in their urge to study in order to find methods of doing that, they revealed a pull towards the future.

Yin Wei-cheng is a fifty-year-old poor peasant from Yellow Earth Commune, south of Peking. At thirteen Yin was a hired hand for a landlord and ate chaff and wild vegetables. Today he is party secretary of his 35,000-strong commune and he is a member of the city's municipal party committee. He first heard of Mao in 1945. 'I was told he was a bandit and his Eighth Route Army would come and set fire to my village and share out our wives. But when the army came they were kind and called us peasant brothers. They said they had been sent by Mao to liberate the poor. They got up early and helped us sweep the courtyard and carry water.

'After liberation, during the land reform in 1950-1, we threw out the landlords. I organised some co-operatives, as Mao said we should, though revisionists branded me as "impetuous and hasty". I was illiterate and others had to read Mao's *Analysis of the Classes in Chinese Society* to me. I wanted to read more of Mao, so I learnt some characters. Up to April 1954 I had learnt only 270. In August 1954 I met Mao at the National People's Congress. He asked what our production was like. I was so excited I just said 'Good!' I was ashamed of my backwardness so I took four months off work and learnt 2,000 characters. By then I could read *Serve the People*. It wasn't until 1960 that I started to read through the four volumes of the *Selected Works*. It took me two years. I can't say I understood it thoroughly. I suffered enough in the past and learnt how to fight the landlords, so I reckoned I was fairly politically conscious. But to be really conscious you need theory as well.

'In 1961 I was dismissed from the commune leadership for resisting the new policy of "fixing output quotas on the basis of individual households". I advised the peasants that this meant a retreat to individual farming. I checked my actions with Mao's teachings and firmly believed I was right. Later I found the policy was not Mao's and I had been correct to resist it. I read the *Selected Works* again during the cultural revolution. Now I have gone on to Marx, Engels and Lenin. It is very difficult but we can learn.

'What I've gained most from Mao is the understanding that contradictions are everywhere. Contradictions exist, for example, between me, as a leader, and the commune members, as led. If we leaders are wrong, we must criticise ourselves. When we talk about democracy, we must remember centralism; when we speak of discipline, we must remember freedom. If problems crop up, consult the masses. We put our heads together. Where there are more people, there are more ideas. Three shoemakers will make a sage. If we do things together, we can change nature. The landlords used to say we poor peasants were "destined" to serve them like beasts of burden. Then how is it that we are able today to run the country as masters of the state? In fact, it is the slaves who make history. All this I have learnt from Chairman Mao.'

If the slaves were to be masters, Mao saw that 'the arming of the people with philosophy' — with the tools of Marxist analysis and criticism — was something that would help prevent the rebureaucratisation of the party. It would mean the workers and commune members were more conscious, and, being more conscious, held more initiative in their living hands to counter the dead hand of the bureaucracy.

But the effectiveness of these tools depends in turn upon the consciousness with which their use is learnt. For some workers, Mao's thought is still in the nature of a revelation. 'I had difficulties in my work and the brilliance of Mao Tse-tung Thought gave me courage' is a typical attitude of idealistic enthusiasm, by no means restricted to the youth.

For others Mao has given a dimension to history. This, too, may be expressed in terms which are part ideal and romantic, and part severely practical. A machine-tool worker said, 'After I studied Chairman Mao's works, I realised I must work for man's emancipation from the past — from poverty, superstition, injustice. As I stand in front of my machine, I cherish the whole world in my heart. I have also learnt that our liberation, as workers, comes in stages. It can't be achieved all at once. Neither is there final victory. There is only development, or slipping back. The third thing Mao has taught me is that I belong to a class — the working class. I now see that after the revolution, classes do not automatically disappear. I have to continue to see things from the point of view of my class and examine whether they really conform to our interests.'

This sense of class brotherhood is strong and Mao's ideas feed it. A cadre in a cotton mill responsible for propaganda among the workers said, 'What kind of skill a worker has, whether it's great or small, is not the most important thing.

It is the spirit of working for his fellow men that makes his work noble, whatever his ability. I have learnt this from Mao. We can forge a true union of the masses on those grounds.' And he gave his own interpretation of the worker-peasant alliance: 'Peasants feed us. With our cloth, we workers clothe them. We are not yet very well off. But to grow rich by taking others' wealth is not for us, either as a class or a country. Our living standard should rise equally step by step, by our own efforts. Mao has said that equality is not in itself a virtue; it is just that equality comes naturally to those who have not lost contact with their fellow workers.'

This spirit informs the outlook of much of the new generation. A young girl machinist described her hopes for China's future, 'Whom should we live for? I am a worker and therefore inherit a worker's way of seeing things. Chairman Mao hopes we young people will go on building. How can we do otherwise when so many have lost their lives in that struggle? A duty to those dead is a duty to us who live. But it isn't easy. I don't yet know enough. I must study hard. I should also work hard. My machine is a tool for changing the objective world. I want to change the world in favour of my class.'

Her loyalty to the dead may be ancestor worship in a new form, but the immensity of the sacrifice — perhaps 50 million dead — is alone enough to command respect. So great a killing might be thought to presage a very great change. Yet Lu Hsun, who remained Mao's favourite modern writer, said in 1923 that in China 'just to move a table or overhaul a stove probably involves shedding blood.' With such a cost, he added, 'even so, the change may not get made.'

It is because Mao knew, with Lu Hsun, that 'unfortunately China is very hard to change' that he has been so concerned to teach its people the opposite lesson — the idea of 'persistent, tenacious struggle' to change their conditions. In such a land, with feudalism breathing down your neck and death not far behind, such doggedness is the first requirement. If you do not have it, the table will stay in its place and the stove will go out.

References

Further Reading

Notes on Editions and Sources

References

CHAPTER 1

1. Emi Siao, *Mao Tse-tung: His Childhood and Youth*, Bombay, People's Publishing House Ltd., 1953, p. 1.
2. Edgar Snow, *Red Star over China*, Harmondsworth, Penguin, 1972, p. 157. Except where otherwise stated, quotations in the main body of the text in Chapter 1 are from Mao's 'autobiography' as told to Edgar Snow and published in *Red Star over China* in 1936.
3. Siao, *op. cit.*, p. 15.
4. Snow, *op. cit.*, p. 156.
5. *Ibid.*, p. 159.
6. *Ibid.*, p. 160.
7. Siao, *op. cit.*, pp. 20–1.
8. Snow, *op. cit.*, pp. 160–1.
9. Han Suyin, *The Morning Deluge*, London, Jonathan Cape, 1972, p. 49.
10. Snow, *op. cit.*, p. 165.
11. *Ibid.*, pp. 166–7.
12. *Ibid.*, pp. 169–70.
13. *Ibid.*, pp. 170–1.
14. Siao, *op. cit.*, pp. 41–2.
15. Translated in Stuart R. Schram, *The Political Thought of Mao Tse-tung*, Harmondsworth, Penguin, 1969, pp. 152–4.
16. Han Suyin, *op. cit.*, p. 74.
17. Snow, *op. cit.*, pp. 177–8.
18. Schram, *op. cit.*, pp. 162–4, 239–41.
19. *Ibid.*, pp. 296–7.
20. Jerome Ch'en, *Mao*, Englewood Cliffs, N.J., Prentice-Hall, 1969, p. 98. From *Hsin-min Hsüeh-hui hui-yüan t'ung-hsun-chi* (Correspondence of the members of the New Citizens' Study Society), Hunan li-shih tzu-liao, No. 4, 1949, p. 76.

CHAPTER 2

1. Schram, *op. cit.*, p. 241.
2. *Ibid.*, p. 245.

3. *Ibid.*, pp. 245—6.
4. *Ibid.*
5. *Ibid.*, p. 249.
6. Mao Tse-tung, *Selected Works*, (hereafter *SW*), Vol. 1, Foreign Languages Press (hereafter FLP), Peking, 1967, pp. 23—4.
7. *Ibid.*, p. 25.
8. *Ibid.*, pp. 27—8.
9. *Ibid.*, pp. 46—7.
10. *Ibid.*, p. 56.

CHAPTER 3

1. Stuart R. Schram, *Mao Tse-tung*, Harmondsworth, Penguin, 1966, p. 121.
2. Agnes Smedley, *The Great Road: The Life and Times of Chu Teh*, New York, Monthly Review Press, 1956, p. 227.
3. *Ibid.*
4. *SW*, Vol. 1, pp. 97—8.
5. Agnes Smedley, *Chinese Destinies*, New York, Vanguard Press, 1933, p. 85.
6. *Ibid.*, pp. 86—7.
7. Smedley, *The Great Road*, p. 236.
8. *Ibid.*, p. 247.
9. *SW*, Vol. 1, p. 124.
10. Smedley, *The Great Road*, pp. 256—7.
11. *Ibid.*, pp. 257—8.
12. *Ibid.*, p. 266.
13. *SW*, Vol. 1, p. 106.
14. *New Left Review*, No. 65, January—February 1971, p. 68.
15. Smedley, *The Great Road*, pp. 270—1.
16. *Ibid.*, p. 271.
17. Mao Tse-tung, *Selected Readings*, FLP, Peking, 1971, pp. 40—9.
18. Smedley, *Chinese Destinies*, pp. 269—72.
19. *Ibid.*, pp. 300—2, 305—9, 311.
20. Conrad Brandt, Benjamin Schwartz and John K. Fairbank, *A Documentary History of Chinese Communism*, New York, Atheneum, 1971, p. 235.
21. *Ibid.*, p. 236.
22. Anna Louise Strong, *China Fights for Freedom*, London, Lindsay Drummond, 1939, p. 83.
23. Snow, *op. cit.*, pp. 247—8.
24. Charles Hodges, *Asia Magazine*, May 1934. Quoted in Strong, *op. cit.*, p. 83.

25. Snow, *op. cit.*, p. 209.
26. Chen Chang-feng, *On the Long March with Chairman Mao*, FLP, Peking, 1972, pp. 5–6.
27. *Ibid.*, pp. 8, 10.
28. Dick Wilson, *The Long March, 1935*, London, Hamish Hamilton, 1971, p. 74.

CHAPTER 4

1. Smedley, *The Great Road*, pp. 311–2.
2. *The Long March: Eye-witness Accounts*, FLP, Peking, 1963, p. 208.
3. Snow, *op. cit.*, p. 222.
4. *The Long March: Eye-witness Accounts*, pp. 213–15.
5. Chen Chang-feng, *op. cit.*, pp. 46–9; and *The Long March: Eye-witness Accounts*, p. 126.
6. *The Long March: Eye-witness Accounts*, p. 215.
7. Chen Chang-feng, *op. cit.*, pp. 50–5.
8. *Stories of The Long March*, FLP, Peking, 1960, pp. 109–10.
9. *The Long March: Eye-witness Accounts*, pp. 215–16.
10. Smedley, *The Great Road*, pp. 321–2.
11. Chen Chang-feng, *op. cit.*, pp. 60–1.
12. *Stories of The Long March*, pp. 7–8.
13. Chen Chang-feng, *op. cit.*, pp. 66–73.
14. *Ibid.*, pp. 78–82.
15. *Ibid.*, pp. 83–6. See also *The Long March: Eye-witness Accounts*, p. 129.
16. Chen Chang-feng, *op. cit.*, pp. 91–3.
17. *SW*, Vol. 1, pp. 159–60.

CHAPTER 5

1. 15 July 1936. Translated in Schram, *The Political Thought of Mao Tse-tung*, p. 261.
2. *SW*, Vol. 1, p. 279.
3. *SW*, Vol. 1, pp. 187–91.
4. Smedley, *The Great Road*, pp. 355–6.
5. Nym Wales, *Inside Red China*, New York, Doubleday, Dorman and Co., 1939, p. 211.
6. Jerome Ch'en, *Mao Papers*, London, Oxford University Press, 1970, p. 13.
7. Snow, *op. cit.*, pp. 110, 112.
8. Agnes Smedley, *Battle Hymn of China*, London, Gollancz, 1944, pp. 121–3.

9. Wales, *op. cit.*, pp. 275—6.
10. Smedley, *Battle Hymn of China*, p. 135.
11. General Li Tien-yu, in *Saga of Resistance to Japanese Invasion*, FLP, Peking, 1959, pp. 18—19.
12. Strong, *op. cit.*, pp. 134—5.
13. Smedley, *The Great Road*, p. 360.
14. Strong, *op. cit.*, pp. 139—40.
15. Jen Pi-shih, in Strong, *op. cit.*, pp. 145—7.
16. Strong, *op. cit.*, p. 155.
17. *SW*, Vol. 2, FLP, Peking, 1967, pp. 219—20.

CHAPTER 6

1. *Saga of Resistance to Japanese Invasion*, p. 79.
2. Smedley, *The Great Road*, pp. 376—7.
3. *Saga of Resistance to Japanese Invasion*, pp. 36—7.
4. Chen Yao, *Comrade Chang Szu-teh As I Knew Him*, Foreign Languages Department, Wuhan University, 1972, pp. 2—42. Translation revised.
5. *SW*, Vol. 3, FLP, Peking, 1965, p. 178.
6. Boyd Compton (Ed.), *Mao's China: Party Reform Documents, 1942—44*, Seattle, University of Washington Press, 1966, pp. 21—2.
7. Robert Payne, *China Awake*, New York, Dodd, Mead and Co., 1947, p. 372.
8. *Ibid.*, p. 384.
9. *Ibid.*, p. 379.
10. *SW*, Vol. 3, p. 73.
11. Mao Tse-tung, *Four Essays on Philosophy*, FLP, Peking, 1966, p. 106.
12. *SW*, Vol. 3, p. 119.
13. Graham Peck, *Two Kinds of Time*, Boston, Houghton Mifflin, 1950, pp. 202—7.
14. Theodore H. White and Annalee Jacoby, *Thunder Out of China*, New York, William Sloane Associates Ltd., 1946, pp. 167—74.
15. Chalmers A. Johnson, *Peasant Nationalism and Communist Power*, Stanford, Stanford University Press, 1970, p. 59.
16. Gunther Stein, *The Challenge of Red China*, New York, McGraw-Hill, 1945, pp. 110—8.
17. Payne, *op. cit.*, p. 371.
18. Stein, *op. cit.*, pp. 115—7.
19. Translated in Mark Selden, *The Yenan Way in Revolutionary China*, Cambridge, Mass., Harvard University Press, 1971, pp. 237—9.

20. Selden, *op. cit.*, pp. 244, 249.
21. *Saga of Resistance to Japanese Invasion*, p. 167.

CHAPTER 7

1. K.A. Abbas, *In the Image of Mao Tse-tung*, People's Publishing House, Bombay, 1953, pp. 68—70.
2. Yen Chang-lin, *In His Mind a Million Bold Warriors*, FLP, Peking, 1972, pp. 2—7, 41—2.
3. Translated in William Hinton, *Fanshen*, New York, Monthly Review Press, 1966, p. 615.
4. Hinton, *op. cit.*, pp. 608—10.
5. *SW*, Vol. 4, FLP, Peking, 1961, p. 374.

CHAPTER 8

1. Peter Townsend, *China Phoenix*, London, Jonathan Cape, 1955, p. 219.
2. Translated in Ch'en, *Mao*, p. 115. From *Shih-chieh chih-shih*, No. 20, 20 October 1958.
3. *Ibid.*, pp. 79—80. From a collection of statements by Mao, no title, n.d. (probably 1967), pp. 19—28.
4. Quoted in Mao, *Four Essays on Philosophy*, p. 90.
5. 'On the Question of Agricultural Co-operation' in *Selected Readings*, pp. 411—12.
6. *Socialist Upsurge in China's Countryside*, FLP, Peking, pp. 257—62.
7. *Five Documents on Literature and Art*, FLP, Peking, pp. 8—9.
8. *Four Essays on Philosophy*, pp. 79—87.
9. *Speech at CCP National Conference on Propaganda Work*, FLP, Peking, 1966, pp. 12—13, 20—8.
10. *Quotations from Chairman Mao Tse-tung*, FLP, Peking, 1972, p. 288.

CHAPTER 9

1. *Selected Readings*, pp. 499—500.
2. Rewi Alley, *China's Hinterland in the Leap Forward*, New World Press, Peking, 1961, pp. 273, 276—7.
3. Edgar Snow, *Red China Today: The Other Side of the River*, Harmondsworth, Penguin, 1970, pp. 172—7.
4. 'The Story of Tachai' by Pien Hsi, in *The Seeds and Other Stories*, FLP, Peking, 1972, pp. 184—5.

5. Ch'en, *Mao Papers*, pp. 86–7.
6. *Ibid.*, p. 94.
7. *Ibid.*, p. 98.
8. *Five Documents on Literature and Art*, pp. 10–11.
9. *Ibid.*, p. 11.
10. *Peking Review*, No. 23, 2 June 1967.

CHAPTER 10

1. Ch'en, *Mao Papers*, p. 102.
2. *Ibid.*, pp. 24–5.
3. *Ibid.*, pp. 27–8.
4. *Peking Review*, No. 33, 11 August 1967.
5. *Important Documents of the Great Proletarian Cultural Revolution in China*, FLP, Peking, 1970. Also, Ch'en, *Mao Papers*, pp. 120–1, 124.
6. Ch'en, *Mao Papers*, pp. 42–4.
7. *The Great Power Struggle in China*, Hong Kong, Asia Research Centre, 1969, pp. 52–5.
8. Jan Myrdal and Gun Kessle, *China: the Revolution Continued*, London, Chatto and Windus, 1971, pp. 106–8.
9. Instructions of 12 June and 8 August 1967 in Ch'en, *Mao Papers*, pp. 141, 143.
10. *Ibid.*, p. 146.
11. Mao's *In Memory of Norman Bethune*, *Serve the People* and *The Foolish Old Man who Removed the Mountains*.
12. *The Ninth National Congress of the CCP* (*Documents*), FLP, Peking, 1969, pp. 64–5.
13. Ch'en, *Mao Papers*, p. 139.
14. *People's Daily*, 1 August 1972.

Further Reading

In addition to those mentioned in the text or listed in the References, the following are some of the works whose help in writing this book I am happy to acknowledge and which I think will repay readers' study.

Ascher, Isaac, *China's Social Policy*, London, Anglo-Chinese Educational Institute, 1972.

Asia Research Centre, *The Great Cultural Revolution in China*, Rutland and Tokyo, Charles E. Tuttle, 1968.

Beauvoir, Simone de, *The Long March*, New York, World Publishing Co., 1958.

Belden, Jack, *China Shakes the World*, Harmondsworth, Penguin, 1973.

Bianco, Lucien, *Origins of the Chinese Revolution, 1915–1949*, Stanford, Stanford University Press; London, Oxford University Press, 1971.

Boorman, Howard L., 'Mao Tse-tung: The Lacquered Image', *The China Quarterly*, No. 16, October–December 1963.

Boorman, Scott A., *The Protracted Game: A Wei-ch'i Interpretation of Maoist Revolutionary Strategy*, London, Oxford University Press, 1969.

Brulé, Jean-Pierre, *China Comes of Age*, Harmondsworth, Penguin, 1971.

Building a New Life: Stories about China's Construction, Peking, FLP, 1955.

Burchett, Wilfred, *China's Feet Unbound*, Melbourne, World Unity Publications, 1952.

Centre for International Affairs and the East Asian Research Centre, *Communist China, 1955–1959: Policy Documents with Analysis*, Cambridge, Harvard University Press, 1965.

Chen, Jack, *New Earth*, Peking, New World Press, 1957.

Ch'en, Jerome, *Mao and the Chinese Revolution*, London, Oxford University Press, 1965.

———— 'Resolutions of the Tsunyi Conference', *The China Quarterly*, No. 40, October–December 1969.

Chen Po-ta, *Notes on Mao Tse-Tung's 'Report on an Investigation of the Peasant Movement in Hunan'*, Peking, FLP, 1954.

Chesnaux, Jean, *Peasant Revolts in China, 1840–1949*, London, Thames & Hudson, 1973.

Chiang Ching, *On the Revolutionisation of Peking Opera*, Peking, FLP, 1968.

Ch'ien Tuan-sheng, *The Government and Politics of China*, Stanford, Stanford University Press, 1950.

China Now (Journal of the Society for Anglo-Chinese Understanding).

China Reconstructs, Writers of. *China in Transition: Selected Articles, 1952-6*, Peking, China Reconstructs, 1957.

Chow Tse-tung, *The May Fourth Movement*, Cambridge, Harvard University Press, 1960.

Clubb, O. Edmund, *Communism in China: A Report from Hankow in 1932*, New York, Columbia University Press, 1968.

————— *Twentieth-Century China*, New York, Columbia University Press, 1964.

Cohen, Arthur A., *The Communism of Mao Tse-tung*, Chicago, University of Chicago Press, 1964.

Crook, Isabel and David, *The First Years of Yangyi Commune*, London, Routledge & Kegan Paul, 1966.

————— *Revolution in a Chinese Village*, London, Routledge & Kegan Paul, 1959.

Davidson, Basil, *Daybreak in China*, London, Jonathan Cape, 1953.

Degras, Jane (Ed.), *The Communist International, 1919–43. Documents*, 2 vols, London, Oxford University Press, 1956.

Domes, Jürgen, *The Internal Politics of China, 1949–1972*, London, C. Hurst & Co., 1973.

Forman, Harrison, *Report from Red China*, London, Robert Hale, 1946.

Gittings, John, *The Role of the Chinese Army*, London, Oxford University Press, 1967.

Griffith, William E., *The Sino–Soviet Rift*, Cambridge, M.I.T. Press, 1964.

Guillermaz, Jacques, *A History of the Chinese Communist Party, 1921–1949*, London, Methuen, 1972.

Gurley, John G., 'Capitalist and Maoist Economic Development', *Monthly Review*, February 1971.

Hinton, William, *Hundred Day War: The Cultural Revolution at Tsinghua University*, New York, Monthly Review Press, 1972.

Ho Kan-chih, *A History of the Modern Chinese Revolution*, Peking, FLP, 1959.

Ho Lung, *The Democratic Tradition in the Chinese People's Liberation Army*, Peking, FLP, 1965.

Hsia, Dr. Adrian, *The Chinese Cultural Revolution*, London, Orbach & Chambers, 1972.

Hsiao Chien, *How the Tillers Win Back their Land*, Peking, FLP, 1951.

Hsiung, James Chieh, *Ideology and Practice: The Evolution of Chinese Communism*, New York, Praeger, 1970.

Hu Chiao-mu, *Thirty Years of the Communist Party of China*, London, Lawrence & Wishart, 1951.

Hunter, Neale, *Shanghai Journal*, New York, Praeger, 1969.

Isaacs, Harold R. (Ed.), *Five Years of Kuomintang Reaction*, Shanghai, China Forum, May 1932.

───────── *The Tragedy of the Chinese Revolution*, Stanford, Stanford University Press, 1961.

Karanjia, R.K., *China Stands Up*, Bombay, People's Publishing House, 1952.

Karnow, Stanley, *Mao and China*, London, Macmillan, 1973.

Klein, Donald W. and Clark, Anne B., *Biographic Dictionary of Chinese Communism, 1921–1965*, 2 vols, Cambridge, Harvard University Press, 1971.

Liang, Y., *Village and Town Life in China*, London, George Allen & Unwin, 1915.

Lin Piao, *Long Live the Victory of People's War*, Peking, FLP, 1965.

Liu Shao-chi, *How to be a Good Communist*, Peking, FLP, 1965.

MacFarquhar, Roderick, *The Origins of the Cultural Revolution*, Vol. 1, London, Oxford University Press, 1974.

MacNair, Harley Farnsworth, *China in Revolution*, Chicago, University of Chicago Press, 1931.

Mallory, Walter H., *China: Land of Famine*, New York, American Geographical Society, 1926.

Mao Tse-tung, *Basic Tactics*, Tr. Stuart R. Schram, New York, Praeger, 1966.

───────── *Poems*, Tr. Andrew Boyd and Gladys Yang, Peking, FLP, 1959.

───────── *Poems*, Tr. Wong Man, Hong Kong, Eastern Horizon Press, 1966.

───────── *Poems*, Tr. Hua-ling Nieh Engle and Paul Engle, New York, Dell, 1972.

───────── *Poems*, Tr. Willis Barnstone, London, Barrie & Jenkins, 1972.

───────── *Ten More Poems*, Hong Kong, Eastern Horizon Press, 1967.

───────── 'Ten Poems', *Chinese Literature*, No. 5, 1966.

Meisner, Maurice, *Li Ta-chao and The Origins of Chinese Marxism*, Cambridge, Harvard University Press, 1967.

Myrdal, Jan, *Report from a Chinese Village*, London, Heinemann, 1965.

Nearing, Scott, *Whither China?*, New York, International Publishers, 1927.

Nee, Victor, *The Cultural Revolution at Peking University*, New York, Monthly Review Press, 1971.

Neuberg, A., *Armed Insurrection*, London, New Left Books, 1971.

Peking Review, Weekly Journal.

Ransome, Arthur, *The Chinese Puzzle*, London, George Allen & Unwin, 1927.

Robinson, Joan, *The Cultural Revolution in China*, Harmondsworth, Penguin, 1969.

Rossanda, Rossana, 'Mao's Marxism', *The Socialist Register, 1971*, London, Merlin Press, 1971.

Rue, John E., *Mao Tse-tung in Opposition, 1927–1935*, Stanford, Stanford University Press, 1966.

Schram, Stuart R. (Ed.), *Mao Tse-tung Unrehearsed*, Harmondsworth, Penguin, 1974.

Schurmann, Franz, *Ideology and Organisation in Communist China*, Berkeley, University of California Press, 1971.

Schwartz, Benjamin I., *Chinese Communism and the Rise of Mao*, Cambridge, Harvard University Press, 1958.

———— *Communism and China: Ideology in Flux*, Cambridge, Harvard University Press, 1968.

Shapiro, Michael, *Changing China*, London, Lawrence & Wishart, 1958.

Smedley, Agnes, *China's Red Army Marches*, New York, Vanguard Press, 1934.

Snow, Edgar, *The Long Revolution*, New York, Random House, 1972.

Solomon, Richard H., *Mao's Revolution and the Chinese Political Culture*, Berkeley, University of California Press, 1971.

Soong Ching Ling, *The Struggle for New China*, Peking, FLP, 1952.

Sun Tzu, *The Art of War*, London, Oxford University Press, 1963.

Swarup, Shanti, *A Study of the Chinese Communist Movement, 1927–1934*, Oxford, Clarendon Press, 1966.

Tang Leang-li, *China in Revolt*, London, Noel Douglas, 1927.

Taylor, George E., *The Struggle for North China*, New York, Institute of Pacific Relations, 1940.

Tenth National Congress of the Communist Party of China (Documents), Peking, FLP, 1973.

Thomson, George, *From Marx to Mao Tse-tung*, London, China Policy Study Group, 1971.

Tretyakov, S., *Chinese Testament: the Autobiography of Tan Shih-hua*, London, Gollancz, 1934.

Union Research Institute, *The Case of Peng Teh-huai*, Hong Kong, 1968.

———— *Index to the Selected Works of Mao Tse-tung*, Hong Kong, 1968.

Van Slyke, Lyman P., *The Chinese Communist Movement*, Stanford, Stanford University Press, 1968.

Wales, Nym, *Red Dust: Autobiographies of Chinese Communists*, Stanford, Stanford University Press, 1952.

Wheelwright, E.L. and McFarlane, Bruce., *The Chinese Road to Socialism*, New York, Monthly Review Press, 1970.

Yakhontoff, V.A., *Chinese Soviets*, New York, Coward-McCann, 1934.

Yao Wen-yuan, *The Working Class Must Exercise Leadership in Everything*, Peking, FLP, 1968.

Yen, Hawkling L., *A Survey of Constitutional Development in China*, New York, Columbia University Press, 1911.

Zagoria, Donald S., *The Sino—Soviet Conflict, 1956—61*, New York, Atheneum, 1969.

Notes on Editions and Sources

In most cases I have quoted the versions of Mao's writings that have been published in the *Selected Works* and in other recent Peking editions. These are the versions familiar to most Chinese. However, where there are substantial differences in content between the versions published today and those published originally or unofficially, I have used the original or unofficial translation. This is the case with, for example, *An Analysis of the Various Classes of the Chinese Peasantry* of January 1926, which Mao rewrote and published a month later as *An Analysis of the Classes in Chinese Society*; and the *Letter to Comrade Lin Piao* of January 1930 which appears in the *Selected Works* in an abridged version as *A Single Spark Can Start a Prairie Fire*.

In some cases, where the colour of Mao's original speech has been lost in the official version, as in his epithets against dogmatism in *Rectify the Party's Style of Work* (1942), I have used an unofficial translation of the original. In one case, the article of 15 April 1958, where neither official nor unofficial translation seemed to me satisfactory, I have used my own version. In cases where there are no official translations as in many early and late writings and speeches, I have, of course, used those that exist. For the cultural revolution directives I have, in the main, relied on Jerome Ch'en's invaluable *Mao Papers*. In general, then, I have hoped to strike a balance between official and unofficial editions.

Since the late 1930s, Mao's works have usually been through a process of intra-party discussion and emendation before being passed on for publication and it is at that stage that decisions are made on what to publish, how much to publish and with what changes. There are indications that on a number of occasions Mao was put in a position of having to tailor his editions to the officials' prudence both politically and in toning down his sometimes scabrous language.

A more important deficiency in the officially translated works is their selectivity. A mass of material by Mao — speeches, articles, essays, letters — awaits translation. Some of this material has reached other countries but what has so far been read by western scholars does not seem to alter very greatly previous impressions of the man, though it helps to clarify details and shades of emphasis at various stages of Mao's struggle. The *Collected Works*, promised by the new leadership under

Hua Kuo-feng, will no doubt fill those gaps. Meanwhile, Volume 5 of the *Selected Works*, covering the years 1949 to 1957, was published in Peking in 1977.

On the question of the attitudes expressed in the other Chinese communist publications I have used as sources, I see no reason to be more suspicious of what some western scholars call 'the official Chinese line' on the events of Mao's life than of any interpretations from other sources. The face provides a measure of the reality behind. Moreover, the face that the Chinese Communist Party projects is an accumulation of viewpoints in whose formation the Chinese people have certainly played a part.

It is equally a duty to examine instances where face and reality have diverged. I have mainly concentrated on one area where such divergence seems to me to hold meanings of great significance for the future. As I make plain, in the post-liberation period, Mao increasingly, in my view, became estranged from officials who only too readily claimed for their own interests the imprimatur of 'Chairman Mao's revolutionary line'. While I do not think they should be under-estimated, I regard their existence as a spur to others to release Mao's words from their clutches. In that future task western and Chinese Marxists would certainly benefit from each other's work.

Index